CIVIL LITIGATION: A CASE STUDY

R. Pierce Kelley, Jr.

Copyright © 2001
All Rights Reserved.
Pearson Publications Company
Dallas, Texas

Website: Pearsonpub-legal.com

ISBN: 0-929563-61-1

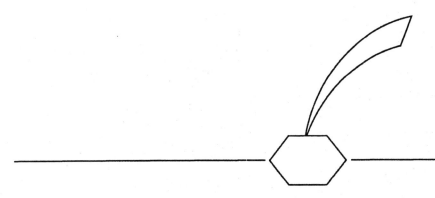

Civil Litigation: A Case Study is designed as a textbook for classroom use. The information contained herein is intended only for educational and informational purposes.

We cannot teach anyone anything. We can only help them discover it within themselves.

Galileo

Centuries later learning specialists confirm what Galileo guessed. They don't phrase it exactly the same way. Instead, they tell us that memory works on strings and that one remembers something that hooks onto something that one already knows. That all of the educational process is essentially working with a double-sided Velcro. This sticks to this which sticks to that which sticks to…. well, you get the idea.

So, Galileo was correct—we only learn those things that we are equipped or at least prepared to learn. Sometimes as a paralegal educator, it has seemed to me that I spend my professional life preparing my students for the real learning that takes place on that vital first job. For no matter how many times we talk about how something works, the sterile classroom discussion simply does not convey the process in the same way that experiencing the process does.

Practicums—classroom exercises that replicate the real life experience—take the student as close as education safely can (without jeopardizing a client) in the learning process. Enter Miss Scarlett Rose. This real life case with all the minutiae and conflicts that accompany real life can give students a taste of the complexity of preparing a client's case for trial. Add to that the role-play opportunity that allows a student to understand what an attorney needs during the pleading process as the issues are set, during discovery as the details come to light, and at trial to be an effective advocate.

This process brings not only a fuller understanding to the student but, perhaps more important, to the student on an immediate clock and working your way through the sorrows and travails of Scarlett Rose and Nickel and Dime is just more fun. Nothing is more memorable than fun.

Susan Demers

ACKNOWLEDGMENTS

First and foremost, I thank Susan Demers, who is, and has been for many years, the head of the legal assistant program at St. Petersburg Junior College. Susan supported and encouraged me in this project from the time I first had the idea to write a textbook for civil litigation. Susan also reviewed the initial draft of the text and placed me in contact with Enika Pearson Schulze, of Pearson Publications Inc., who agreed to publish the book.

Second of all, I thank Enika for her willingness to publish this book, and for the time and energy, as well as that of her staff and editorial team, expended in completing all of the tasks necessary to finally conclude the process of producing the book. It was, and it remains, our mutual belief that this book offers students a more practical approach to civil litigation than the texts currently available for students. We have additional goals and aspirations for further books and projects that I hope to achieve.

Next, I thank the various students who have given me their advice and suggestions as to how to make the book more worthwhile, from their perspective, especially Mike Earle and Annette Kurtz. This book is the result of several years of effort, and I had the benefit of testing my book on several groups of students who have taken a civil litigation class with me. My intent was to create a book that fairly presents a typical personal injury lawsuit, without putting any more emphasis on either the plaintiff's or the defendant's side, so that the students will be better prepared to successfully enter a law firm once they are ready to begin to utilize the education they have received and become legal assistants.

Finally, I thank my family and friends for their patience and support.

Pierce Kelley

INTRODUCTION

It is my hope that this textbook can be useful to educators in a variety of ways. At St. Petersburg Junior College, it is intended for students who have successfully completed an introductory course in civil litigation. It provides students with a practical application of the theories they learned from the first semester. If civil litigation is not offered as a two-semester topic, it can be used as a stand-alone text to teach civil litigation. It can also be used as a trial practice text. I expect that it will have other possible applications as well, depending upon the curriculum at the various schools across the country.

The book's premise involves two students who have successfully completed a legal studies program and are beginning to work on their first case in a law office. One student works for a firm that handles only plaintiff cases; the other works for a defense law firm. The text is presented from the perspective of each student.

This book offers students an opportunity to develop and analyze a trip-and-fall case. The first chapters address pretrial activity, and the later chapters concentrate on the trial proceedings, testimony, and dialogue. Acting as a jury, the class will vote to determine the outcome of the case.

The rules of procedure in the fictitious state of Atlantis will differ from the rules of some other states. I suggest that students compare their jurisdiction's rules of procedure to those of Atlantis.

I intended to provide students with a practical example of what to expect in a law firm that handles civil litigation cases in general, and personal injury cases in particular. I hope the hands-on approach used in this book will be thought-provoking and enjoyable.

TABLE OF CONTENTS

The Incident

A Trip and Fall Accident

On January 31, 2000, Scarlet Rose entered the Nickel & Dime store in Clearwater, Atlantis, to exchange a pair of shorts. While walking to the customer service department at the rear of the store, she turned off the main aisle and tripped over a box in the middle of the aisle of the accessories department. She experienced immediate back pain that was severe enough that paramedics were called. Ms. Rose was taken to the emergency room of a local hospital.

The Injuries and Damages

Ms. Rose was unable to work for several months. Her injury required surgery in March. The surgery involved the insertion of two titanium rods in her back to repair a disk condition and some unstable disks. The medical bills totaled $44,000, of which insurance paid 80%.

Ms. Rose returned to work in May. She received some of her wages from her employer by way of sick leave benefits, vacation, and personal days, but because she was unable to work, she lost income in the amount of $6,000.

Ms. Rose felt that she is entitled to compensation for her out-of-pocket expenses and the pain and suffering she experienced. So, she decided to consult with an attorney.

Entering a Law Office

Marlene Mertz and Chris Walden have just graduated from St. Petersburg Junior College, in St. Petersburg, Atlantis, each with an associate of science degree for paralegals. They both found jobs and are anxious to begin their new careers.

The first day on the job can make anyone nervous. Meeting new people, learning their names, finding out everyone's job responsibilities, and discovering where the new employee fits in is all part of the experience. In a law office, it is even more challenging for recent graduates, who finally have the opportunity to put into action all they have learned from their years of study.

On May 1, 2000, Marlene entered the office of Bruce K. Franklin for her first day of work. Bruce is a sole practitioner, a lawyer who practices law without any partners or associates. Marlene will be required to work with one other person, a legal secretary, Mayda Maloney. Bruce limits his practice to representing plaintiffs in personal injury matters. He needs help managing all of his case files, so he has decided that it would be economical and practical to hire a paralegal instead of an associate attorney. He wants Marlene to prepare the case files either for settlement or for trial.

Chris, on the other hand, will be working for a law firm of over 30 attorneys. Although he will work primarily with one attorney, he may be called upon to assist other attorneys in the office. The firm for which Chris will be working is Sullivan and Jagger, whose practice is limited exclusively to representing defendants in personal injury lawsuits. The firm represents either insurance companies, or businesses that are large enough not to need insurance, or companies that only have coverage for catastrophic claims over a specified amount, typically in excess of $100,000. Chris will be working in a large office and will interact with a number of other employees.

It is difficult for the employer and employee to gauge how well they will work together. Everyone has a unique personality and not all personalities blend well. It may be easier for Marlene to adjust to her job because she will only have to adjust to two new personalities, whereas Chris will be working with dozens of people. A number of things will be the same, however, for both Marlene and Chris. Both law firms will perform similar tasks, and each law firm has the same goals, which are to provide high-quality legal representation to its clients and to make money. No matter how skilled the attorney, if the firm is not financially successful, it will not survive.

Learning About Benefits and Rights and Responsibilities

Because all lawyers are different, every law firm is different. There is no exact way for a law firm to operate, and each law firm creates its own internal operating procedures. For Marlene, there may not be formalized procedures. For Chris, an employee's manual describes and details his benefits and responsibilities as an employee of Sullivan and Jagger. Chris and Marlene will need to learn what their employers expect of them to fit in as quickly as possible and become productive employees of their firms.

Chris' employee manual is quite exhaustive and requires him to be aware of his rights and responsibilities as an employee of the firm. He will have to make decisions about health benefits, life insurance benefits, participation in a retirement program such as a 401(k) plan, and a disability plan. Marlene does not have a formal procedure in her new office.

Attire

Every law office has its own personality, which begins with the personality of the most senior attorney. The personality of the office is determined, in part, by the location of the office and whether it is in a building all by itself, a large office building with other attorneys, a mall, or some other area. The office could be located on a large commercial street, next to the courthouse, or miles away in a quiet neighborhood. The personality of the office is also affected by the furnishings, the furniture, the decorations, the size of the office, the employees' work stations, or even by whether the firm owns the building or rents office space. It will also be determined by whether clients come to visit the office on a regular basis. To be sure, each office will want to put forth an image to its clients, and the legal community, which reflects both professionalism and success.

The atmosphere of the law firm is reflected in the attire of those who work in the office. Marlene's employer is a man in his mid-thirties, who has been out of law school and practicing law for over ten years. He is married and has two children, and he wants to present a youthful and energetic image. He dresses stylishly, but not always in a coat and tie, unless he has to make an appearance in court that day. There are magazines such as *Sports Illustrated* and *Travel* in the reception area. He owns a building in an area a few blocks from the courthouse, and his is the only office in the building. The paintings on his wall are of beautiful landscapes and outdoor activities.

On the other hand, Chris' law firm is located in a large, downtown office building. The firm occupies two floors of a ten-story building in which several other law firms are located. Attorneys come to the office dressed in business suits, and male attorneys wear ties. In the reception area, the *Wall Street Journal*, the *New York Times* and *Business Today* are displayed. There are four senior partners: two men in their late fifties, who have practiced together for thirty years, and two women in their late forties, who joined the firm twenty years ago. The firm wishes to present a businesslike and professional image. The wall decorations are of historical significance, such as a copy of the Declaration of Independence, the Constitution of the United States, or some law-related topic.

Naturally, Marlene and Chris are apt to choose different wardrobes to wear to work. Both must choose professional apparel, but the clothes Marlene can wear to work might not be acceptable at Chris' place of work. Still, if either paralegal wears inappropriate clothing, that person's chances of making a good first impression and fitting in at the office will be reduced.

Behavior

Bruce's legal secretary, Mayda, is in her early forties. She has been Bruce's secretary since he opened his own firm and a legal secretary her entire adult life. She is organized, skilled at her job, and convinced that she can do anything that Marlene can. Rather than explaining the new technology and resources that were available to her at St. Petersburg Junior College, Marlene would be wise to seek Mayda's advice as to how things should be done. At the right time, and in the right spirit, Marlene can introduce some new skills and equipment to Mayda that will make her job a little easier; but in the beginning, Marlene should be respectful and solicitous.

On the other hand, Chris will be working with one of the younger associates in the firm. His name is Alan Richards, and he has been out of law school for about five years. Alan recently joined the firm after spending four years with the state's attorney's office. He has a secretary, Barbara, who joined the firm after graduating from high school and has been there for about a year. Both Alan and Barbara will look to Chris for assistance. They will assume that he has acquired a large amount of knowledge in school that will help them do their jobs better. Chris will want to behave in a way that reflects competence and professionalism.

Virtually everyone who begins a new job upon graduation will work in a different office environment. There is no precise way to behave. What would be acceptable behavior in one office may not be acceptable in another. Paralegals must behave professionally — especially in the beginning —to fit into the office where they will be working.

Formal and Informal Office Procedures

Every office will have similar equipment and supplies. Each will have stationery, telephones, photocopiers, fax machines, postage machines, computers, printers, transcription equipment, file folders, storage facilities, and so forth. There may be a lunchroom or break room with a refrigerator and coffee or snack machines. There will be both formal and informal office procedures to adjust to or, perhaps, create. In Marlene's situation, she will be creating new ways to perform jobs that Mayda had been doing herself before Marlene arrived.

In Chris' situation, there is an office manager whose job is to make sure that everything is done properly, and this office manager will tell Chris what he needs to do about any aspect of office routine. As with dress and behavior, both Marlene and Chris will have to adjust to completely different office environments. Both will be given a reasonable amount of time to learn the procedures, but the sooner they learn, the easier it will be for them to become productive employees of the firm.

Both will have to learn quickly and understand how daily costs of office maintenance are paid for. If possible, every expense will be billed to the file for which the work is done. If long distance calls are required, both must know how the charges are to be billed to a file. When photocopies are made, the file for which the copies are made must be billed. The same is true for faxes and postage. Both Chris and Marlene will need to account for exactly what they did and the amount of time they took to perform each task.

Every office will have a different way of recording information. Marlene is asked to record her hours on time sheets. She must write down the total number of copies, telephone calls, letters and postage, and other expenses. At the end of each day, she enters all costs in the computer and keeps the paper in a separate file marked "daily logs." Chris is told to enter items in the computer by using a code that is assigned to each file. In fact, Chris can't make a telephone call, send a fax, or make a copy without entering a file code.

In Marlene's office, each case is put in a separate file folder and is alphabetically arranged by the client's last name. There are no file numbers and only two large file cabinets. Bruce gives all new files to Mayda, who organizes and maintains the files. The filing system is simple, yet neat and professional.

At Sullivan and Jagger, each attorney's new case is assigned to him or her by a senior partner. By the time Chris sees the file, it is already in a file folder and has a file number assigned to it. His firm has a procedure by which the first two numbers reflect the year the case was first assigned, and the last four numbers reflect the order in which the case was received by the firm for that particular year. The first case of the year 2000 was given the number 00-0001 and so forth. After the first documents were put in a file folder, all subsequent papers were put in a color-coded file, depending upon the type of record. Pleadings are kept separate from correspondence, and all medical records, depositions, subpoenas, and other records are kept in separate files within a large expandable file.

Understanding a Paralegal's Role in the Office

Both Marlene and Chris know what a paralegal can and cannot do. They know that paralegals cannot practice law, give legal advice, solicit clients for their respective firms, or accept or negotiate legal fees. Paralegals can provide services to a client. Under the guidance and supervision of an attorney, they can draft pleadings, conduct research, interview witnesses and clients, conduct investigations and, in general, be an enormous benefit to a law office.

Investigating the Claim

A few weeks after Marlene started working, Bruce handed her a file entitled *Scarlet Rose v. Nickel & Dime, Inc.,* and said, "I met with Scarlet Rose yesterday, and she has asked me to represent her on a case against the Nickel & Dime store. I told her that you would be calling her to arrange a time for her to come into the office to discuss the matter. A copy of our standard retainer agreement is in the file. I want you to work this case up for me. Please complete the initial client interview form and prepare a summary of your conversation with her."

"At this point," Bruce continued, "we have agreed only to investigate the claim. We have not agreed to file suit on her behalf. Please contact Ms. Rose and arrange to conduct a detailed initial interview. Do all things necessary, including drafting the complaint, to allow me to file suit on her behalf as quickly as possible, if we decide the case is worth pursuing. I'll be busy working on another case that is set for trial next month, but I'll be available at any time to answer questions you might have."

The retainer agreement that Mayda had prepared, anticipating the signature of Scarlet Rose, was included in the file Bruce handed to Marlene.

Contacting the Client

Marlene had her first real case, and she couldn't wait to begin. Marlene immediately called Ms. Rose to schedule a meeting, telling her to bring everything related to the case that she had in her possession, such as medical records, tax returns, correspondence, names and addresses of witnesses. In addition, Marlene wrote the following letter to Ms. Rose:

Bruce K. Franklin, P.A.
Attorney At Law
616 Turner Street
Clearwater, Atlantis 34616

May 1, 2000

Ms. Scarlet Rose
1111 Pine Street
Tarpon Springs, Atlantis 34689

Re: *Scarlet Rose v. Nickel & Dime, Inc.*

Dear Ms. Rose:

This is to confirm the meeting scheduled for Monday, May 8, 2000, at 10 a.m. at our office. The purpose of the appointment is to discuss in detail the incident that occurred at the Nickel & Dime store in Clearwater on January 31, when you tripped and fell over a box that was left in the aisle way. The appointment is for an hour, or more if necessary.

If they are available, please bring the following items with you:

- Your Social Security card
- Your insurance policy, address, and phone number of agent
- Your medical insurance policy, address and phone number of agent
- Any information you have about Nickel & Dime, including names of employees
- Photos of incident scene, injuries, or other damage
- Diagram of incident and location
- Newspaper clippings about the incident or any similar incidents
- Names, ages, and birth dates of your spouse and dependents
- Medical bills, attending physicians
- Medical insurance, medical history
- Occupation and salary information, plus records reflecting time lost from work
- Records relating to any accidents or injuries subsequent to this incident
- Records relating to any accidents or injuries prior to this incident
- Any correspondence regarding this incident

- Names, addresses, and phone numbers of other witnesses, such as friends and family
- Any other records, such as a diary you may have kept, or other papers or documents you believe may be significant.

Thank you for taking the time to gather as much of the information as you can before we meet. It will help us get to work on your case as quickly as possible. I look forward to meeting you. In the meantime, contact me at 462-1000 if you have any questions or need to reschedule for any reason.

Sincerely,

_____

Marlene Mertz
Paralegal

The Initial Interview

On the designated day, Scarlet Rose arrived at the office. She was of average height and build and made a nice physical presentation. She was dressed nicely but not extravagantly. She was nervous, but smiling. Marlene took her into the law library, which also serves as a conference room. After exchanging pleasantries with Ms. Rose and getting her a cup of coffee, Marlene asked Ms. Rose to tell what had happened that day at Nickel & Dime. Marlene did not take many notes while Ms. Rose was talking. After the interview was concluded, Marlene would have time to write a summary for Bruce. Marlene wanted to give Ms. Rose her undivided attention.

After Ms. Rose completed her narrative, Marlene asked Ms. Rose a number of questions from an initial client interview form that had been provided to her. She had Ms. Rose sign several authorizations for release of information, so she could get records from former employers and all doctors who treated her. Since Ms. Rose had been unable to locate all of her tax records, Marlene asked her to sign a form that would allow the IRS to release tax records.

Form 1.1 — Initial Client Interview

Background

- Name: Scarlet Rose
- Address: 1111 Pine Street, Tarpon Springs, Atlantis 34689
- Telephone: 727-786-6060 (home); 727-466-4444 (work)
- Social Security No: 234-34-4567
- Age: 38
- Date of Birth: 2/8/1962
- Marital Status: Divorced
- Spouse's Name: N/A
- Children: Sarah, age 13
- Education background, beginning with high school: (State name of institution, dates of attendance, and degree obtained): East Lake High School, 1979; St. Petersburg Junior College, 1982, A.A. in criminal justice
- Military Service: None
- Have you ever been arrested? No
- If yes, explain: N/A
- Employment History (State name, address, and telephone number of employer, length of employment, position held and salary): Pineapple County Public Defender's Office, 100 Main Street, Clearwater,

Atlantis 33759. 727-425-6821. 1982-present. Investigator, $36,000; Miscellaneous employment while in school at restaurants
- Client Income: $36,000
- Spouse: N/A
- Assets: Home, car and personal property

Nature of Claim/Liability

- Reason for seeking legal advice: Trip-and-fall incident at the Nickel & Dime store
- Date of incident: 1/31/2000
- Time: 12:45 p.m.
- Statute of Limitations: 1/31/2004
- Description of accident by client: I was walking down an aisle in the slippers department of the Nickel & Dime store, and I tripped over a box that I didn't see that had been placed in the middle of the aisle by an employee of Nickel & Dime.
- Description of accident scene: It was just off the main aisle. The aisle ran through the accessories department, which included slippers. It was several feet wide and 20 or 30 feet long.

Parties

- Names of potential defendant: Nickel & Dime, Inc.
- Address: 714 Main Street, Clearwater, Atlantis, 33759
- Phone: 727-753-6764
- Identify all parties to the incident: Only Nickel & Dime
- Information about other potential parties: None known of
- Have you discussed the incident with anyone else? Yes
- If yes, with whom have you discussed this incident? My mother, Jane Morris, and a few friends

Name of Medical Insurance Carrier

- Blue Cross/ Blue Shield
- Address: 2468 Meadow Street, Clearwater, Atlantis 34567
- Have you submitted a claim to your insurance carrier concerning this incident? Yes
- When was the claim submitted: 2/5/2000
- Have you received any response? Yes
- Has anyone attempted to contact you to discuss the incident? No
- If so, who? N/A
- Have you applied for workers compensation? No
- When? N/A
- Any response? N/A
- If so, what? N/A

Damages

- What injuries did you sustain? I hurt my back and required surgery.
- Were you treated for the injuries? Yes
- If so, when? 1/31/2000
- Where did you receive treatment? Please list all doctors & hospitals:

> Community Hospital
> 200 Main Street
> Clearwater, Atlantis
> 727-754-0373
> Treatment: emergency room treatment and surgery a month later

Period of Treatment: four hours and four days after surgery

Dr. Brendan Patrick
2244 Eagle Drive
Clearwater, Atlantis
727-861-8642
Treatment: He referred me to Dr. Beebe for surgery.
Period of Treatment: one visit

Dr. Michael Conor Mullan
700 Green Street
Clearwater, Atlantis
727-764-4444
Treatment: He is my primary care physician. I have seen him for years.
Period of Treatment: ongoing

Dr. Von N. Beebe
777 Coconut Street
Clearwater, Atlantis
727-777-7777
Treatment: He operated on me in March
Period of Treatment: about two months.

- Injuries are: Temporary ___ Permanent <u>Yes</u>
- Restrictions of Activities in Work, Sports, etc.? I wasn't able to work for three months. I haven't been able to play tennis in a long time. There were some other inconveniences too.
- Prior Medical Treatment, Doctors & Hospitals:

  Dr. Mullan:
  Treatment: see above

  Dr. Patrick: operated on my ankle in 1998

- Prior injuries related to present injuries? My back was bothering me a little before the incident, but nothing like it did after the incident. I fell and broke my ankle on a tennis court in 1998, and my back bothered me a little for a while.
- Any prior lawsuits? Yes, divorce, nothing else.
- Did you suffer any property damage? No
- If so, what damage? N/A
- Loss of Earnings: Yes. Two months not paid for by sick leave or vacation pay
- Days Hospitalized: Four days
- Days at Home: Three months
- Date Returned to Work: 5/1/2000
- Pain & Suffering? Yes
- How has the injury affected your life? I was hurt, in pain, unable to work, or to do numerous things for a couple of months. I was just about ready to start playing tennis again, but this set me back.
- Loss of Consortium: N/A

Defenses and Counterclaims

- What do you think the other party will say to its lawyer about the incident? I expect that they will say it was entirely my fault, and the store did nothing wrong.

Comparative Negligence

- Client in a hurry? A little. My mother was waiting for me.
- Distracted? No
- Vision obstructed? Yes
- If so, explain: The racks blocked my vision.
- Any potential claims by other parties against client? No
- If yes, what are the potential claims? N/A

Witnesses

- Were there any witnesses to the incident? Two store employees came up to me after the incident.
- If so what are their names? Marjorie and Caitlin, I think.
- Address if known: c/o Nickel & Dime
- Were any statements by the witnesses given to anyone? I don't know.
- If so, to whom? N/A
- Were any other parties injured to your knowledge? No
- If so, who was injured, and what was the extend of the injuries? N/A

Records/Physical Objects

- Are there any records concerning the incident? Yes
- If so, what records exist? Hospital records, employment records, EMT records, doctors' records
- Are there records that are not in the client's possession? Yes
- If so, where are the records located? With the doctors and the hospitals
- Were photos taken of the client's injuries? Yes
- If so, where are these photos located? I have some, and Nickel & Dime took some after the incident.
- Are there physical objects involved in the incident? Yes
- If so, what are the physical objects? The box I tripped over.

Other Law Firms

- Why did the client choose this office? Recommended by a friend
- Have any other law firms been consulted on this matter? No
- If so, what other firms have been consulted? N/A

Client's Goals

- What disposition of the matter does the client want? I think I deserve to be compensated for the pain and suffering I have endured and may endure in the future, plus pay all my medical bills and other expenses.
- Favorable to settlement? Yes
- Prefers trial? No
- Seeks vindication/revenge/specific performance? No
- Expectations of client realistic? Yes

Form 1.2 — The Client Retainer Agreement

General Contingent Fee Agreement

1. I, Scarlet Rose, having been injured on January 31, 2000, hereby retain Bruce K. Franklin, of the law firm of Bruce K. Franklin, P.A., as my attorney to make claims or bring suit against anyone necessary.

2. My attorney is to receive 33 1/3% of the gross settlement for legal services. This percentage will increase to 40% of the final judgment in the event of a trial. This agreement does not cover an appeal

of the final judgment to the court of appeals or supreme court. My attorney is hereby given a continuing lien in my claim and the proceeds thereof for the amount of the contingent fee.

3. I understand that I could retain the attorney to represent me in this action and compensate him on an hourly basis, but expressly decline to do so, subject to paragraph 8.

4. I also have been informed that I am responsible to pay for costs and disbursements including, but not limited to, court filing fees, court reporter fees, expert witness fees and expenses, long-distance telephone charges, and photocopying charges, in addition to postage.

5. Mr. Franklin may, but is not obligated to, advance these and other costs he believes are reasonable and necessary for preparing and presenting any claim. Any costs advanced by Mr. Franklin for which he was not reimbursed shall be paid by me.

6. I understand that if no recovery is obtained for me, no attorneys' fees shall be due; however, I will remain responsible for costs and disbursements. I also understand that no settlement shall be made without my approval.

7. I understand that Mr. Franklin may notify me, in writing, within 30 days of today's date, if he believes my case lacks merit or is not fiscally responsible to pursue, and he will have no further obligation to me or to my case at that point.

8. I understand that in the event that, even if it is contrary to the advice of my attorney, Mr. Franklin, I instruct Mr. Franklin to discontinue the matter, the matter shall be discontinued and I shall pay the law firm a reasonable hourly rate, plus expenses, for the time it has expended on my behalf.

9. It is expressly agreed and understood by me that no promises, assurances, or guarantees as to the outcome of this matter have been made by the attorney. Payment of costs is not contingent upon the outcome of this matter.

10. I agree to pay all costs for which I am responsible within 30 days of receiving a written statement thereof.

11. I have read and my attorney has explained the above ten points of this agreement, and I understand the same.

Dated: _____   Client: _____
                                                                                      Scarlet Rose

                                                             Witness: _____
                                                                                     Bruce K. Franklin

Form 1.3 — Statement of Client's Rights

Statement of Client's Rights

Before you, the prospective client, arrange a contingency fee agreement with a lawyer, you should understand this statement of your rights as a client. This statement is not a part of the actual contract between you and your lawyer, but as a prospective client, you should be aware of these rights:

1. There is no legal requirement that a lawyer charge a client a set fee or percentage of money recovered in a case. You, the client, have the right to talk with your lawyer about the proposed fee and to bargain about the rate or percentage as in any other contract. If you do not reach an agreement with one lawyer, you may talk with other lawyers.

2. Any contingency fee contract must be in writing, and you have three business days to reconsider the contract. You may cancel the contract without any reason if you notify your lawyer in writing within three business days of signing the contract. If you withdraw from the contract within the first three days, you do not owe the lawyer a fee, although you may be responsible for the lawyer's actual costs during that time. But if your lawyer begins to represent you, your lawyer may not withdraw from the case without giving you notice, delivering necessary papers to you, and allowing you time to employ another lawyer. Often, your lawyer may obtain court approval before withdrawing from a case. If you discharge your lawyer without good cause after the three-day period, you may have to pay a fee for the work the lawyer has done.

3. Before hiring a lawyer, you, the client, have the right to know about the lawyer's education, training and experience. If you ask, the lawyer should tell you specifically about his or her actual experience dealing with cases similar to yours. The lawyer should also provide information about special training or knowledge and give you this information in writing if you request it.

4. Before signing a contingency fee contract with you, a lawyer must advise you whether he or she intends to handle your case alone or whether other lawyers will be helping with the case. If your lawyer intends to refer the case to other lawyers, he or she should tell you what kind of fee-sharing arrangement will be made with the other lawyers. If lawyers from different firms will represent you, at least one lawyer from each law firm must sign the contingency fee contract.

5. If your lawyer intends to refer a case to another lawyer or counsel with other lawyers, your lawyer should tell you about that at the beginning. If your lawyer takes the case and later decides to refer it to another lawyer or to associate with other lawyers, you should sign a new contract that includes the new lawyers. You, the client, also have the right to consult with each lawyer working on your case. Each lawyer is legally responsible to represent your interests and is legally responsible for the acts of the other lawyers involved in the case.

6. You, the client, have the right to know in advance how you will need to pay the expenses and the legal fees at the end of the case. If you pay a deposit in advance for costs, you may ask reasonable questions about how the money will be or has been spent and how much of it remains unspent. Your lawyer should give a reasonable estimate about future necessary costs. If your lawyer agrees to lend or advance your money to prepare or research the case, you have the right to know periodically how much your lawyer has spent on your behalf. You also have the right to decide after consulting with your lawyer, how much money is to be spent to prepare a case. If you pay the expenses, you have a right to decide how much to spend. Your lawyer should also inform you whether the fee will be based on the gross amount recovered or on the amount recovered minus the costs.

7. You, the client, have the right to be told by your lawyer about possible adverse consequences if you lose the case. Those adverse consequences might include money that you might have to pay as attorney's fees to the other side.

8. You, the client, have the right to receive and approve a closing statement at the end of the case before you pay any money. The statement must list all of the financial details of the entire case, including the amount recovered, all expenses and a precise statement of your lawyer's fee. Until you approve the closing statement, you need not pay any money to anyone, including your lawyer. You also have the right to require every law firm working on your case to sign this closing statement.

9. You, the client, have the right to ask your lawyer at reasonable intervals how the case is progressing and to have these questions answered to the best of your lawyer's ability.

10. You, the client, have the right to make the final decision regarding settlement of a case. Your lawyer must notify you of all offers of settlement of a case. Your lawyer must notify you of all offers of settlement before and after the trial. Offers during the trial must be immediately communicated to you,

and you should consult with your lawyer regarding whether to accept a settlement. You, however, must make the final decision to accept or reject a settlement.

11. If at any time you, the client, believe that your lawyer has charged an excessive or illegal fee, you, the client, have the right to report the matter to the Atlantis Bar, the agency that oversees the practice and behavior of all lawyers in Atlantis. For information on how to reach the Atlantis Bar, call 352-561-5600, or contact the local bar association. Any disagreement between you and your lawyer about a fee can be taken to court, and you may wish to hire another lawyer to help you resolve this disagreement. Usually, fee disputes must be handled in a separate lawsuit, unless your fee contract provides for arbitration. You can request, but may not require, that a provision for arbitration (under Chapter 682, Atlantis Statutes, or under the fee arbitration rule of the Rules Regulating the Atlantis Bar) be included in your fee contract.

_____	_____
Attorney Signature	. Scarlet Rose
_____	_____
Date	Date

After Marlene finished meeting with Ms. Rose and taking all of the information she could think to obtain, she gave the file to Bruce, who spoke to Ms. Rose for a half hour. Marlene also prepared a memorandum to Bruce in which she summarized her meeting with Ms. Rose.

Inter-Office Memorandum

TO: Bruce Franklin
FROM: Marlene Mertz
RE: Summary of meeting with Scarlet Rose
DATE: May 8, 2000

Statement of Ms. Scarlet Rose:

Ms. Rose is a 38-year-old woman who stands five feet, five inches in height and weighs about 135 pounds. Her address is 1111 Pine Street, Tarpon Springs, Atlantis 34689. She says that her weight is about the same now as it was when the incident occurred on January 31, 2000. She graduated from East Lake High School in 1979 and completed an Associate of Arts curriculum at the St. Petersburg Jr. College with a degree in criminal justice. Ms. Rose was married to Bob Benjamin for 11 years from 1978 to 1990. There was one child born of the marriage, Sarah, who is now 13. Ms. Rose has decided to use her maiden name.

Ms. Rose acknowledges that she is better off now, following back surgery in March 2000, than she has been since her fall on the tennis court in January 1998. She says, however, that the fall at Nickel & Dime further aggravated her back condition. According to her, surgery was necessary because of this incident. She was unable to work for three months after the incident.

Ms. Rose says that she had driven from her home in Tarpon Springs to Clearwater to return a Christmas present from her daughter, a pair of jean shorts. According to her, the main aisle was blocked with a table and merchandise on display. She made a "judgment call" to take an alternative route to the area of the store where she was trying to go. She said that she took one step off the main aisle and landed inside a plastic box from which merchandise was being placed on the shelves. She has no idea how she got inside the box, but she said that both knees were inside the box, and she could not get herself out. She said that the box was open and she landed inside the box. As she was falling into the box, with both knees, she grabbed a rack in order to break her fall and pulled it down on top of her, twisting her back in the process.

She said that the box was in the middle of the aisle between two racks that were about three feet apart. She made her decision to take an alternative route because the aisle was blocked. Her eyes were looking in the general direction of where she was going and not down at the floor. She says that she may have seen the box out of her peripheral vision.

She remembers two Nickel & Dime employees coming to her aid. One had a bunch of keys on her wrist, and the other came from the front of the store. She did not see any salespersons anywhere near where she fell.

After the fall, she was taken to the emergency room of Community Hospital by EMTs. They conducted tests over several hours and discharged her to follow up with her treating physician, Dr. Mullan. She went to see him the next day, but he was not there. She was given pain medications and saw Dr. Mullan the following week. A week later, Dr. Mullan sent her to see Dr. Patrick, an orthopedic doctor. Dr. Mullan has treated her primarily for her general medical condition, but she considers him her primary treating physician, and he makes referrals for her to other doctors.

Plaintiff is an investigator for the Pineapple County Public Defender's office. The public defender's name is Robert Forest. Her salary is $36,000 per year. Because of this incident, she lost $6,000 of income, two months of salary that was not covered by her sick leave benefits or vacation pay.

There is a lien from Blue Cross/Blue Shield, her group health insurer through her employer. She had an 80/20 co-pay and had to pay 20% of all bills. The total of all medical bills is approximately $44,000. She owes $8,000 of those bills and has paid some portion of it already. There are outstanding bills against her.

As far as her current ailments are concerned, she blames her back problems entirely upon the fall at Nickel & Dime. She says that, in addition to the pain, she was having some degree of numbness all of the time. Dr. Patrick told her to see Dr. Beebe, who ultimately performed back surgery, involving the insertion of two titanium rods in her back in March 2000. Since the surgery, she says her back is much better. She has not seen any other doctor for her back since she was released by Dr. Beebe in April.

Regarding her prior medical condition and pre-existing back problem, she says she had a few problems with her back after a fall on the tennis court in 1998. Although she is not back to playing tennis, she feels as she did before the 1998 fall. She had no back problems for six months before the accident. She has not seen Dr. Beebe since April 2000, and she has no plans to go back and see him. Her back is the only problem that she attributes to this incident and, again, she says that the surgery was caused entirely by the incident at Nickel & Dime.

Gathering Information About the Claim

To get all medical records and billing information, Marlene wrote letters to the doctors and medical providers, enclosing authorizations Ms. Rose had signed for release of information. She also wrote to all the doctors who had seen Ms. Rose before the incident at Nickel & Dime, since Bruce would need to review those records.

She wrote letters to all known witnesses, telling them that Bruce represented Ms. Rose and their assistance and cooperation would be necessary. Marlene went to the Nickel & Dime store where the incident occurred and took photographs of the inside of the store and, in particular, the accessories department. Even though the scene was, in all likelihood, not the same as it was on the day of the incident, and the photos were not admissible, they helped Marlene get a better understanding of the case. She thought they would help Bruce as well.

Witness Statements

Marlene knew the store employees would probably refuse to talk to her about the case, either because they did not want to get involved or because they did not want to help a case against the store. If Marlene had been able to talk to any witnesses, statements would have been taken and summarized, not reported verbatim. Marlene would not have recorded the statements unless Bruce told her to do so. Marlene knew that if she did record the statements that she could be required to turn over, through discovery, each such statement to the defense attorney.

The only witness statement she was able to obtain was from Ms. Rose's mother, Jane Morris, which Marlene summarized in a memorandum to Bruce.

Inter-Office Memorandum

TO: Bruce Franklin
FROM: Marlene Mertz
RE: Witness statement of Jane Morris
DATE: May 15, 2000

Jane Morris

Ms. Morris is the mother of Ms. Scarlet Rose, our client. She remarried after the death of her husband (Scarlet Rose's father) to a man named Frederick Morris. She is 58 years old and speaks with a heavy southern drawl. She is a sweet and demure woman. She took care of her daughter for a month or so after the 1998 incident and served her every meal in bed on a tray during that period. Ms. Morris said that she did all of the laundry, vacuuming, took care of her granddaughter, Sarah, drove her every place — basically waiting on Mr. Rose hand and foot. Ms. Morris said that Ms. Rose gradually returned to her own home and was doing better, but Ms. Rose and Sarah returned to Ms. Morris' home after the Nickel & Dime fall for another month or so. Once again, Ms. Morris did many of the same things to help her.

Ms. Morris stated that she went with Ms. Rose to the Nickel & Dime on the day in question, but she stayed in the car. She said that someone came out of the store, walked up to her car, and told her that her daughter had been in an incident. When she walked into the store, she found her daughter lying on the floor complaining of pain. She said that she saw a plastic box in the aisle and that the aisle was blocked, but she did not see the racks pulled down. The racks were standing when she got there. She was more concerned about her daughter's medical condition than she was about who was at fault, and she did not speak to anyone at the scene about why the incident occurred or how.

Ms. Morris will be able to testify about Ms. Rose's medical condition before and after the incident and about what she saw when she entered the store after the incident had occurred. She will be a good witness for Ms. Rose.

Obtaining Medical Records

Knowing that she could not rely entirely upon everything that Scarlet Rose had told her, Marlene began to obtain medical records directly from the doctors and hospitals that had treated Ms. Rose, especially records from the doctor who had been treating her before the incident. She sent the following authorization for release of medical records to all doctors identified by Ms. Rose.

Authorization for Release of Medical Records

Name: Scarlet Rose
Social Security No.: 234-34-4567
Date of Birth: 2/8/1962
Age: 38
Address: 1111 Pine Street, Tarpon Springs, Atlantis 34689
Phone: 727-786-6060

By my signature below, I hereby authorize and request that Michael Mullan, M.D., provide my attorney, Bruce K. Franklin, access to all my medical records and copies thereof as may be requested.

I request that this information remain valid until further notice from me. This authorization includes, but is not limited, to the following:

> All medical and hospital records, including medical history, tests, test results, diagnoses, treatment, x-ray reports, current medical status, prognosis, bills, and any other information designated in the attached letter relevant to treatment occurring from 1990 to the present.
>
> All medical insurance records, including plan name, plan number, claim number, service description, dates, covered expenses and non-covered expenses, total benefits paid, and provider.

```
                                              _____
                                                                  Scarlet Rose
                                              _____
                                                                          Date
```

Marlene sent the authorization to all of Ms. Rose's doctors, including Dr. Von N. Beebe, who performed the surgery, and Dr. Brendan Patrick, her prior treating physician. She prepared a transmittal letter.

Bruce K. Franklin, P.A.
Attorney At Law
616 Turner Street
Clearwater, Atlantis 34616

May 24, 2000

Von N. Beebe, M.D.
777 Coconut Street
Clearwater, Atlantis 33759

Re: Request for Medical Records

Dear Dr. Beebe:

This office represents Scarlet Rose with regard to a potential claim for personal injuries sustained in a slip-and-fall accident that occurred on January 31, 2000, at the Nickel & Dime store in Clearwater. As stated in the attached Authorization, you are hereby requested to provide the undersigned with all records in your possession relating to any care and treatment that you have provided Scarlet Rose at any time.

Please bill us for all reasonable costs of copying and mailing the records. We appreciate your assistance and cooperation.

Sincerely,

_____
Marlene Mertz
Paralegal

cc: Scarlet Rose

To the Community Hospital, Marlene sent a slightly different letter.

Bruce K. Franklin, P.A.
Attorney At Law
616 Turner Street
Clearwater, Atlantis 34616

May 24, 2000

Clearwater Community Hospital
Medical Records Department
1000 Main Street
Clearwater, Atlantis 33759

Re: Request for Medical Records

Patient: Scarlet Rose, 1111 Pine Street, Tarpon Springs, Atlantis 34689
Soc. Sec. No: 234-34-4567
Date of Birth: 2/8/1962
Dates of Care: 1/31/2000 to 2/10/2000; 3/17/2000 to 3/21/2000

Scarlet Rose has retained this office to represent her interests with regard to a personal injury matter. Enclosed is a current Authorization to Release Medical Information executed by our client. Please send a copy of the following records to the address listed above:

(X)   Discharge summary
(X)   ER and outpatient reports
(X)   Patient's chart
(X)   History and physical
(X)   Operative and pathology reports
(X)   X-ray reports
(X)   Lab reports
(X)   Progress noted by physicians and nurses
(X)   Doctors' orders
(X)   Consultation reports
(X)   Nurses' notes

On receipt of the records, our firm will submit reasonable payment for any preparation fee. Thank you for your assistance.

Sincerely,

_____

Marlene Mertz,
Paralegal

cc: Ms. Scarlet Rose

Obtaining Records

Employment Records

In letters to Ms. Rose's former employers, Marlene used the format above but substituted a request for employment records with a description of Ms. Rose's position, her length of employment, her compensation and benefits, her record of absences, her performance record, and her accumulated sick leave.

School Records

In her letter to St. Petersburg Junior College requesting academic records, she asked for academic and school records showing attendance dates, evaluations, grade performance, results of psychological, aptitude, and achievement tests, class ranking, and teachers' names.

Locating the Defendant

Marlene knew that the local Nickel & Dime store was just down the street, but she wasn't sure who owned it or who should be served. Since Nickel & Dime was a corporation, she searched for information about it online at the web page of the Atlantis Secretary of State. She also wrote to the office of the Atlantis Secretary of State's corporations section for a report of current directors, officers, and registered agent. A form was available for use, so Marlene simply filled out the form and mailed it.

Analyzing the Claim

Summarizing Medical Records

After a few weeks, Marlene began to receive the requested medical records. She summarized the records for Bruce and created a memorandum to the file.

Inter-Office Memorandum

TO: Bruce Franklin
FROM: Marlene Mertz
RE: Medical Records Summary
DATE: May 27, 2000

Michael Conor Mullan, M.D.

Dr. Mullan is a general practitioner who has been treating Ms. Rose since 1989. He has seen her for different problems, including various injuries from playing tennis. None were serious until the ankle fracture in 1998. Ms. Rose went to see Dr. Mullan shortly after this incident.

Dr. Mullan's charts show that he referred Ms. Rose to an orthopedic specialist, Dr. Patrick, for the ankle fracture of 1998. He was aware that during that time an MRI was performed because of her complaints of back pain. Before the incident, he prescribed anti-inflammatory medications and pain relievers for minor aches and pains of muscular over-use relating to Ms. Rose's tennis playing. Dr. Mullan's notes reflect that Ms. Rose had improved since the back surgery in March 2000, and he has not treated her back since the ankle incident. Dr. Mullan is not an orthopedist. He is a specialist in general medicine.

Von N. Beebe, M.D.

Dr. Beebe is a neurosurgeon. He first saw Ms. Rose on March 3, 2000, when she was referred to him by Dr. Patrick. He diagnosed her problem as intractable low back pain with radiating pain into the right leg. His notes say that he was told by the plaintiff that she had fully recovered from the first accident involving the ankle fracture but became worse because of the incident at Nickel & Dime.

Dr. Beebe ordered an MRI when he first saw Ms. Rose. His notes indicate that he offered Ms. Rose two options: conservative treatment or an aggressive dual rod stabilization surgery. Ms. Rose opted for surgery, which took place on March 17.

Surgically, Dr. Beebe inserted two rods into the L4-L5 level. He indicated in a letter to Dr. Patrick, who referred Ms. Rose to Dr. Beebe, that the problem was a severe collapse and disruption due to disc disease. There is a discussion of a disk either bulging or being herniated, but Dr. Beebe's conclusion is unclear. There is reference to degenerative disc disease and scoliosis. He reports that Ms. Rose is doing well after the surgery. After a few weeks of physical therapy, he discharged her from his care in late April.

Brendan Patrick, M.D.

Dr. Patrick is an orthopedic specialist. He treated Ms. Rose for approximately six months in early 1998 for an ankle fracture and some related back problems that apparently resulted from her ankle injury. Ms. Rose was first referred to Dr. Patrick by Dr. Mullan. In June 1998, Dr. Patrick ordered an MRI of Ms. Rose's back, which was negative. Ms. Rose also went to see him after the fall at Nickel & Dime, but his records reflect that Dr. Patrick referred Ms. Rose to Dr. Beebe because Dr. Patrick does not operate on backs.

Physical Therapist

Ms. Rose was referred to physical therapy for approximately three weeks after the March 17 surgery. The physical therapist's bill totals approximately $1,000. There is nothing noteworthy in the records other than the fact that Ms. Rose was very cooperative and did very well.

Community Hospital Emergency Room Records

Ms. Rose was taken to the emergency room of the Community Hospital for the 1998 ankle injury, and the January 31, 2000, incident at Nickel & Dime. The records reflect that x-rays were not taken. After several hours, Ms. Rose was released and told to see an orthopedic specialist as soon as possible. She was given some muscle relaxants and pain medications. The diagnosis was lumbar sprain/strain.

Emergency Medical Technicians

The records reflect that at approximately 1:15 p.m. on January 31, 2000, Ms. Rose was transported on a stretcher from Nickel & Dime to the Community Hospital. She was in acute pain and discomfort in her lower back because of a trip-and-fall incident. Otherwise, her vital signs and medical status were normal.

Community Hospital Records

Records were also received for the four days that plaintiff spent in the hospital while undergoing the surgery performed by Dr. Beebe. The records reflect that her hospital stay was unremarkable and that she was discharged with instructions to go to physical therapy.

Determining the Value of the Claim

Marlene obtained all the medical bills and other damages, such as lost wages, to determine the "special damages" in the claim.

Dr. Beebe (surgery)	$25,000
Community Hospital (surgery)	$16,000
Emergency Physicians	$250
Community Hospital (emergency room)	$550
Dr. Patrick	$100
Dr. Mullan	$100
Physical Therapists	$1,000
Radiology Consultants (MRI)	$1,000
Amount paid by Scarlet Rose personally:	$8,000
Medical bills paid by Blue Cross/Blue Shield	$36,000
Total of all medical bills:	$44,000
Amount of wage loss:	$6,000
Total amount of special damages:	$50,000

Research

Marlene took the facts provided to her by the client and Ms. Morris and conducted research to determine whether the applicable law would support Ms. Rose's claim. She conducted research on her computer using a legal database. By analyzing Atlantis cases, she determined that, in order for Ms. Rose to prevail, she would have to prove that Nickel & Dime either knew, or should have known by the exercise of reasonable diligence that a dangerous condition existed and that Nickel & Dime failed to correct the dangerous condition. She located a number of cases. The *Butte* case was the most on point.

JUDITH L. BUTTE,
    Appellant,

v.   District Court of Appeal of Atlantis, Second District. July 25, 1986.

MART CORPORATION,
    Appellee

Customer brought negligence action against store for injuries sustained when struck by an oversized garden cart pushed by an unknown customer. The Circuit Court, Charlotte County, Michael Earle, J., granted store summary judgment, and customer appealed. The District Court of Appeal, Schoolmaster, J., held that: (1) store was not an insurer of customer's safety, but it did have a duty to exercise ordinary care and to keep its aisles and passageways in a reasonably safe condition, this included eliminating dangerous conditions of which it had actual or constructive notice, and (2) question of fact precluding summary judgment was raised as to whether store knowingly left an oversized float, which it knew to be unwieldy and not easily controlled by someone unfamiliar with it, in a place where the float could be and was frequently and customarily used by customers.

Reversed and remanded.

Gary L. Gorday for appellant.

Darryl Stewart for appellee.

SCHOOLMASTER, Judge.

Appellant, Judith L. Butte, appeals from a final summary judgment entered against her. We reverse.

Butte brought a negligence action against appellee, Mart Corporation, because of injuries she sustained in one of its stores. While shopping in the garden department of a Mart store in Charlotte County, Atlantis, Butte was struck by an oversized garden cart. An unknown customer had pushed the cart between two display tables, and as it entered the aisle in which Butte was standing, it struck her on the back of her leg, causing her to fall onto and across the cart.

Mart moved for summary judgment on the grounds that its negligence, if any, was not the proximate cause of the accident and that there was an independent intervening cause of Butte's injuries. Depositions of three store employees were submitted at the hearing on Mart's motion. According to the deposition of the manager, the carts, referred to as "floats," were approximately three feet wide, five feet long, and one and one-half-feet high. They were unwieldy and not easily controlled by someone who was unfamiliar with their operation. Some of the floats were customarily kept in the garden department area, but they were not to be used by customers because merchandise would be damaged as the floats were moved through the aisles. According to the deposition of an assistant store manager, the floats were used by employees in the storeroom, within the store to move merchandise, and in the garden department to assist stockpersons in loading large bags of fertilizer into customers' cars. The store did not want customers to use the floats because, in attempting to load bags of fertilizer onto floats, customers would pick up the bags incorrectly and would rip the bags and destroy merchandise. The cashier employed in the garden department, Linda Myers, testified by deposition that the floats were frequently and customarily used by customers to cart bigger merchandise, such as plants and bags of fertilizer.

In addition to the deposition testimony of all witnesses, the testimony and answers to interrogatories propounded by Mart were filed in support of the motion. In these answers, Butte stated that immediately after the accident the employee who took her statement told her that the accident was not the fault of the customer who had moved the float but was the fault of the employees who had placed the float in the store. The trial court granted Mart's motion for summary judgment, and Butte filed a timely notice of appeal.

We agree that Mart did not carry its burden of proving the nonexistence of a genuine issue as to any material fact and its entitlement to a judgment as a matter of law.

As Butte was a business invitee, Mart owed her a duty to exercise reasonable care for her safety. Although Mart is not an insurer of its customers' safety, Mart does have the duty to exercise ordinary care to keep its aisles and passageways in a reasonably safe condition, and this includes eliminating dangerous conditions of which it has actual or constructive notice. A store may be held liable on the basis of constructive notice if the condition is one that has existed for a sufficient length of time such that the owner should have known of it, regardless of whether the condition was created by a store employee or by an outsider. The evidence would support a finding that Mart knowingly left an oversized float, which it knew to be unwieldy and not easily controlled by someone unfamiliar with it, in a place where the float could be, and was, frequently and customarily, used by customers.

This was done even though the store had knowledge that its use by customers would likely result in damage to property and in spite of its policy not to allow customers access to the floats.

The trial court ruled that, as a matter of law, Butte's injuries were not the reasonably foreseeable consequence of Mart's negligence. Mart concedes that it could be foreseen that an injury "might" occur to a patron because of the floats but contends that foreseeability is not what "might" possibly occur. In support of its argument, Mart relies upon *Shep v. Store, Inc.*, a case where a customer was injured on an escalator when another customer pushed a baby stroller into her. The court found there was nothing inherently dangerous about a mother conveying a child in a stroller and refused to require an owner of a public building to anticipate such injury. The court indulged itself in the presumption that those who use escalators will conduct themselves as ladies and gentlemen. We agree that no liability exists when the act complained of involves a sudden, unexpected action by a tortfeasor where there is no prior indication that the tortfeasor is engaging in the type of conduct that causes the injury.

Here, however, evidence would support a finding that a dangerous condition was created by Mart itself, and the store knew that use of the floats by customers had caused property damage in the past. The fact that the act resulted in injury to a person rather than property does not, as a matter of law, change the result. The question of foreseeability was for the trier of fact to decide.

We also disagree with Mart's contention that the unknown customer was an independent, intervening cause that operated to relieve Mart from liability for any alleged negligent act or omission. In order for injuries to be a foreseeable consequence of a negligent act, it is not necessary that the initial tortfeasor be able to foresee the exact nature and extent of the injuries or the precise manner in which the injuries will occur. It is only necessary that the tortfeasor be able to foresee that some injury will likely result in some manner as a consequence of its negligent act. If the harm that occurs is within the scope of danger created by a defendant's negligent conduct, then such harm is a reasonably foreseeable consequence of the negligence. The question of foreseeability, as it relates to proximate cause, and whether an intervening cause is foreseeable is for the trier of fact. The question of the extent of Mart's responsibility to anticipate the consequences of making the floats accessible to customers, in spite of its policy of not allowing customers to use them, was therefore the province of the trier of fact and should not have been summarily resolved in favor of either party. We, accordingly, reverse and remand for proceedings consistent herewith.

Chang, J., and Anderson, J., concur.

Finding Out About Insurance

Marlene decided to determine if Nickel & Dime was covered by insurance, was self-insured, or able to pay any judgment from its capital or cash reserves and operating accounts. She wrote the following letter, pursuant to an applicable Atlantis Statute, asking Nickel & Dime if there was insurance to cover Ms. Rose's claim.

Bruce K. Franklin, P.A.
Attorney At Law
616 Turner Street
Clearwater, Atlantis 34616

June 14, 2000

Nickel & Dime Department Store
714 Main Street
Clearwater, Atlantis 33759

RE: *Scarlet Rose v. Nickel & Dime, Inc.*

Dear Sir or Madam:

Our office represents Scarlet Rose with regard to a potential claim for personal injuries sustained in a trip-and-fall accident that occurred on January 31, 2000, at the Nickel & Dime store in Clearwater. Pursuant to the applicable statute, you are hereby requested to provide the following information:

- The name of your insurer
- The name of each insured
- The limits of the liability coverage
- A copy of the policy
- A statement of any policy defense or coverage issue that such insurer reasonably believes is available to disallow any coverage for the incident described above.

Your immediate attention to this matter is appreciated.

Sincerely,

_____

Marlene Mertz
Paralegal

cc: Scarlet Rose

Evaluating the Claim

At this point, Marlene had done everything she could think of to analyze and assemble the claim. Now her job was to assess the claim and decide what to recommend to Bruce. Marlene knew that there were three aspects of this particular claim. These aspects, which exist in every lawsuit or claim, are 1) liability; 2) damages; and 3) ability to collect. She recognized immediately that there was, in all probability, an ability to collect a judgment against Nickel & Dime if Ms. Rose could convince a jury that Nickel & Dime was negligent. Based on the *Butte* case, Marlene felt that Nickel and Dime was negligent in leaving the box unattended in a walkway; therefore, Nickel and Dime was liable for the injury.

Because Ms. Rose had undergone major back surgery involving fusion of two disks and the insertion of rods in her back, Marlene felt that the damages were substantial. The medical bill for the neurosurgeon alone was $25,000.

The next step was to decide what the claim was worth. Since Marlene had no previous experience with juries or jury verdicts, she was at a complete loss as to how to evaluate the claim. She remembered being told about *Jury Verdict Reporter*, which reported jury verdicts and provided information about trials occurring throughout the state. This service is available online for a fee or could be used without charge at the local law library. Marlene decided to find what juries were awarding for a disk problem that required the insertion of rods and the fusion of disks. She found the following case:

Carrie Lauth v. Grocery Store, Inc.

FACTS: Plaintiff fell in a department store on a banana peel that had been left in an aisle. Plaintiff presented testimony from other patrons that the banana peel had been in the aisle for at least 15 minutes. Someone else had complained about it to the manager, but the area had not been cleaned. Defendant argued that the plaintiff was partially at fault for not being more careful.

NATURE OF INJURY: Compression fracture at L4-L5. Five months before this accident, plaintiff fractured her clavicle and rib and had low back complaints. X-rays taken from the first accident did not show a compression fracture. Plaintiff underwent surgical diskectomy. Medical bills were $30,000. Defendant alleged that plaintiff's condition was pre-existing. Dr. Robers was plaintiff's treating physician.

VERDICT: $236,952 for plaintiff on July 2, 1997.

Plaintiff's Negligence: 5%
Defendant's Negligence: 95%

(Editor's Note: Defendant offered $95,000; Plaintiff's demand was $125,000.)

Marlene thought *Lauth* was strikingly similar to Scarlet Rose's case. Therefore, the major obstacle to recovery of monetary damages from Nickel & Dime in this case seemed to be whether Nickel & Dime would be found negligent or if a jury would decide that Ms. Rose should have been more careful. Since the state of Atlantis is a pure comparative negligence state, Marlene thought that if a jury would decide by a preponderance of the evidence (*i.e.*, more likely than not) that Nickel & Dime was even partly responsible for the injury, then the lawsuit was worth pursuing.

Recommendation as to Whether to Pursue the Claim

Since Scarlet Rose was fully recovered from surgery and not still under a doctor's care, nor did she have anymore scheduled visits, she was at maximum medical improvement (MMI). Although she was not quite as good as she was going to be, as far as the injury and damage sustained in the trip-and-fall incident at Nickel & Dime was concerned, it was the right time to file suit.

The Demand Letter

Once Marlene completed her analysis, she scheduled a time to discuss her evaluation with Bruce. Bruce told Marlene that it was his customary practice and procedure to draft a demand letter and prepare a settlement demand before drafting the complaint and filing suit to see if the case could be settled without filing suit. He wouldn't send it out until he was sure Ms. Rose was at MMI and he had completely discussed the situation with Ms. Rose. Since Marlene had told him that Ms. Rose was at MMI, Bruce asked Marlene to draft a demand letter. After discussing the situation with Ms. Rose, Bruce sent the following letter to Nickel and Dime.

Bruce K. Franklin, P.A.
Attorney At Law
616 Turner Street
Clearwater, Atlantis 34616

June 19, 2000

Director
Loss Prevention Department
Nickel & Dime Inc.
Post Office Box 2000
Boston, Massachusetts 01267

Re: Claim for injuries and damages submitted on behalf of Scarlet Rose
Date of Incident: January 31, 2000
Place of Incident: Clearwater, Atlantis

Dear Director:

Scarlet Rose fell in the Nickel & Dime store located in Clearwater, Atlantis, on January 31, 2000. She sustained a very serious injury to her back that ultimately required surgery to alleviate her pain. At this time, I hereby submit the following materials to you for consideration in an attempt to settle this claim without the necessity of litigation. The enclosed materials and this letter are to be considered for settlement purposes only.

Facts

At the time of the incident, my client was a business invitee on the premises of Nickel & Dime. Ms. Rose went to the store to exchange an item that had been purchased at that store. While walking in an aisle within the accessories department, she tripped over a box of merchandise that was on the floor in the middle of the aisle. The box was partially hidden from view due to a large rack next to the box. Ms. Rose fell forward and attempted to break her fall by grabbing onto the display rack, which then toppled down on her. As she fell to the floor, she twisted her back and felt severe pain and discomfort in her low and mid-back areas.

As you know, if the owner of a store such as yours, or its agents and employees, creates a dangerous condition on the premises or had either actual or constructive notice of a dangerous condition, an owner is liable for damages sustained in a trip-and-fall resulting from the condition. In this case, employees and agents of Nickel & Dime placed a box on the floor in an aisle. Specifically, the box restricted the walk areas between display racks and created a hazardous condition.

There were no warning signs in the store to put my client on notice to be aware of the possible dangerous condition. I enclose several pictures that were taken a few days after the incident, clearly depicting the cluttered nature of the store and the resulting dangerous condition.

Liability

In our view, liability clearly rests upon the store for creating the hazardous condition that directly and proximately caused the incident. As a direct result of the store's negligence, my client suffered severe injuries and significant damages. Based on the facts in this case, it is reasonable to conclude that a jury would find Nickel & Dime 100% responsible for this accident.

Injuries and Damages

Immediately after the accident, Ms. Rose, complaining of low back pain, was taken to the Community Hospital emergency room via ambulance. Ms. Rose was examined and discharged with instructions to follow up with her regular doctor. Copies of the ER records are enclosed.

In February, Ms. Rose saw Dr. Mullan with complaints of low back and knee pain. Ms. Rose attributed the increased pain and discomfort to her recent fall at Nickel & Dime. Ms. Rose was homebound at this point, and Dr. Mullan prescribed pain medications and referred Ms. Rose to Dr. Patrick for consultation regarding the injury. Dr. Mullan continued to treat Ms. Rose on a regular basis for other problems and remained knowledgeable of her condition. Dr. Patrick immediately referred Ms. Rose to Dr. Beebe, a neurosurgeon. Copies of Dr. Mullan's records and Dr. Patrick's records are enclosed.

After conducting numerous tests, including an MRI, on March 17, Dr. Beebe performed on Ms. Rose surgery that involved the placement of two titanium rods in her back and a laminectomy at L4-L5. Copies of Dr. Beebe's records are enclosed.

The care and treatments, including the back surgery, were causally related to the injury of January 31, 2000. Copies of the hospital records and records for rehabilitation and home health services are enclosed for your review.

As a direct and proximate result of Nickel & Dime's negligence, Ms. Rose has incurred past medical bills of $44,000. Enclosed are copies of medical bills and a damage printout. In addition to these damages, Ms. Rose has experienced pain and suffering related to her injury and the medical procedures required to address her problems. She required home assistance during the period before the surgery and immediately thereafter. She missed three months of work and has a wage loss of $6,000.

Due to the clear negligence of Nickel & Dime, and the substantial damages that have resulted, a demand of $300,000 is hereby made. Please contact me within 30 days of the date of this letter if you desire to resolve the matter amicably. I look forward to hearing from you.

Very truly yours,

_____
Bruce K. Franklin

cc: Ms. Scarlet Rose

Chapter Two

THE PLEADINGS STAGE
FROM THE
PLAINTIFF'S PERSPECTIVE

Drafting the Complaint

Nickel & Dime decided not to settle the claim, and Bruce instructed Marlene to draft a complaint. Marlene had never drafted a complaint before. She asked Bruce if he had filed similar cases that she could review. Bruce suggested that she look at a few closed cases in his office and also visit the courthouse to review pleadings filed by other attorneys in similar cases.

Marlene remembered that the basics of a pleading were a caption, the body; a prayer for relief, and the subscription. Drawing upon her training, and after reviewing other complaints, Marlene drafted the following complaint.

Form 2.1 — Compliant

IN THE SIXTH JUDICIAL CIRCUIT COURT
IN AND FOR PINEAPPLE COUNTY, ATLANTIS

SCARLET ROSE,
      Plaintiff,

v.   Civil Action No.:

NICKEL & DIME, INC.,
      Defendant.

Complaint

Plaintiff, Scarlet Rose, sues defendant, Nickel & Dime, and alleges the following:

1. This is an action for damages for an unspecified amount of money in excess of $15,000.

2. Plaintiff, Scarlet Rose, resides in Pineapple County, Atlantis.

3. Defendant, Nickel & Dime, Inc., is an out-of-state corporation authorized to do business in the State of Atlantis and has a place of business in Clearwater, Atlantis.

4. On January 31, 2000, Scarlet Rose entered the Nickel & Dime store located at 714 Main Street, Clearwater, which was and is owned by the defendant, Nickel & Dime, Inc., to exchange a pair of shorts that had been purchased at the Nickel & Dime store on a prior date.

5. On that date, and at that location, plaintiff tripped and fell over a box or boxes that had been left in the aisle where patrons, such as Scarlet Rose, would walk.

6. As a result of the incident complained of, plaintiff was seriously injured, requiring extensive medical care and treatment, and incurred substantial bills, expenses, and other financial loss, in addition to pain, suffering, mental anguish, loss of past wages, loss of ability to earn wages in the future, loss of income earning ability, and a permanent injury that will require continuing care and treatment in the future.

7. Plaintiff alleges that the incident and all subsequent injury and damages she sustained were a direct result of the negligence of the defendant, Nickel & Dime, Inc., in failing to maintain the premises properly.

8. Plaintiff further alleges that the defendant, Nickel & Dime, Inc., had an affirmative duty to maintain its stores in a fashion that patrons, such as the plaintiff, could reasonably expect the walkways and aisles to be free from hazards such as the box that injured the plaintiff when she tripped and fell.

9. Plaintiff further alleges that the defendant breached the duty of care it owed her by negligently placing the box in the aisle and failing to keep the aisles free from debris and other objects, such as the box that the plaintiff tripped over and, as a result of the negligence of the defendant or its employees and agents for whom defendant is legally responsible, plaintiff suffered injury and damages.

WHEREFORE plaintiff, Scarlet Rose, demands judgment for damages against defendant, Nickel & Dime, for an unspecified amount of money in excess of $15,000 to compensate her for her loss, including all costs and interest, and for such other and further relief as this court may deem just and proper.

Furthermore and finally, plaintiff demands a trial by jury on all issues so triable.

Bruce K. Franklin
Attorney for Plaintiff

Bruce approved the draft Marlene had prepared and instructed her to prepare discovery to file with the complaint.

Discovery Available to Plaintiff at the Time the Complaint Is Filed

Although there was plenty of time before the four-year statute of limitations for negligence actions expired, Bruce knew that Scarlet Rose, like virtually everyone who files a lawsuit, hoped to settle the case, or to win a money judgment, as soon as possible. Attaching discovery requests to the complaint would force the defendant to respond more quickly than if Marlene had sent the discovery requests after filing the complaint, so Bruce told Marlene to attach them to the complaint. Filing these requests promptly might speed up the amount of time necessary to get the case to trial.

Interrogatories

Marlene remembered there was a limit to the number of questions that could be asked of an opposing party through written interrogatories. She looked at the interrogatories approved by the Supreme Court of Atlantis, found in the appendix to the rules, and drafted a set of interrogatories for Bruce to review. Since she could ask only 30 questions, including subparts, she also looked at the negligence section of the *Proof of Facts* volume in the law library to decide what questions to ask.

Form 2.2 — Interrogatories

IN THE SIXTH JUDICIAL CIRCUIT COURT
IN AND FOR PINEAPPLE COUNTY, ATLANTIS

SCARLET ROSE,
     Plaintiff,

v.   Civil Action No.:

NICKEL & DIME, INC.,
     Defendant.

Plaintiff's First Interrogatories to Defendant Nickel & Dime

1.   Please state the names, addresses, and job titles and, if an officer of a corporation, identify such office or position, of all persons participating in the answering of these Interrogatories.

2.   Were you aware, before the filing of the Complaint in this action, that the plaintiff, Scarlet Rose, was injured while in Nickel & Dime located in Clearwater, Atlantis, on January 31, 2000?

3.   State the name, address, and job titles of any and all persons who were responsible for the maintenance of the area where the incident occurred.

4.   Plaintiff, Scarlet Rose, alleges that the boxes placed in the customer walkway caused her to fall. Do you contend that the boxes were not located in the aisle, nor did they impede the path of the customer, or cause the plaintiff to fall and sustain injuries? If so, state the reasons for said belief and what you contend did cause injuries to the plaintiff.

5.   Did you, or anyone on your behalf, conduct a formal investigation of the facts and circumstances surrounding the incident? If so, state the date it was made; the name, address, occupation of each person who made it; and whether any report was made of it.

6.   Were any statements obtained by you, or in your behalf, from any person concerning the accident? If so, state the date and time it was obtained; the name, address, occupation of the person who made it; and whether it was written or oral. If written, the name and address of the person who has custody of it.

7.   Did any person witness the accident? If so, state the name or other means of identification, address, occupation and name of employer, and the location from which he or she witnessed the accident.

8.   Do you know of anyone who took, or claims to have taken, photographs of the scene of the accident, the persons, or objects involved? If so, state the subject matter of the photographs, the date each was taken, the identity and address of the persons taking the photographs, and the name and address of each person who has possession or control of the photographs.

9.   Are you protected by any insurance company indemnifying you against the type of risk on which plaintiff's claim is based? If so, state the name and address of each insurer, the number of each policy, and the type of coverage.

10.   Did you have an agent or employee whose duties included the cleaning, maintenance, or care of the subject area? If so, please state the name, address, job title, and a description of his or her duties.

11. List all accidents that occurred before January 31, 2000, involving the customer walkway, aisles and surrounding area. Specifically, list the date, type of accident, and the persons involved.

12. For every allegation in plaintiff's Complaint that you will or have denied, state the specific grounds for the denial.

13. State whether any representative, agent, or employee of Nickel & Dime has received any complaints concerning boxes being placed in the aisles. (Yes or No)

14. If the answer to No. 13 is "Yes," list the date of the complaint, the nature of the complaint and the actions taken by Nickel & Dime, Inc., to remedy the complaint.

15. Is a diary, log book, or similar written record maintained containing the day-to-day happenings at Nickel & Dime? If the answer is in the affirmative, where and in whose custody are the above referenced records for the months preceding January 31, 2000?

16. What statements were made in your presence by plaintiff or anyone else after the accident on January 31, 2000?

17. If you would do so without a motion to produce or inspect, please attach copies of such statements to your answers to these interrogatories.

18. List any other persons or entities, including their addresses, that you feel are responsible for plaintiff's injuries. For each person or entity listed, specifically describe the actions, inactions, or conduct that makes them responsible.

19. Please state the names of all employees who were working at Nickel & Dime on the date of the incident.

STATE OF ATLANTIS
COUNTY OF PINEAPPLE

BEFORE ME, the undersigned authority, personally appeared, _____, who being by me first duly sworn, on oath, deposes and says that the foregoing Answers to Interrogatories are true and correct to the best of his or her knowledge, and that he or she has read the foregoing Answers to Interrogatories and knows the contents thereof.

SWORN TO AND SUBSCRIBED before me this _____ day of _____, 2____.

Notary Public, State of Atlantis at Large
My Commission Expires:

_____

CERTIFICATE OF SERVICE

I HEREBY CERTIFY that a true copy of the foregoing Interrogatories have been furnished to the defendant, together with the summons and complaint filed in this action.

_____
Bruce K. Franklin, Esq.
616 Turner Street
Clearwater, Atlantis 34616

Requests for Admissions

As far as the requests for admissions were concerned, most of the requests were issues that would not be disputed, such as ownership of the corporation, that the store was open to the public, and that Scarlet Rose was lawfully on the premises.

Form 2.3 — Requests for Admissions

IN THE SIXTH JUDICIAL CIRCUIT COURT
IN AND FOR PINEAPPLE COUNTY, ATLANTIS

SCARLET ROSE,
     Plaintiff,

v.   Civil Action No.:

NICKEL & DIME, INC.,
     Defendant.

Requests for Admissions

1. Plaintiff, Scarlet Rose, by and through undersigned counsel and pursuant to Rule 1.370 of the Atlantis Rules of Civil Procedure, hereby requests that defendant, Nickel & Dime, admit the truth of the following statements, within the applicable time period required by said rule, to wit:

2. Jurisdiction and Venue of this matter properly lies in Pineapple County, Atlantis.

3. The incident stated in the complaint occurred on January 31, 2000, in the slipper department of the Nickel & Dime store located in Clearwater, Atlantis.

4. Defendant, Nickel & Dime, Inc., owned the Nickel & Dime store in which plaintiff was injured in January 2000 at the time the incident occurred.

5. Plaintiff sustained injuries to her back as a result of the incident.

6. Plaintiff, as a member of the general public, was an invited guest of Nickel & Dime at the time of the incident complained of and had a legal right to be in the place where she was when the incident occurred.

7. Plaintiff was within a section of the Nickel & Dime store, where she had a legal right to be at the time of the incident.

8. Boxes should not be left in an aisle where patrons of Nickel & Dime might inadvertently trip over them.

9. Nickel & Dime knew or should have known that a box was left in an aisle within the slipper department of the Nickel & Dime store at the time plaintiff tripped and fell over the box.

10. Nickel & Dime owed a duty to plaintiff, and all other members of the general public who patronized their store, not to leave a box in an aisle where patrons, such as plaintiff, might fall over the box.

11. Nickel & Dime breached the duty of care that it owed plaintiff when it allowed a condition to exist, namely a box in an aisle, which was potentially hazardous to patrons such as plaintiff.

12. Plaintiff was injured as a result of Nickel & Dime's failure to keep the aisle in the slipper department clear of a box.

13. Nickel & Dime is legally responsible for all injuries that plaintiff sustained when she tripped and fell over the box that was left in the aisle of the slipper department.

CERTIFICATE OF SERVICE

I HEREBY CERTIFY that a true copy of the foregoing Requests for Admissions has been furnished to the defendant, together with the summons and complaint filed in this action.

Bruce K. Franklin, Esq.
616 Turner Street
Clearwater, Atlantis 34616

Requests for Production

The request for production of documents could yield interesting information, such as other people who have fallen in similar situations or in the same part of the store, or if other trip-and-fall lawsuits have been filed against Nickel & Dime. This information could allow Marlene to view the files, learn the outcome, and read depositions given in the other lawsuits by employees and corporate representatives, all of which would make her job easier. Other documents requested would not prove the case against the defendant; however, they would document ownership of the building and provide a copy, among other things, of an insurance policy.

Form 2.4 — Requests for Production

IN THE SIXTH JUDICIAL CIRCUIT COURT
IN AND FOR PINEAPPLE COUNTY, ATLANTIS

SCARLET ROSE,
      Plaintiff,

v.   Civil Action No.:

NICKEL & DIME, INC.,
      Defendant.

Plaintiff's First Requests for Production to Defendant

COMES NOW plaintiff, Scarlet Rose, by and through undersigned counsel, and hereby requests the defendant to produce the following:

1. Any and all photographs both prior to and subsequent to plaintiff's injury-incident that depict the area where plaintiff alleges she tripped and fell, including the area where the box impeded the walkway.

2. Any and all documents, including employee training manuals, pertaining to the inspection and warning procedures for dangerous conditions.

3. A copy of any and all insurance policies, liability, health, medical, or otherwise, that could afford the plaintiff coverage for any expenses, medical or otherwise, sustained or incurred as a result of the alleged fall that is the subject matter of the plaintiff's Complaint.

4. All licenses or any permit authorizing you to operate the business known as Nickel & Dime, Inc., in Clearwater, Pineapple County, Atlantis.

5. All accident or incident reports concerning any accident of persons falling at Nickel & Dime, Inc., located in Clearwater, Pineapple County, Atlantis, on or before January 31, 2000, and any other dates pertinent hereto.

CERTIFICATE OF SERVICE

I HEREBY CERTIFY that a true copy of the foregoing Requests for Production has been furnished to the defendant together with the summons and complaint filed in this action.

Bruce K. Franklin, Esq.
616 Turner Street
Clearwater, Atlantis 34616

Filing the Complaint With Attachments

After drafting the discovery requests and the complaint, Marlene presented them to Bruce for his approval and signature. She revised the summons to reflect that interrogatories, requests for admission, and requests for production had been served upon the defendant, along with a copy of the complaint, and that they were to be answered within 45 days of service of process. Bruce told Marlene to file the complaint.

Marlene knew she had to have 1) an original and a copy of the complaint; 2) a summons; 3) a civil cover sheet; and 4) the filing fee, which included a fee for service of process on defendant by the sheriff's office. Marlene called the clerk's office to confirm the amount of the filing fee and the service of process fee. These fees required two separate checks.

The Civil Cover Sheet

Form 2.5 — Civil Cover Sheet

The civil cover sheet and the information contained herein neither replaces nor supplements the filing and service of pleadings or other papers as required by law. This form is required for the use of the Clerk of Court for reporting judicial workload data pursuant to Atlantis Statute 25.075.

I. CASE STYLE

SCARLET ROSE,
 Plaintiff,

v.   Civil Action No.:

NICKEL & DIME, INC.,
 Defendant.

Judge:

II.   TYPE OF CASE

(Place an X in one box only. If the case fits more than one type of case, select the most definitive.)

Domestic Relations	Torts	Other Civil
Simplified Dissolution Support/IV-D Support /No IV-D URESA/IV-D URESA/Non IV-D Domestic Violence Other Domestic Relations	Professional Malpractice Products Liability Auto Negligence Other Negligence XXX	Contracts Condominium Real Property/Mortgage Foreclosure Eminent Domain Other

III. IS JURY TRIAL DEMANDED IN THIS COMPLAINT?
            YES X   NO___

Date: July 1, 2000

Bruce K. Franklin, Esq.
616 Turner Street
Clearwater, Atlantis 34616
727-462-1000

Marlene then took the entire package, with a copy of the complaint and the various discovery requests, to the Clerk's Office, civil division, and filed the complaint. She gave one of the two checks to the clerk to pay the filing fee. She gave a second check to the clerk for the fee to have the sheriff serve the complaint upon the defendant's registered agent. All corporations in Atlantis are required to have an agent registered with the secretary of state who can be served with process, if necessary. The clerk assigned a case number: 00-125 (the year, 2000, and a specific case ID number). When the case would be assigned to a judge, that judge's initials would be placed behind the number.

Chapter Three

THE PLEADINGS STAGE
FROM THE
DEFENDANT'S PERSPECTIVE

The Defendant's Case

Receiving and Reviewing the Assignment

On Chris' first day at work, Alan gave him a file marked *Scarlet Rose v. Nickel & Dime, Inc.* Chris was told to work on the case immediately because there was only one week remaining to respond to the complaint. Carol Sullivan, one of the senior partners of the firm, had received the assignment from Nickel & Dime the day before and assigned the case to Alan. The first thing Chris found in the file was a form showing the client's name, address, personal information and the billing arrangements.

Form 3.1 — New Defense Assignment Case Form

If New Client, Check Here: N/A
Client #: 254
File/Matter #: 00160
Style of Case: *Scarlet Rose v. Nickel & Dime, Inc.*
Court: Circuit   County: Pineapple
Division: Civil   Circuit: Sixth
Judge's Name: Patrick D. Doherty
W/C Division District: N/A
Client's Name: Nickel & Dime, Inc.
Address: P.O. Box 1000, Boston, Massachusetts 01670
Mandatory Corporate Contact: Louise Mallet
Insurance Company's Name: National Insurance Co. (only over $500K)
Assigned By/Adjuster: Louise Mallet
Address: Same as above
Claim #: 2000-0001-ND-01
Phone: 202-455-5000
Additional Defendant: N/A
Address: N/A
Phone: N/A
Date of Accident or Loss: 1/31/2000
Policy Limits: $500,000
Place of Accident: Clearwater, Atlantis
Opposing Counsel: Bruce Franklin
Phone: 727-462-1000
Address: 616 Turner Street, Clearwater, Atlantis 34616
Date of Service on Company: 7/5/2000
Date of Service on Insured: Same
Statute of Limitations: 1/31/2004
Information/Action to be Taken: Respond to Complaint
Answer By: 7/25/2000
Completed By: Carol Sullivan

Date: 7/20/2000
Attorney Information: None
Assigned Billing Attorney: Alan Richards
Attorney #: 030
Billing Information: Quarterly
Type of Case: Premises liability/negligence
Hourly: Yes
Rate: $125/hr.
Fixed Fee: No
Retainer Amount: None
Billing Cycle:
Monthly: ___ Quarterly: X Six Months: ___ Yearly: ___ End of Case: ___
Date Opened: 7/20/2000
Entered on Computer By: BWB
Opened By: CKS
Assigned Attorney Initials: AR

Another document that Chris found in the file was a formal retainer agreement.

Form 3.2 — Legal Representation Agreement

Nickel & Dime, Inc., hereby employs the law office of Sullivan and Jaggar to represent Nickel & Dime, Inc., and provide legal services for Nickel & Dime, Inc., in connection with the trip-and-fall negligence action, *Scarlet Rose v. Nickel & Dime, Inc.* Nickel & Dime, Inc., authorizes the firm to defend this matter as may be advisable in the judgment of its attorneys, subject to the approval of Nickel & Dime, Inc.

Attorneys' Fees and Expenses

Nickel & Dime, Inc., agrees that the following method is to be used for determining the proper amount of legal fees:

Fees

The fees for services performed under this agreement will be based upon an hourly rate of $150 for partners, $125 for associates, and $65 for paralegals. Hourly billing will be to the tenth (1/10th) of an hour.

Retainer

In order to secure the time and services of the firm for this matter, Nickel & Dime, Inc., agrees to make an initial, nonrefundable payment in the amount of $5,000 toward its attorneys' fees and expenses. It understands this is the minimum fee it will be charged for services and expenses.

Costs

Nickel & Dime, Inc., authorizes the firm to retain any individual and entities to perform services necessary for investigation or completion of legal services. Nickel & Dime agrees to pay the fees or charges of every person or entity hired by the attorney to perform necessary services. Nickel & Dime, Inc., acknowledges that its attorney may incur various expenses in providing services. It agrees to reimburse the attorney for all out-of-pocket expenses paid. If Nickel & Dime, Inc., is billed directly for these expenses, it agrees to make prompt direct payments to the originators of the bills. Such expenses may include, but are not limited to, service and filing fees, courier or messenger services, recording and certifying documents, depositions, transcripts, investigations, witnesses' fees, long-distance telephone calls, copying materials, overtime clerical assistance, travel expenses, postage, notarial attestations, and computer research.

Billing

Nickel & Dime, Inc., agrees to the following schedule of billing: Fees, charges, and expenses will be billed on a quarterly basis as they accrue. The retainer, if any, shall be paid in full upon the execution of this agreement. The retainer shall be a credit against monthly bills.

Nickel & Dime, Inc., agrees to make prompt payments. It understands that failure to make payments is sufficient reason for the firm to withdraw from representing Nickel & Dime, Inc., in this matter, whether litigation has been commenced. Nickel & Dime, Inc., will be notified in writing before any withdrawal. It agrees that a letter to its business address is sufficient notice.

Consultations

Nickel & Dime, Inc., understands that telephone consultations with authorized agents of the firm shall be part of its representation, and that it will be billed by the firm for the time spent on such consultations.

Discharge of Firm

Nickel & Dime, Inc., may, if unsatisfied with the service for any reason, discharge the firm at any time; however, it is understood that the firm will be paid or arrangements will be made for the payment of all fees and costs.

Representation

It is expressly agreed and understood by Nickel & Dime that no representations in this matter have been made by the firm other than contained herein. Payment is not contingent upon the outcome of this matter. Nickel & Dime has read this fee agreement and has had an opportunity to discuss it with authorized representatives of the firm or any other attorney of its choice. Nickel & Dime, Inc., understands, agrees, and accepts all of the terms within this agreement.

Dated this 21st day of July, 2000

Attorney _____   Client _____
          Alan Richards, Esq.   Nickel & Dime, Inc.
          For the Firm   By an authorized representative

As Chris found out, it is not unusual for a defense firm to receive an assignment only days before an answer is due. Once the registered agent was served, Nickel & Dime, by the applicable rule of civil procedure, had 20 days to respond. The registered agent called the company, alerted it to the lawsuit, and put the papers in the mail. A few days later, the documents arrived at the office of the company. Once the papers were routed to the litigation department, they were placed on the desk of the claims manager, who reviewed the claim and within a day or two assigned the claim to a specific claims adjuster for handling. The claims manager instructed the claims adjuster to send this case to the law firm of Sullivan and Jagger. By the time the claims adjuster reviewed the file, copied the file, and dictated an assignment letter, almost two weeks had passed before the file actually reached the law firm. In this case, due to the potential exposure, the claims manager kept the case herself. She called the law firm and spoke directly with Carol.

Acknowledgment of Assignment Letter

Alan sent an acknowledgment letter to the client.

Sullivan and Jagger
Attorneys At Law
515 Maple Street
Clearwater, Atlantis 34616
727-462-8888

July 22, 2000

Louise Mallet, Director
Loss Prevention Department
Nickel & Dime, Inc.

P.O. Box 1000
Boston, Massachusetts 01670

RE: *Scarlet Rose v. Nickel & Dime, Inc.*
     Your Claim No.: 2000-0001-ND-01
     Date of loss: 1/31/2000

Dear Ms. Mallet:

This will confirm your telephone call on July 20 to this office during which the above-referenced case was assigned to this firm. I am the attorney who will be handling this case on your behalf. I thank you for allowing us this opportunity to work with you on this case. A copy of the Notice of Appearance, which I have filed in this cause, is enclosed. Once I am able to locate and speak with the store personnel, I will promptly file an answer to the Complaint. I will visit the store in question as soon as possible and meet with the individuals within the store who have knowledge of the matter.

Also, in accordance with your guidelines, I will serve discovery requests upon plaintiff at the time the answer is filed. I will not initiate any research or further discovery without your specific authorization to do so.

Again, I thank you for providing us with the opportunity to work with you on this case. I ask that you contact me immediately if you have any questions or comments with regard to this matter.

Very truly yours,

_____

Alan Richards, Esq.

Enc: Notice of Appearance

Form 3.3 — Notice of Appearance

IN THE SIXTH JUDICIAL CIRCUIT COURT
IN AND FOR PINEAPPLE COUNTY, ATLANTIS

SCARLET ROSE,
     Plaintiff,

v.   Civil Action No. 00-125-PDD

NICKEL & DIME, INC.,
     Defendant.

Notice of Appearance

Comes now the law firm of Sullivan and Jagger, P.A., and respectfully serves notice to this Honorable Court, and counsel for the plaintiff, Scarlet Rose, that henceforth it will represent the defendant, Nickel & Dime, Inc., in this matter and that all pleadings and correspondence should be addressed to undersigned counsel. All issues relating to jurisdiction are hereby reserved and preserved.

Respectfully submitted,

_____
Alan Richards, Esq.
Attorney for Defendant

CERTIFICATE OF SERVICE

I hereby certify that a true and accurate copy of the foregoing notice of appearance was sent to Bruce K. Franklin, the attorney for Plaintiff, by regular mail, to his office address of 616 Turner Street, Clearwater, Atlantis, 34616, on this 20th day of July 2000.

_____
Alan Richards

Analyzing the Complaint

This was the first case Chris would be handling from start to finish. He took the booklet on the rules of civil procedure from his credenza and read the rules on commencement of a civil action, service of the summons and complaint, time limitations, how the complaint must be captioned, and when and how an answer must be filed. He also read rule 1.140 on Motions to Dismiss the complaint, and affirmative defenses. He noticed that some defenses were waived unless raised by motion to dismiss or affirmative defense.

At that point, Chris examined the complaint. He read every word carefully and scrutinized it to determine whether it contained any technical flaws or improper allegations. He checked to see if the Pineapple County Circuit had jurisdiction over the matter and if venue was proper in that county. It seemed to Chris that the complaint was short and to the point, and he could find no flaws in it.

Motions by the Defendant

Chris knew that in a negligence action the plaintiff must prove duty, breach of duty, proximate causation, and damages. He looked to see what he could do before answering the complaint. He determined that he had three options:

1. to file a motion to dismiss the complaint
2. to file a motion to strike
3. to file for a bill of particulars.

After considering the matter, Chris concluded that the complaint was technically sufficient and that no motions were available to him in this case. But, before answering the complaint, he needed to talk to a representative of Nickel & Dime and find out its position regarding the claim. Chris would have to investigate the facts of the case.

Investigating the Claim

Chris hoped there would be an employee or two who still worked at the store and who knew about the incident. He called the store manager, explaining who he was and why he was calling, and asked for an appointment to meet at the store to discuss the matter. The store manager referred Chris to the loss control director. The loss control director obtained the name and telephone number of the claims adjuster at the company who was assigned to this claim. After speaking to the claims adjuster and confirming that Chris was someone with whom employees of Nickel & Dime could talk freely, the loss control director called Chris back and made the appointment.

Meeting with Witnesses

Fortunately for Chris, two employees of Nickel & Dime had witnessed the incident. One of the employees was still working for Nickel & Dime and would be at work later that day. The other person no longer worked at the store, but she lived nearby, had left on very good terms, and would be happy to cooperate. Chris went to the store that afternoon to meet with the loss control director, Kate Frechette, and the employees, Caitlin Palmer and Marjorie Murphy. He brought his camera.

Just as Marlene had done, Chris took pictures of the scene. He made thorough notes of his conversation with Ms. Frechette, Ms. Murphy, the former selling supervisor who had witnessed the incident, and Ms. Palmer.

Witness Statements

Chris prepared a memorandum to Alan in which he summarized the statements given to him.

Interoffice Memorandum

TO: Alan Richards
FROM: Chris Walden
DATE: July 21, 2000
RE: Summary of statements taken from Marjorie Murphy and Caitlin Palmer

Statement of Marjorie Murphy

Marjorie Murphy, a 12-year employee of Nickel & Dime, was a supervisor of the lingerie, accessories, jewelry, and women's department. As have all Nickel & Dime employees, over the years Ms. Murphy has received a great deal of training with regard to safety. Part of this training included stocking procedures.

Ms. Murphy was working at the time of the incident. Although she did not witness the alleged fall, she arrived at the scene within minutes after it occurred. The plaintiff, Ms. Scarlet Rose, was still on the floor when she got there. She remembers talking to Ms. Rose and preparing the incident report. Within five to ten minutes after the incident occurred, Ms. Murphy took a picture of the area where Ms. Rose fell.

Most significantly, Ms. Murphy remembers that Caitlin Palmer told her (Ms. Murphy) that Ms. Rose said she (Ms. Rose) was in a hurry and thought she could step over the box in the aisle from which merchandise was being taken and placed on the display racks. The box is called a tote. Ms. Murphy thought that Ms. Rose said she was on her way to the bathroom, but Ms. Murphy wasn't certain. Ms. Murphy also stated that she did not think there was anything wrong with how the stocking was done and did not criticize Carol Westwoman, the employee doing the stocking.

According to the incident report and Ms. Murphy's recollection, Ms. Rose said she had fallen and broken her ankle a year or so before this incident, that at the same time she had hurt her back, and that she felt she may have injured her back again. Ms. Rose also complained of pain in her left leg, which was cut, and in her knee.

Ms. Murphy stated further that Ms. Rose's knees were inside the tote, which suggested to Ms. Murphy that Ms. Rose attempted to step over the tote and lost her balance. Ms. Murphy called 911. Paramedics responded and took Ms. Rose to the hospital on a stretcher.

Ms. Murphy is unaware of any prior similar incidents.

Statement of Caitlin Palmer

On the date of the incident, Ms. Palmer was a selling supervisor. She was a little vague and ambiguous in her physical description of Ms. Rose. Ms. Palmer told me, "I saw her [Ms. Rose] walk down the aisle, and I saw her try to step over the tote and fall." Ms. Palmer could not remember much of the mechanics about the fall, but she did remember that Ms. Rose fell forward. Ms. Palmer remembers that Ms. Rose was in a hurry and was rushing to get to the bathroom.

Ms. Palmer went back to work and did not complete the incident report. She did not speak about the incident to any one other than Ms. Murphy. That was the extent of her involvement. She may have spoken to Ms. Rose, but she wasn't sure.

Except for the fact that Ms. Palmer couldn't describe Ms. Rose well, Ms. Palmer positively stated that Ms. Rose appeared to be in a hurry and attempted to step over the tote.

While at the store where Ms. Frechette and Ms. Palmer were working, Chris asked Ms. Frechette to assist him in responding to the plaintiff's numerous discovery requests. To do so, Ms. Frechette had to locate all the files reflecting which employees were working at the store when the incident occurred, all employees who were actually on duty at the time, and all other claims and lawsuits.

Since Ms. Frechette had been at the store for only the last six months, she did not have personal knowledge of the facts and had to get assistance from the store manager. As Chris explained to Ms. Frechette, for purposes of deposition and at trial, someone from the store would have to be the contact person for Chris' law firm as the corporate representative for Nickel & Dime. That person would, more than likely, be Ms. Frechette.

Obtaining Medical Records, Employment Records and Other Information

Unlike Marlene, Chris could not simply write letters to the doctors and medical providers in order to get all of the medical records and bills. He would have to obtain those records pursuant to a subpoena. Some records were, however, provided to Chris by Ms. Mallet, because they were contained within the demand letter sent to Ms. Mallet by the plaintiff's attorney. Chris could review those records and summarize them for Ms. Mallet and Alan.

Contacting Other Witnesses

Chris wrote letters to all employees who were on duty the day of the incident. He told them that Sullivan and Jagger was representing Nickel & Dime, that Alan was the attorney for the matter, that their assistance would be appreciated, and that, if they cooperated, a deposition might not be necessary. After a few weeks, Chris had heard from only two employees, both of whom said they had no knowledge of the incident.

Initial Report Letter

Sullivan and Jagger
Attorneys At Law
515 Maple Street
Clearwater, Atlantis 34616
727-462-8888

Louise Mallet, Director
Loss Prevention Department
Nickel & Dime, Inc.
P.O. Box 1000
Boston, Massachusetts 01670

Re: *Scarlet Rose v. Nickel & Dime, Inc.*
    Your Claim No.: 2000-0033-ND-01
    Date of Loss: 1/31/2000
    Our File No.: 00-0160

Dear Ms. Mallet:

I write to inform you of our progress on this case and to provide you with our initial analysis of the claim. After receiving the assignment, my paralegal immediately contacted Marjorie Murphy, who had filled out the incident report, and Caitlin Palmer, a selling supervisor who saw plaintiff fall. Carol Westwoman, the salesperson who was working out of the tote in question that day, did not see the plaintiff fall, and she no longer works at the store. Ms. Murphy gave us a last known address for Ms. Westwoman, and I will try to get in touch with her as quickly as possible.

Ms. Murphy recalls the incident clearly. She also recalls the conversation she had with the plaintiff after the incident in which she asked the plaintiff if the plaintiff saw the tote that was in the aisle. Ms. Murphy told us that the plaintiff told her, "I was in a hurry, and I thought I could step over it." Ms. Murphy also remembers the plaintiff saying something to the effect that she [the plaintiff] thought she could walk over the tote.

Furthermore, the plaintiff told the ambulance personnel, or fire rescue people, that she had a pre-existing back condition after she fell and broke her ankle a year or so ago. Ms. Murphy remembers thinking that this was a ridiculous occurrence and that the plaintiff had no one else to blame for the incident but herself.

As far as the tote itself is concerned, Ms. Murphy explained that the sales clerk, Carol Westwoman, was emptying the tote and putting slippers on the "A-frame" display shelves. Ms. Westwoman was doing this work at the time the plaintiff fell. Ms. Murphy said that stockpersons would take totes, which are about one foot high, three feet long, two feet deep, made of heavy plastic, and stack them inside one another once they were unloaded. She said that sometimes there may be three stacks of totes on the floor at one time. She is positive that stockpersons would not have left the tote on the floor unless they were emptying it.

Ms. Murphy took two photographs of the area with the tote as it had been when the plaintiff fell. Since Ms. Murphy has the greatest knowledge of the situation, I will have her sign answers to the interrogatories that accompanied the complaint.

Should you have any questions or comments with regard to the foregoing, please do not hesitate to contact me. Again, I thank you for allowing us this opportunity to work with you. I look forward to achieving the best possible result on your behalf.

Very truly yours,

_____
Alan Richards, Esq.

Research

Chris didn't understand some of the affirmative defenses, such as collateral sources and joint and several liability, so he consulted a copy of the Atlantis statutes in Alan's office. He made a photocopy of the statutes in question and put those photocopies in a file labeled "research." He also conducted research on his computer in a subscription program to which the law firm subscribed, using the key words "trip," "fall," and "negligence." He located a few cases that explained the law in similar situations in which a patron of a department store tripped and fell over boxes or other obstacles on the floor of a store.

It seemed to Chris that, in this case, Scarlet Rose had failed to pay proper attention to where she was walking and failed to observe what was open and obvious. He did not think that a big box in the middle of an aisle was an inherently dangerous condition. Chris placed photocopies of the cases in the research file.

ADVENTURE MALL,
        Appellant,

v.   District Court of Appeals of Atlantis, Third District

JANE SMITH,
        Appellee.

March 20, 1999

Invitee brought negligence action against mall owner after she fell off a six-inch sidewalk curb. The Circuit Court for Plum County, Rosemary Yiengst Jones, J., entered judgment on jury verdict for invitee, and owner appealed. The District Court of Appeal, Geagan, J., held that owner had no duty to warn invitee of step-down from ordinary curb and manner in which curb "blended in" with driveway below did not give rise to inherently dangerous condition.

Reversed and remanded with directions.

Gamble, Charles, for appellee.

Rutledge, Hugh, for appellants.

Before GEAGAN, HURLEY and BRENNAN,
GEAGAN, Dennis, Judge.

Adventure Mall appeals from a final judgment entered after an adverse jury verdict in a slip-and-fall negligence action. We reverse based upon our decision that, as a matter of law, Adventure committed no act of negligence in this case.

On a clear day in December 1998, Jane Smith was injured when she slipped and fell from a six-inch sidewalk curb at the Adventure Mall. Smith brought a negligence action against Adventure. Smith alleged that Adventure's failure to paint the "crown" of the sidewalk curb yellow constituted negligence because Smith was not adequately warned of the step-down from the sidewalk. Smith also alleged that Adventure negligently designed and maintained the area surrounding the curb in an unreasonably dangerous condition.

As evidence of the curb's allegedly dangerous condition, Smith introduced photographs taken at other malls in Plum County depicting curbs painted yellow in their entirety.

Adventure asserted as affirmative defenses that it had no duty to warn Smith of the sidewalk curb and that Smith was comparatively negligent because it was an ordinary condition and she was not looking where she was going at the time of the accident. The trial court denied Adventure's motions for directed verdict. The jury returned a verdict against Adventure assessing damages of $230,000.

Adventure contends on appeal that the court erred in refusing to direct a verdict in its favor. Specifically, it argues that there was no duty to warn Smith of the step-down from an ordinary sidewalk curb and that Smith failed to introduce any evidence to demonstrate that the curb was inherently dangerous. We agree.

It is well settled that the duty of a landowner to a customer is to maintain the premises in a reasonably safe condition and to warn the invitee of latent perils that are known or should be known to the owner but are not known to the invitee or, by the exercise of due care, could not be known to him or her.

An owner is entitled to assume that the invitee will perceive that which would be obvious to him upon the ordinary use of his own senses, and is not required to give the invitee notice or warning of an obvious danger.

The curb in question was not a concealed or latent danger. The presence of uneven floor levels in public places does not constitute a hidden and dangerous condition, as a matter of law. Furthermore, this was not the situation in this case. On the day of Smith's accident, according to the testimony, the weather was clear, the lighting around the sidewalk was adequate, and there were no foreign objects on the sidewalk. Had Smith been looking where she was going, she would have seen the curb.

Smith's allegation that the problem with the driveway condition existed because the color of the curb blended with and concealed the existence of the step-down is likewise without merit. It is a matter of common knowledge that sidewalks and the drop-offs from the sidewalks to the streets have the same color as streets in thousands of instances throughout Atlantis. Indeed, Adventure admitted several photographs showing such conditions into evidence.

In a strikingly similar case, the Supreme Court of Mississippi held that a sidewalk that was 7½ inches above the parking lot could not be considered inherently dangerous and was an obvious open and apparent condition. *Stanley v. Morgan & Lindsey, Inc.*, 203 So.2d 473, 477 (Miss. 1967). Stanley, the appellant in that case, slipped off the sidewalk at the curb and was seriously injured when she fell. In *Stanley*, as here, a portion of the curb was painted yellow, but none of the painted area was visible to customers going south from the store where the trip-and-fall occurred. *Id.* at 475. Stanley testified that "it just looked like one big solid slab of concrete, all on the same level." *Id.* The court concluded that the step-off was not inherently dangerous and that there was no evidence of negligence. *Id.* at 477.

Smith encountered a condition that was permanent, in place, and obvious. There was no proof of any defect in the sidewalk curb that caused Smith to fall. In other words, there was no evidence of negligence. Some conditions are simply so open and obvious that they can be held as a matter of law not to constitute a hidden dangerous condition. The condition complained of here represents such a case. To hold that an ordinary sidewalk curb, without more, is inherently dangerous would make every municipality and business establishment the virtual insurer of the safety of every pedestrian. Accordingly, we find, as a matter of law, that Adventure committed no act of negligence in this case.

The judgment appealed is reversed, and this cause is remanded with directions to enter judgment in accordance with the appellant's motion for directed verdict.

Reversed and remanded with directions.

Chris also found another case, decided in 1974, that discussed the duty of a customer to exercise care when contributory negligence was a bar to recovery in a lawsuit.

DIXIE, INC.,
          Appellant,

v.   District Court of Appeals of Atlantis, First District

JEAN MARIE FERRARA and
TERENCE B. FERRARA,
          Appellees.

February 14, 1974
Rehearing Denied April 8, 1974

Action for injuries sustained by customer who fell on sidewalk near front door of defendant's supermarket. The Circuit Court, Pineapple County, Steve C. Riley, J., entered judgment for plaintiff, and defendant appealed. The District Court of Appeal, Neely, Armistead, J., held that, in absence of showing that waxy paper came upon sidewalk in front of defendant's grocery store as a result of negligence of defendant's employees, that employees saw the paper on sidewalk before plaintiff slipped on it while leaving store, or that paper had been on sidewalk for so long a time that defendant or its employees in exercise of reasonable care should have seen it and removed it, defendant was not liable for injuries sustained by plaintiff in fall.

Reversed.

Robert P. Nickel, of Nickel and Nickel P.A., for appellant.

Patrick Wilkie, of Patrick Wilkie, P.A., for appellees.

NEELY, Judge.

Appellant, the owner and operator of a supermarket located in a shopping center, seeks reversal of a final judgment, entered pursuant to jury verdict, awarding appellees money damages for injuries sustained when Jean Ferrara fell on the sidewalk near the front door to appellant's store. It is contended by appellant that its motion for a directed verdict should have been granted, inasmuch as there was no evidence from which a jury could conclude that negligence on the part of appellant caused appellee's fall.

The facts of this slip-and-fall case are not in dispute. The appellee, Ms. Ferrara, accompanied by her mother, went to appellant's store to buy groceries. As they approached the front door to the premises, Ms. Ferrara noticed a good bit of waxy white paper on the sidewalk. They shopped in the store for about two hours. When they left the store, they were accompanied by a bag boy who pushed two shopping carts of groceries that appellee had purchased. Appellee was first to the front door, which she held open with her back so that the bag boy could exit. She then looked around, saw her mother reaching for the door, and began to exit. She took about two steps, slipped on a piece of paper, and received injuries from the fall.

Her mother testified that the sidewalk in front of the store was littered with waxy, white paper used to wrap hotdogs or hamburgers. There was a hotdog stand down the sidewalk to the right of appellant's store. That hotdog stand was not a part of appellant's store. After a trial by jury, appellees were awarded some $4,485 in damages as a result of the fall.

In this appeal, appellant contends that a storekeeper is not liable to his customers for transitory conditions on a sidewalk in front of his store. While we cannot approve of this contention for the reason that situations can be envisioned where the storeowner might be held liable for negligence, we are compelled by the facts herein to agree that there was no evidence of negligence on the part of appellant, and its motion for a directed verdict should have been granted.

The duty of one who operates a place of business is to exercise ordinary or reasonable care to see that those portions of the premises that persons may be expected to use are reasonably safe. This duty would extend to the approaches to the premises also.

Here, there was evidence of white, waxy paper on the sidewalk leading to the entrance of appellant's store. There was no evidence that the paper came upon the sidewalk as a result of any act of negligence of any employee of appellant or that any employee actually saw the paper before the accident occurred. In fact, the evidence disclosed that the paper most likely emanated from a hotdog stand further down the sidewalk. Nor was there evidence that the same piece of paper that caused Ms. Ferrara to fall had remained on the sidewalk a sufficient length of time as to put appellant's employees on notice of its existence.

Liability for negligence in failing to maintain premises in a reasonably safe condition, or in failing to warn of existing dangers, must be predicated on the occupant's superior knowledge or means of obtaining knowledge concerning the danger. In order to recover, a plaintiff must show either that the occupant or proprietor had actual notice of the condition or that the dangerous condition existed for such a length of time that in the exercise of ordinary care the occupant should have known of it and taken action to remedy it or guard the plaintiff from harm therefrom. No liability can attach where it is not shown that the owner or proprietor had actual or constructive notice of the dangerous condition. This is especially true where the dangerous condition is traceable to the acts of persons other than himself and his employees. These principles of law briefly recited above have been reaffirmed so many times by the appellate courts of this state that we feel we would achieve no purpose in reiterating the many citations that do so.

Here, as mentioned above, there was no evidence to justify any conclusion that the paper came upon the sidewalk as a result of any negligence on the part of any of appellant's employees or that any employee saw the paper on the sidewalk before the accident. A finding that an employee dropped the paper on the sidewalk or even that he had seen it there before would be purely conjectural. Nor was the evidence such as would warrant a finding that the paper had been on the sidewalk for so long a time that the owner or his employees in the exercise of reasonable care should have seen it and removed it. While appellee and her mother testified that the sidewalk was littered two hours before their exit from the store, there was no evidence to show that the same paper upon which she fell had been there for two hours.

Although we need not touch upon the issue of contributory negligence on the part of appellee, in light of our conclusion of absence of negligence on appellant's part, we feel that it may be useful to briefly recite a few known principles with regard to contributory negligence. First, a customer is obligated to exercise a reasonable degree of care for his own safety, which includes observing the obvious and apparent condition of the premises. The distraction rule, which suggests that a person may not be guilty of comparative negligence even though he had the opportunity to avoid a dangerous condition if his attention is diverted from the known danger by a sufficient cause, would not be applicable to this case. Appellee did not contend that she was distracted, but merely that she forgot about the presence of the paper while she was in the store shopping. Diversion of attention is to be distinguished from a mere lack of attention. The fact that one momentarily forgets the existence of a hazard or fails to pay attention to what he is doing is no excuse for his failure to observe the hazard. We bring this up merely to illustrate that even had there been a justiciable issue as to negligence on the part of appellant, the evidence before this court tends to suggest that recovery would be barred by the appellee's own negligence.

In conclusion, a storekeeper is not an insurer of the safety of all those who come upon his premises. He need only exercise reasonable care to protect his patrons from harm of which he has actual or constructive notice. Here, the evidence shows neither actual nor constructive notice, and it is our conclusion that the evidence in this case was wholly insufficient to raise a jury question as to the negligence of appellant.

Therefore, the final judgment must be, and it is, hereby set aside and reversed, and the trial judge is directed to enter a judgment in favor of appellant.

Reversed.

BRADY, C.J., and SMITH, Brian, Associate Judge, concur.

Chris also found the following case that dealt with the issue of a storeowner's policies and procedures being admissible into evidence at the time of trial. He knew that one of the issues in the case was whether or not store policy and procedure allowed store employees to place a tote in an aisle while stocking shelves during business hours.

JOHN BEGOOD,
      Appellant,

v.   District Court of Appeals of Atlantis, Fourth District

SUPER MARKET, INC.,
      Appellee.

January 29, 1997

Patron who suffered injury in a fall off a scale in a grocery store brought action against store, alleging that store was negligent in placement of scale adjacent to shopping carts in high-volume traffic area of store. The Circuit Court for the Sixth Judicial Circuit, Pineapple County, Rodriquez, Barbara, Judge, entered judgment for store. Patron appealed. The District Court of Appeal, Carole Anne Nickel, Judge, held that patron failed to show that store's manager's procedures manual was relevant to issue of reasonable care in placement of scale, as required for manual to be admissible as evidence. Affirmed.

Issue no. 1: Party's own internal operating manuals are admissible if relevant to issues raised.

Issue no. 2: Party's internal rule does not itself fix legal standard of care in negligence action; party is entitled to appropriate jury instructions to that effect.

Summary of opinion of the Court: Patron who suffered injury in fall off a scale in a grocery store failed to show that store's manager's procedures manual was relevant to issue of reasonable care in placement of scale, as required for manual to be admissible as evidence in patron's negligence action against store; patron conceded that manual made no mention whatsoever of safe situation of scale in store, but merely addressed accumulation of clutter and debris in store aisle.

NICKEL, CAROL ANNE, Associate Judge.

We affirm on all issues raised. We write only to clarify that a party's own internal operating manuals are admissible if relevant to the issues raised.

This appeal arose from a jury verdict and judgment in favor of the defendant in a slip-and-fall case. Appellant Begood brought a personal injury action against Appellee Super Markets, Inc., as a result of injuries he sustained when he fell while stepping off a scale in appellee's store. A shopping cart struck Begood, and the fellow store customer who had been using the shopping cart fled without rendering him any assistance. A central issue was whether appellee was negligent in the placement of the scale. The evidence at trial established that the scale was located in the entranceway of store adjacent to shopping carts and was stationed in a high-volume traffic area of the store. There was also evidence presented, though disputed, that visibility of the scale was obscured by display items located nearby.

Plaintiff sought to introduce into evidence at trial portions of store manager's procedures manual to demonstrate what was reasonable care in placement of the scale for public access. In excluding the manager's manual from evidence, the trial court relied upon *Department Store v. Hall*, 662 So.2d 977 (Atlantis 4th DCA 1995), rev. granted on different grounds, 675 So.2d 120 (1996). The trial judge interpreted the decision to mean that evidence of a business's own internal rules is not admissible. He reasoned that permitting a jury to consider such evidence would unfairly lead the jury to impose a higher legal standard on a party and, thereby, undermine important public policy considerations. At the pretrial hearing on store's motion *in limine* to exclude any reference to the procedure manual, the trial judge stated:

"Let me tell you what I think public policy wise. We want all stores to have internal policies that assure the highest standard of public safety. And God forbid that there be jury instructions that, hey, if you fail to wash your hands or something like that the jury can consider it in evidence against you. In other words, these retail establishments are being held to a higher standard than the reasonable man standard. But by the same token, it seems to me that if they enunciate these policies in some kind of a procedure manual, personnel manuals, safety manuals, but the public policy requires that they not be hammered with those things because they will simply erase them. Right? They will have no polices to assure public safety because it would then hold them to a higher standard. . . I'm granting that you may not refer to the internal rules, in this case, to fix the standard of care."

In *Corp. v. Ladder*, 74 662 A.2d 977 (Atlantis 4th DCA 1995), our court held that it would be improper for the trial court to instruct the jury that a violation of the internal policy or procedure of a party was evidence of negligence. In so ruling, we cited *Stein v. Glass*, 531 A.2d 199 (Atlantis 3d DCA 1988), rev. denied, 539 So.2d 476 (1989). However, the Third District Court of Appeal noted in *Stein* that a party's own rules of conduct are relevant and can be received into evidence with an express caution that they are merely evidentiary and not to serve as a legal standard.

This court has also recognized that safety rules and procedures established by a party to govern the conduct of its employees are relevant evidence of the standard of care. In *Able v. Cain*, 569 A.2d 771 (Atlantis 4th DCA 1990), a slip-and-fall action was brought against a service station owner/operator by a patron who slipped on a greasy substance on the ground. We held that a jury question arose as to whether it would have been reasonable for a gas station's employees, in light of their allegedly established inspection procedures, to have been in the island area of the gas station examining for foreign substances left on the ground by the prior customer before the plaintiff's vehicle entered the full service lane.

We clarify that a party's own internal operating manuals are admissible if relevant to the issues raised. We reiterate, however, that a party's internal rule does not itself fix the legal standard of care in a negligence action, and that the party is entitled to appropriate jury instructions to that effect.

We further emphasize that the manual, or portions thereof, proffered for evidence at trial, must nonetheless meet the test of relevancy. In the instant case, Appellant has not sustained his burden of showing that the internal policies and procedures set forth in the manager's manual were relevant to the issue of reasonable care in placement of the scale. Appellant conceded that the manual made no mention whatsoever of safe situation of the scale in the supermarket but merely addressed the accumulation of clutter and debris in the store aisles. No evidence was adduced at trial pertaining to any violations of these specific policies. Nor was it established that any such violations had any causal connection to the slip-and-fall accident in question. Therefore, we hold that the trial court did not err in excluding the manual from evidence at trial on the basis of relevancy.

AFFIRMED.

Investigating Plaintiff's Background

Chris knew that Alan would want to know as much as possible about Scarlet Rose's history and background. He might want school records, dental records, driving record, employment records, optical records, and all prior medical records. Chris could get some records without subpoena, but most would require subpoenas. Virtually all records would require further identifying information from Scarlet Rose before that information could be obtained.

For driving records, a form is available for use in Atlantis. Chris simply filled out the form and mailed it in with a check made payable to the Department of Motor Vehicles. Much of this information is available via the Internet, but Alan wanted a formal document from the Department of Motor Vehicles instead of a printout. Chris would not be able to obtain much of this information before answering the complaint. He was able, however, to find out much information about Scarlet Rose through a commercial public records service to which the firm subscribed.

Answering the Complaint

At this point, Chris drafted an answer to the complaint and presented it to Alan for review.

Form 3.4 — Answer

IN THE SIXTH JUDICIAL CIRCUIT COURT
IN AND FOR PINEAPPLE COUNTY, ATLANTIS

SCARLET ROSE,
Plaintiff,

v.   Civil Action No.: 00-125-PDD

NICKEL & DIME, INC.,
Defendant.

Answer and Affirmative Defenses

COMES NOW defendant, Nickel & Dime, Inc., by and through undersigned counsel, and hereby submits the following in response to the Complaint filed herein and states:

Answer

1. Defendant admits the allegations of Paragraphs 1, 2, 3, 4, and 5.

2. Defendant is without knowledge as to the allegations of Paragraph 6 regarding injury and damages and, therefore, denies same and will require strict proof thereof. All allegations of negligence and causation are denied.

3. The allegations of Paragraph 7, regarding negligence of defendant and plaintiff's exercise of due care, are denied. It is admitted that plaintiff was a business invitee and guest of Nickel & Dime on January 31, 2000, and that on that date she fell in the store.

4. In response to the allegations of Paragraph 8, Nickel & Dime, Inc., admits that it has a duty to act in a reasonable and proper way in the conduct of its business, and it asserts that it did so in this case. All other allegations, as phrased, are denied.

5. The allegations of Paragraphs 9 are denied.

6. Any allegations of any paragraphs not specifically admitted or denied previously are hereby denied.

WHEREFORE, defendant, Nickel & Dime, Inc., prays that this Honorable Court enter judgment in its favor and against plaintiff and award it all costs incurred in the defense of this case and such other and further relief as this court deems just and proper.

Affirmative Defenses

1. The defendant, Nickel & Dime, Inc., was not guilty of any negligence whatsoever and there was no negligent condition that caused plaintiff to fall.

2. At the time and place in question and immediately prior thereto, the plaintiff was guilty of negligence that contributed proximately to cause the injuries sustained in the incident in question, thereby reducing the claim by the proportion that the negligence aforesaid contributed to the total negligence involved in the accident, or barring the claim entirely.

3. In any event, the injuries and damages complained of may have been caused by the actions of an unknown third party and not of this defendant.

4. The condition of which plaintiff complains was an open and obvious condition for which she was under a duty to exercise due care, and she failed to do so.

5. Defendant had no actual knowledge, before the time that the incident occurred, that there was any dangerous or unsafe condition existing at the time and place as alleged.

6. Any dangerous or unsafe condition, if any such condition is found to have been there, did not exist for such time as to put defendant on constructive notice of said condition.

7. Any judgment should be reduced in accordance with the requirements of Atlantis Statute 768 *et seq.* (collateral sources of indemnity), and this defendant asserts all rights it has under said Statute.

8. The parties' rights shall be controlled by, and judgment if any, entered in accordance with the requirements of Atlantis Statutes 768.31 (contribution among tortfeasors) and 768.81 (comparative fault/joint and several liability) and, therefore, this defendant asserts all rights it has under each Statute.

WHEREFORE, defendant, Nickel & Dime, Inc., prays that this Honorable Court enter judgment in its favor and against plaintiff, and award it all costs incurred in the defense of this case and such other and further relief as this Court deems just and proper.

A TRIAL BY JURY OF ALL ISSUES TRIABLE AS A MATTER OF RIGHT IS HEREBY DEMANDED.

CERTIFICATE OF SERVICE

I HEREBY CERTIFY that a true and correct copy of the above was mailed this 25th day of July, 2000, to:

Bruce K. Franklin, Esq.
616 Turner Street
Clearwater, Atlantis 34616
Attorney for Plaintiff

Respectfully submitted,

_____
Alan Richards
515 Maple Street
Clearwater, Atlantis 34616

Responding to the Discovery Requests Made by Plaintiff

Although more investigation and analysis of the claim was needed, Chris had sufficient information to prepare proposed answers to the interrogatories, requests for admission, and requests for production. Alan had reminded Chris that the store employees were not lawyers, nor had they been trained as paralegals. It would be difficult for them to do all things necessary to respond to the discovery requests. Alan told Chris to draft a response to every request and interrogatory and make it as easy as possible for the client. A client would have to sign the answers to interrogatories, but Alan could respond on behalf of the client to the responses to requests for admissions and requests for production.

Chris went through every question and responded to each one as best he could.

Sullivan and Jagger
Attorneys At Law
515 Maple Street
Clearwater, Atlantis 34616
727-462-8888

July 25, 2000

Marjorie Murphy
2303 Green Street
Clearwater, Atlantis 33759

Re: *Scarlet Rose vs. Nickel & Dime, Inc.*

Dear Ms. Murphy:

I enclose a set of interrogatories submitted by Scarlet Rose's attorney. Your assistance and cooperation in answering each of the questions is absolutely necessary. We will assist you in every way possible. **We must have the information and your answers no later than 15 days from date of this letter**. Failure to return the answers when they are due may be harmful to our case. Should it be necessary for you come to the office to discuss your answers, we will gladly meet with you at a mutually convenient time.

Please begin gathering all of the documents and other information needed to answer the questions. When writing answers to the questions, keep the following in mind:

1. Answer all questions completely, but concisely.
2. Always be truthful.
3. Do not try to withhold information or be evasive. Any evasiveness can affect the outcome of the case. If there is any information that you are reluctant to reveal, please discuss it with us.
4. Look up all dates, amounts, times, and other information requested, even if it is a laborious and time-consuming process. This information is needed by both the plaintiff and your attorneys.
5. You are not required to make an unreasonable search or incur unreasonable expense. If you do not have access to the information, you are not required to provide it. Please let us know of any reasons why you would prefer not to answer a question.

After answering the questions, return them in the enclosed envelope. We will prepare the answers in final form. It will be necessary for you to sign the answers before a notary public. You may come to our office to do so, or we will mail the answers to you and you may sign the answers before a notary public who affixes his or her state seal and return the answers to us. Based on our conversation a few days ago, I have drafted some of the answers for you.

Thank you for your assistance. If you have questions, please call me.

Sincerely,

_____
Chris Walden
Paralegal

Encl.

Further Reporting to the Client and the Excess Insurance Company

Chris told Alan that he had completed his investigation of the claim and had drafted an answer. Chris asked to schedule an appointment to discuss the matter with Alan. Later that afternoon they met and discussed the case at length. After their meeting, the following report was prepared:

Sullivan and Jagger
Attorneys At Law
515 Maple Street
Clearwater, Atlantis 34616
727-462-8888

Louise Mallet, Director
Loss Prevention Department
Nickel & Dime, Inc.
P.O. Box 1000
Boston, Massachusetts 01670

RE: *Scarlet Rose v. Nickel & Dime, Inc.*
    Your Claim No.: 2000-0001-ND-01
    Date of loss: 1/31/2000
    Insured: Nickel & Dime, Inc.
    Our File No.: 00-0160

Dear Ms. Mallet:

Enclosed please find my litigation plan, pursuant to your reporting requirements. Should you have any questions or comment with regard to the report, or any other aspect of this case, please do not hesitate to contact me.

Very truly yours,

_____

Alan Richards, Esq.

Form 3.5 — Nickel & Dime Litigation Plan

- Claim Number: 2000-0001-ND-01
- Defendant(s): Nickel & Dime, Inc.
- Caption: *Scarlet Rose v. Nickel & Dime, Inc.*
- Docket Number: Civil Action No.: 00-125-PDD
- Court/Branch: Circuit Court, Pineapple County, Clearwater, Atlantis
- Date of Occurrence: January 31, 2000
- Date of Suit: July 1, 2000
- Date of Original Report of Claim: 1/31/2000
- Initial Litigation Plan Report Date: 8/25/2000

1. Litigation Plan
   a. Claim Professional: Louise Mallet
   b. Managing Supervisor: Christie Liscomb
   c. Defense Attorney: Alan Richards
   d. Briefly describe the nature of the action.
      Plaintiff tripped over totes that were in the aisle.

2. Venue
   a. Is venue proper for this case? If no, explain: Yes
   b. Is venue proper in more than one location? If yes, is *forum non-conveniens* available? N/A
   c. Is the current venue favorable or unfavorable for a defendant in this type of claim? If unfavorable, explain.
      Favorable in that verdicts are lower in this relatively conservative community

3. Jurisdiction
   a. Does the court have subject matter jurisdiction over the case? Yes
   b. Does the court have personal jurisdiction over this defendant? If so, set forth the manner and date of service of each defendant.
      Yes. Service of process on registered agent.

4. Statute of Limitations
   a. Was suit filed against the defendants(s) within the statute of limitations? Yes
   b. What statutes of limitations apply with respect to cross-claims, counter-claims, third party actions, or defenses that may be brought on behalf of the defendants in this case? N/A

5. Complaint/Cross Complaint/Third Party Complaint or other pleading asserted against defendant? No

6. What are the theories asserted against the defendant(s)? Negligence

7. What are the legal defenses, if any, to the theories of liability asserted?
    Condition was open and obvious.

8. Identify statutes or common law supportive of the legal defenses.
    Comparative negligence statute will apply.

9. Can any of the legal defenses be raised by motion to defeat the action(s) against the defendant(s)? If so, what is the nature of the motion? When can/must it be brought? From 0% to 100%, what is the likelihood of success?
    Summary judgment is probably not feasible. A jury must decide factual issue of whether there was negligence. However, it was an open and obvious situation, and I believe it will be worthwhile to at least present the issue to the judge.

10. What are the factual defenses to the theories? If liability was asserted?
    One former employee saw plaintiff try to step over the tote. A picture of the scene was taken within minutes. The situation was open and obvious.

11. Based upon the factual information known about the occurrence, and the nature of the case, is this a case in which summary judgment could be sought? If so, set forth evidence that could support a motion for summary judgment.
    Yes, but it is unlikely we will prevail because the court will most likely determine that it is a factual issue to be decided by a jury.

12. Please describe what further investigation or discovery (written and depositions, etc.,) is necessary to raise contemplated summary judgment motion.
    Take depositions of all fact witnesses.

13. From 0% to 100%, what is the estimated likelihood of success for the contemplated summary judgment motion?
    Less than 50%.

14. What is the *ad damnum* prayed for by the plaintiff?
    Plaintiff's settlement demand is for $300,000. The prayer for relief is for the jurisdictional minimal limit of $15,000.

15. Does plaintiff seek punitive damages against the defendant(s)? No

16. Is plaintiff's comparative/contributory negligence/fault applicable? Yes

17. Is plaintiff's comparative negligence greater than 50% a complete bar? No

18. Is plaintiff's negligence a complete bar to recovery? No

19. Based upon the facts known at this time, estimate plaintiff's comparative negligence.
    50% - 100%

20. What is the appropriate course of action in response to the complaint/counterclaim/third party complaint asserted against defendant(s)? For example: answer and raise affirmative defenses, counterclaims, etc.; motion to strike or dismiss; other?
    Answer and raise affirmative defenses.

21. Are there potential actions for contribution, indemnity, etc., that may be brought against co-defendants or other third parties? No
    If yes, identify the party or parties. N/A

22. Describe the theories of liability and nature of the recovery sought against each (*e.g.,* partial contribution, complete indemnity, etc.). N/A

23. If a division of fault is sought, estimate the percentage of fault of potentially culpable parties to that of the defendants. N/A

24. What is the statute of limitations for each potential action? N/A

25. Has this case been assigned to one judge for all future handling? If yes, state the name of the judge, and a brief description of any background information you have on this judge.
    Yes. Judge Patrick D. Doherty

26. Who is the opposing counsel?
    Bruce K. Franklin

27. Have you or anyone in your firm had prior dealings with this attorney? Yes

28. Briefly describe any information you know of concerning the skills and ability of opposing counsel.
    He is a sole practitioner. He is in his mid 30s. He will do a competent job at trial.

29. List cases and verdicts of plaintiff's counsel. Attach jury verdicts or other reporting service information.
    None with this firm. All prior cases settled before trial.

30. List the names of the defense team who will be working on the defense of this case. Which of the attorneys will arbitrate or try the case?
    Alan Richards will try the case, if necessary. Paralegal Chris Walden will assist and attend trial.

31. Please list any further investigation you believe should be accomplished and the purpose sought to be achieved by it.
    Locate Carol Westwoman, the store employee who was stocking shelves. Nothing else presently known of.

32. What discovery (written, depositions, etc.) do you believe is necessary, at this time, to prepare this case for trial? Please list each item of discovery and the purpose sought to be achieved by it.
    We will need to fully discover the case: standard negligence interrogatories, requests for production, requests for admission, production from nonparties in order to discover plaintiff's prior medical condition, depositions of plaintiffs, witnesses, former employees who will not cooperate, an IME, depositions of plaintiff's treating physicians, plus experts, if necessary.

33. Do you anticipate the need to hire experts as consultants or testifying witnesses? If so, please identify the areas of expertise in which expert assistance or testimony will be needed.
    Not at this time. We may need a physician to conduct an IME and a case management/nurse rehabilitation expert to assist with analysis of medical records if we cannot settle the case without trial.

34. Briefly describe the anticipated areas of expertise for which legal research is contemplated.
    There will be some substantial evidentiary issues for which research will be necessary, such as whether or not the Nickel & Dime internal procedures are admissible and jury instructions, if necessary.

35. Is alternative dispute resolution appropriate for this case? If so, what type?
    Yes. Mediation, if we cannot settle the case informally.

36. Based upon your experience in this venue, what is the anticipated arbitration or trial date for this case?
    Trial will probably occur within one year from the date suit was filed.

37. Briefly describe plaintiff's injuries.
Plaintiff underwent a diskectomy and two level disk fusions and was unable to work for three months. She has a prior condition in which she broke her ankle as a result of a fall on a tennis court in 2000, which also affected her back.

38. What are plaintiff's economic damages?

39. List medical special damages, if known: $44,000

40. List wage loss, if known: $6,000

41. Does plaintiff claim permanent disability, lost earnings, etc.? If so, please describe.
Yes, due to inability to work while injured, plaintiff has a lost wages claim. She also has an anatomic permanent injury and claims permanent disability as well.

42. Based upon what you know at this time, do you consider this a case of liability? If so, why?
Yes, possibly, because the tote should not have been left in the middle of the aisle, as pictures reflect it was.

43. Based upon what you know at this time, from 0% to 100%, what are the chances of prevailing on the liability issues at trial?
50%-100%, depending on the jury's assessment of plaintiff's failure to avoid an open and obvious condition.

44. Based upon what you know at this time, what is the estimated range of verdict if the plaintiff prevails, without taking into consideration any reduction for plaintiff's own fault?
$75,000-$150,000

Submitted by: Alan Richards
Date: August 15, 2000

Approved by: _____
Claim Professional

_____
Date

Alan was pleased with what Chris had accomplished. He asked Chris to prepare a letter to Excess Insurance Company reporting all that he had found out about this claim. Alan explained that Nickel & Dime was paying the attorneys' fees, had selected the law firm to defend Nickel & Dime, and was the client. The law firm's first obligation was to Nickel & Dime. In this particular situation, Nickel & Dime was responsible for the first $500,000 of any claim, and the Excess Insurance Company wouldn't pay any money until Nickel & Dime had paid the $500,000. Even though Alan did not believe the case had sufficient value to exceed $500,000, it was always a good practice to keep the Excess Insurance Company aware of what was going on in the case on a regular basis.

Chris asked if he should prepare any discovery requests. Alan told Chris to reread the assignment letter from the company, which said that this particular company allowed initial discovery to be undertaken without prior approval of the claims adjuster. The company wanted to know the firm's initial opinion of the suit and then have a telephone conference to agree upon a defense plan. Alan explained that this company, just as every other insurance company or business, wanted to keep costs and expenses to a minimum, which included the amount of money paid to its attorneys to defend cases. He also emphasized that it was extremely important to maintain a constant, although not too frequent, contact with Nickel & Dime, and, on a less frequent basis, with the insurance company. Alan told Chris to mark on his calendar a note to make sure that, at the very minimum, monthly reports were issued.

Chris prepared a letter for Alan's signature that reported all he had learned about this claim, included a copy of the answer to be filed on behalf of Nickel & Dime, and copies of the various discovery requests served upon plaintiff. Chris also included a draft of answers to interrogatories for Ms. Frechette's signature.

Chris thought it was interesting that the response to requests for admission and the response to plaintiff's request for production did not require the signature of Ms. Frechette, although the interrogatories did.

Discovery by Defendant

Within a few days after the report letter was mailed, Alan called Chris into his office and said he had spoken to Ms. Mallet, the claims adjuster on this case. He further explained that no depositions, other than the deposition of the plaintiff, were authorized until after the adjuster had a better understanding of plaintiff's medical condition and the value of this case. A compulsory physical examination of the plaintiff might be necessary, but only if the firm disagreed with the opinions of plaintiff's treating physician, which was likely.

Alan told Chris that Ms. Mallet agreed with his assessment of the liability aspect of the case and that this did not appear to be a case she would want to settle, certainly not for the $300,000 demanded by plaintiff's attorney. No offers of settlement were to be made at this time.

Chris determined that there were at least five discovery requests he could prepare at that time. Other requests could be prepared once the plaintiff provided further information. First, Chris prepared a set of interrogatories.

Negligence Interrogatories

Form 3.6 — Negligence Interrogatories

IN THE SIXTH JUDICIAL CIRCUIT COURT
IN AND FOR PINEAPPLE COUNTY, ATLANTIS

SCARLET ROSE,
    Plaintiff,

v.   Civil Action No.: 00-125-PDD

NICKEL & DIME, INC.,
    Defendant.

Defendant's First Set of Negligence Interrogatories to Plaintiff

Instructions for Use

All information that is in the possession of the individual or corporate party, her attorneys, investigators, agents, employees or other representatives of the party and her attorney is to be divulged.

If answering for another person or entity, answer with respect to that person or entity, unless otherwise stated.

Where the terms "incident" or "the incident" are used, they are meant to denote the occurrence that is the basis of this lawsuit, unless otherwise specified.

1. Please state the name and address of all persons answering or assisting in the answering of these Interrogatories:
    a. Please state your full name, address, Social Security number, and date and place of birth.
    b. Please state your height and weight.

2. Are you presently employed? If so, please state the following:
    a. The name and address of your employer, the dates of employment, and your position.
    b. The salary you earned as of the date of the accident sued upon.
    c. The amount of any time lost from work as a result of the accident sued upon.

3. Please state whether you or your attorneys, agents, servants, have obtained any statements, written or oral, from any person relating to the facts of your injuries and, if so, state:
    a. Whether written or oral and the name and address of the person obtained from
    b. Date or dates obtained.

4. Please state whether you or your agents or attorneys have any photographs of the scene of the incident complained of and, if so, state:
    a. The name and address of the photographer
    b. The date or dates such photographs were taken
    c. The name and address of the custodian thereof.

5. Please state whether you have obtained any expert to examine the scene of the incident in question and, if so, state the name and address of such expert.

6. Please describe in detail your version of how the accident occurred.

7. Please state, with particularity:
    a. All injuries known to you to have been sustained at the time of the accident
    b. Which of the foregoing injuries have you fully recovered from, giving the date of recovery
    c. Which injuries you believe to be permanent

8. List any permanent scars, disfigurement, or disability, if any, arising from the incident and state, with particularity, to which portions of the body.

9. Have you suffered from any pre-existing mental or physical infirmity, condition, disease, or injury, which you allege to have been aggravated by this accident? If so, please state:
    a. The complete name, address and specialty, if any, of each physician or other healthcare provider
    b. Who examined and/or administered treatment to you prior to this accident for same
    c. The approximate date or dates of such treatment or examination.

10. Please state the name and address of all hospitals, clinics or institutions in which you have been a patient as a result of the incident; the exact dates of such confinement, the expenses or bills paid or incurred to date therefrom for which you seek compensation in this case, specifying, with particularity, for what services or items the said charges were made.

11. Please state the full name, address and specialty, if any, of all doctors who have examined and/or treated you as a result of the subject accident along with the date or dates of such treatment, the nature of the treatment received, whether you have been discharged from said medical care, whether any doctor has given you a permanent impairment or disability and the type of treatment received from said doctors for each visit.

12. List each item of expense that you claim to have incurred as a result of the injuries sued on in this action, giving for each item the date incurred, to whom owed or paid and the goods or services for which each was incurred.

13. Have any benefits been paid or are any payable for the expenses listed in your answers to Interrogatories 11 and 12? If so, which expenses are covered by insurance, what type of insurance, and who paid the premium for the insurance?

14. Describe each injury for which you are claiming damages in this case, specifying the part of your body that was injured; the nature of the injury; and any injuries you contend are permanent.

15. Give the complete name and present addresses of all witnesses to this accident known by you, your attorneys, agents or representatives, and the names and addresses of all persons who are known to you, your attorneys, agents or representatives who have any knowledge of the facts or circumstances surrounding this accident, and whether they are eye witnesses, medical witnesses, or expert witnesses.

16. Do you intend to call any nonmedical expert witnesses at the trial of this case? If so, identify each witness; describe his or her qualifications as an expert; state the subject matter upon which the expert witness is expected to testify; state the substance of the facts and opinions to which the expert witness is expected to testify; and give a summary of the grounds for each opinion.

17. Please state the exact date and time of day or night when the accident complained of herein occurred and the conditions at the time. Give the exact location of defendant's premises, so that time can be readily identified where it is alleged the accident occurred, and set forth any alleged defect that is claimed to have caused the alleged accident.

18. If you claim you were injured by any defect of any nature, please describe in detail said defect and how in your own words this defendant would be responsible for such a defect and what you claim was dangerous about it.

19. Please state in your own words why you feel that this defendant was negligent.

20. Please state whether you had ever been on the premises prior to the date of the incident in question and, if so, for each such instance, please state:
    a. The date(s) you were upon the premises
    b. The circumstances surrounding your being upon the premises
    c. The length of time you were on the premises.

21. Do you wear glasses? If so, please state:
    a. The name and address of the physician who prescribed the eyeglasses
    b. The date said eyeglasses were prescribed
    c. The date the prescription was filled and the name and address of the person or firm filling the prescription
    d. The last time your eyes were examined and the name and address of the physician examining them.

22. Describe in detail the type of shoes that you were wearing at the time of the accident.

23. At any time prior or subsequent to, the date of the alleged occurrence did you sustain any injury, illness, or disability other than those that you have described in response to Interrogatory No. 18?

24. If your answer to the preceding interrogatory is in the affirmative, please state:
    a. A full and detailed description of each injury, illness or disability
    b. Where and when you sustained each such injury, illness or disability
    c. For what period of time, giving dates, you suffered from such injury, illness or disability

d. The name and address of each medical practitioner or other person or hospital, clinic, sanitarium, rest home or other institution visited by you or in which you were confined for the purpose of consultation, diagnosis, x-rays, treatment, or other care, specifying the dates of such visits or the period of time of such confinement.

25. Please list all physicians or other healthcare providers whom you saw for any medical reason or purpose for the last ten years before this accident.

STATE OF ATLANTIS
COUNTY OF PINEAPPLE

BEFORE ME, the undersigned authority, personally appeared Scarlet Rose, who after first being duly sworn, deposes and says that the foregoing Answers to Interrogatories are true and correct to the best of her knowledge, and she has read the foregoing Answers to Interrogatories and knows the contents thereof.

_____
Scarlet Rose

SWORN TO AND SUBSCRIBED before me, this_____ day of _____, 2___.

NOTARY PUBLIC, STATE OF ATLANTIS
My Commission Expires:
_____

CERTIFICATE OF SERVICE

I HEREBY CERTIFY that a true and correct copy of the above was mailed this 25th day of July, 2000, to: Bruce K. Franklin, Esq., attorney for Plaintiff, 616 Turner Street, Clearwater, Atlantis, 34616.

Respectfully submitted,

_____
Alan Richards, Esq.
515 Maple Street
Clearwater, Atlantis 34616

Collateral Source Interrogatories

Chris propounded collateral source interrogatories to find out about health insurance or payments from other sources, such as government assistance or workers compensation benefits.

Form 3.7 — Collateral Source Interrogatories

IN THE SIXTH JUDICIAL CIRCUIT COURT
IN AND FOR PINEAPPLE COUNTY, ATLANTIS

SCARLET ROSE,
　　　　Plaintiff,

v.   Civil Action No.: 00-125-PDD

NICKEL & DIME, INC.,
　　　　Defendant.

Defendant's Collateral Source Interrogatories to Plaintiff

Plaintiff, Scarlet Rose, is requested to answer, separately and fully, in writing and under oath, within 30 days after service of the following Interrogatories:

Instruction for use

Unless otherwise indicated, these Interrogatories refer to the time, place, and circumstances of the occurrence mentioned or complained of in the Complaint.

Where the name or identity of a person, or persons, is requested, please state full name, home address, and also business or employment address.

Where knowledge or information or possession of a party or parties is requested, such request includes knowledge of the party's agents, representatives and, unless privileged, her attorneys.

The pronoun "you" refers to the party to whom these Interrogatories are addressed and the persons mentioned in the previous paragraph.

Collateral Source Interrogatories

1. Pursuant to Atlantis Statute 627-7372, please state any and all amounts of money that you have been paid, contributed or forfeited by you to secure any rights to collateral source payments of which sums are payable from collateral sources.

2. Please list all sums paid to you or that are payable to you from Social Security, disability, and any other public program providing medical expenses, disability payments or other similar benefits.

3. Please list all sums paid to you or which are payable to you from health, sickness or income disability insurance.

4. Please list all sums paid to you or which are payable to you from any auto accident insurance that provides health benefits or income disability insurance.

5. Please list all sums paid to you or which are payable to you from any other similar insurance benefits (except life insurance) being available to you.

6. Please list any contract or agreement with any group, organization, partnership or corporation that would provide payments or reimbursements for costs of hospitalization, medical/dental expenses, or other healthcare services.

7. Please list any voluntary wage, contribution plan provided by employer(s) or any other system, intended to provide wages during a period of disability.

8. Please list any other source of collateral indemnification payments. Indicate whether these amounts have already been paid or are to be paid in the future.

STATE OF ATLANTIS
COUNTY OF PINEAPPLE

BEFORE ME, the undersigned authority, personally appeared Scarlet Rose, who after first being duly sworn, deposes and says that the foregoing Answers to Interrogatories are true and correct to the best of her information, knowledge and belief.

NOTARY PUBLIC, STATE OF ATLANTIS
My Commission Expires:

_____

CERTIFICATE OF SERVICE

I HEREBY CERTIFY that a true copy of the above has been furnished by first class U.S. Mail, postage prepaid, to Bruce K. Franklin, Esq., attorney for the Plaintiff, on this 25th day of July, 2000.

_____
Alan Richards, Esq.
Attorney for the Defendant

Requests for Admissions

Next, Chris prepared requests for admissions.

Form 3.8 — Requests for Admissions

IN THE SIXTH JUDICIAL CIRCUIT COURT
IN AND FOR PINEAPPLE COUNTY, ATLANTIS

SCARLET ROSE,
　　　Plaintiff,

v.　　　　　　　　　　　　　　　　Civil Action No.: 00-125-PDD

NICKEL & DIME, INC.,
　　　Defendant.

Requests for Admissions

Defendant, Nickel & Dime, Inc., by and through undersigned counsel, pursuant to Rule 1.370 of the Atlantis Rules of Civil Procedure, hereby requests Plaintiff, Scarlet Rose, to admit the truth of the following statements within 30 days of service.

1. Plaintiff had sustained injuries to her back and her ankle from an incident that occurred while she was playing tennis in 1998.

2. The total medical expenses incurred in this case, which are potentially recoverable, as of this date are $44,000.

3. The total amount of money that plaintiff has lost due to inability to work, as of this date is $6,000.

4. The amount of the lien from all collateral sources as of this date is $36,000.

5. The box over which plaintiff fell was approximately three feet long by one foot high by two feet deep.

6. The box was visible if the plaintiff had been looking where she was walking and paying proper attention.

7. The reason this incident occurred is because the plaintiff was not paying proper attention and did not notice the box, which was an open and obvious condition.

CERTIFICATE OF SERVICE

I HEREBY CERTIFY that a true copy of the foregoing Requests for Admissions has been furnished by first class U.S. Mail to Bruce K. Franklin, Esq., attorney for the plaintiff, 616 Turner Street, Clearwater, Atlantis 34616, on this 25th day of July, 2000.

Alan Richards, Esq.
Attorney for Defendant
515 Maple Street
Clearwater, Atlantis 34616
727-462-8888

Request for Production from Plaintiff

Then, Chris prepared a request for production.

Form 3.9 — Request for Production

IN THE SIXTH JUDICIAL CIRCUIT COURT
IN AND FOR PINEAPPLE COUNTY, ATLANTIS

SCARLET ROSE,
            Plaintiff,

v.   Civil Action No.: 00-125-PDD

NICKEL & DIME, INC.,
            Defendant.

Defendant's Request for Production

Defendant, Nickel & Dime, Inc., by and through its undersigned attorneys, and pursuant to Atlantis Rules of Civil Procedure 1.350, requests the plaintiff to produce the following for inspection and/or copying the materials and items described below, at the offices of defendant's counsel within 35 days from the date hereof.

1. Copies of federal income tax returns, W-2 withholding tax statements, any and all other business records and/or income records, and any other evidence of income for the five years prior to the subject incident or occurrence together with evidence of any other income to date.

2. Any and all photographs, graphs, charts, and other documentary evidence of the scene, parties, if applicable, involved in or pertaining to the subject incident or occurrence of issues in this cause, which the plaintiff intends to use at the trial of this action, including photographs of the scene.

3. Any and all chiropractic records, osteopathic records, faith healer's records, x-ray reports, MRI Scan reports, CT Scan reports, nurses notes, physical therapy records, including copies of any radiographic materials such as x-ray films, CT films, MRI films, etc., for this accident and any and all prior or subsequent accidents.

4. Any and all reports or records concerning any prior or subsequent accidents.

5. Any and all medical reports, doctors' reports, or reports rendered by experts applicable to any and all issues in this cause, for which the plaintiff intends to use the author of said report as an expert witness at trial.

6. Any and all written or recorded statements from the defendants on any witness concerning this action or a stenographic, mechanical electrical, or other recording or transcription of a statement that is a substantial verbatim recital or an oral statement, the date taken, and the means of recording or preserving same.

7. Any and all copies of any applications for insurance, including health, disability, casualty, automobile, hospital, business interruption or umbrella liability policies. Plaintiff may comply by providing a listing of each and every insurance policy applied for, the name of the agent who took the application if applicable, whether the policy was issued, the effective dates of the policy and a listing of any claims submitted under the policies. This request is limited to the period subsequent to 1990.

8. Any and all copies of all other medical and/or disability insurance policies, including all booklets concerning any group policies, that provide or may provide medical or disability payments to plaintiff regarding damages alleged to have been incurred as a result of the subject incident, together with the relevant declarations or face sheet reflecting available coverage and deductibles.

9. Any and all medical records from all medical providers that the claimant has seen in the last five years, including hospital emergency rooms and walk-in clinics.

10. Any and all medication records, whether prescription or not, that the claimant is now taking on a regular basis.

11. Any and all employment records of the plaintiff whether as a regular employee or independent contractor for the last ten years.

12. Any and all medical records from all medical providers who have rendered any care or treatment to the plaintiff as a result of the incident complained of, or for any reason whatsoever, subsequent to the incident complained of.

I HEREBY CERTIFY that a true and correct copy of the above was mailed this 25th day of July, 2000, to Bruce K. Franklin, Esq., 616 Turner Street, Clearwater, Atlantis 34616.

Alan Richards, Esq.
515 Maple Street
Clearwater, Atlantis 34616

Expert Witness Interrogatories

Alan told Chris to send out expert witness interrogatories at this early stage to see if plaintiff had already retained an expert. This would be somewhat unusual, but not unheard of.

Form 3.10 — Expert Witness Interrogatories

IN THE SIXTH JUDICIAL CIRCUIT COURT
IN AND FOR PINEAPPLE COUNTY, ATLANTIS

SCARLET ROSE,
    Plaintiff,

v.   Civil Action No.: 00-125-PDD

NICKEL & DIME, INC.,
    Defendant.

Defendant's Expert Witness Interrogatories to Plaintiff

Pursuant to Rule 1.350 of the Atlantis Rules of Civil Procedure, defendant hereby propounds the following expert witness interrogatories, which are to be answered within 30 days

1. Please state the name and address of each person expected by you, your attorney, or any representative of yours, to testify as an expert witness during the trial of this matter.

2. Please state the following information for each expert witness listed in No. 1 above:
    a. His or her profession or occupation, and the field in which he or she is allegedly an expert
    b. The name and address of each school he or she attended and a description of each degree received
    c. The name of any professional trade association of which he or she is a member
    d. The title, subject matter, publisher and date of publication of any books, papers, or articles on subjects in his or her field and that were relied upon by the expert in determining the facts, conclusions or opinions pertinent to this litigation
    e. The number of years each has practiced or worked in this field
    f. His or her places of employment for the past ten years
    g. The subject matter on which he or she is expected to testify.

3. Please state whether any of your experts listed in No. 1 have determined any facts or formed any opinions concerning any issues involved in this case. If so, please indicate:
    a. The name of the expert or experts, and the issue about which he or she has an opinion
    b. The fact or facts determined and the opinion or opinions formed by each expert
    c. The substance of the facts relied on by such expert in arriving at his or her opinion or opinions
    d. A summary of the grounds relied on by each expert in reaching his or her opinion.

4. Please state whether any item or object relevant to this lawsuit has been tested, analyzed, examined or inspected by any of the experts listed in No. 1. If so, please describe in detail:
    a. Each item or object that was tested, analyzed, examined or inspected, and the name of the expert
    b. The facts or information you were seeking in having these tests, examinations, or inspections made the steps used in each test, examination or inspection of any object or item material to this lawsuit
    c. The findings resulting from each inspection, analysis, examination or test conducted
    d. The facts or opinions derived from the tests
    e. The date of each test, the name and address of the person conducting the test, and the name of each test performed.

5. Did any expert listed in No. 4(a) submit a report setting forth his or her opinions or conclusions reached from any test, analysis, examination or inspection that he or she may have conducted? If so, state:
    a. The date his or her report was submitted and who submitted it
    b. The name or other means of identification of the person to whom this report was submitted
    c. The name and address of the person who has present custody of this report
    d. A summary of contents of the report.

6. Have any experts listed in No. 1 submitted any other reports with regard to any issues relevant to this lawsuit? If so, state:
    a. The name of each such expert
    b. A description of each report that was made
    c. The date that each report was made
    d. The name, or other means of identification of the person to whom each report was submitted
    e. The name and address of the person who has present custody of each report
    f. A summary of the contents of each report.

7. If you will do so without a Request to Produce, please attach a copy of all reports, writings, memoranda, recordings, or any other material submitted to you by any expert listed in No. 1.

STATE OF ATLANTIS
COUNTY OF PINEAPPLE

BEFORE ME, the undersigned authority, personally appeared Scarlet Rose, who being duly sworn, deposes and says that the above Answers to Interrogatories are true and correct to the best of her knowledge, information and belief.

_____
Scarlet Rose

SWORN TO AND SUBSCRIBED before me this _____ day of _____, 2000.

NOTARY PUBLIC, STATE OF ATLANTIS
My Commission Expires:

_____

CERTIFICATE OF SERVICE

I HEREBY CERTIFY that a true copy of the foregoing Defendant's Expert Witness Interrogatories to Plaintiff has been furnished by first class U.S. Mail to Bruce K. Franklin, Esq., attorney for the plaintiff, on this 25th day of July, 2000.

_____
Alan Richards, Esq.
Attorney for the Defendant
515 Maple Street
Clearwater, Atlantis 34616

Notice of Serving Discovery Requests

Chris remembered what Alan had told him about the court and clerk's office trying to reduce the amount of paper that was placed in the court files. Interrogatories were not to be filed with the court. The answers might be filed with the court at a later time, if trial were necessary, or if the answers were necessary for the judge to consider a motion for summary judgment. Instead, Chris filed a document that simply informed the court that interrogatories had been served. That way the court was made aware of the fact that the case was proceeding, and there was activity of record, but the court file did not become too voluminous. He filed the following document that was used with all such discovery requests.

Form 3.11 — Notice of Serving Discovery Requests

IN THE SIXTH JUDICIAL CIRCUIT COURT
IN AND FOR PINEAPPLE COUNTY, ATLANTIS

SCARLET ROSE,
     Plaintiff,

v.   Civil Action No.: 00-125-PDD

NICKEL & DIME, INC.,
     Defendant.

Notice of Service of Defendant's First Set of Negligence Interrogatories,
Collateral Source Interrogatories, Expert Interrogatories,
Requests for Production and Requests for Admission

COMES NOW the defendant, Nickel & Dime, Inc., by and through its counsel, and pursuant to Rule 1.340, Atlantis Rules of Civil Procedure, and hereby gives notice to the court that it has served the plaintiff, Scarlet Rose, Defendant's First Set of Negligence Interrogatories, numbered 1 through 25, to be answered in writing under oath within 30 days of service, in addition to collateral source interrogatories, expert witness interrogatories, Requests for Admission, and Requests for Production.

CERTIFICATE OF SERVICE

I HEREBY CERTIFY that a true copy of the foregoing has been furnished by first-class U.S. mail to Bruce K. Franklin, Esq., attorney for the plaintiff, on this 25th day of July, 2000.

_____

Alan Richards, Esq.
Attorney for the Defendant
515 Maple Street
Clearwater, Atlantis 34616

Request for Production From Nonparties

Since Chris could not obtain medical records or any other records without a signed authorization from the plaintiff, he prepared a notice of intent to subpoena the records, as required by the rules of civil procedure. He used the list of names he obtained from the medical records that were attached to the demand letter sent to Ms. Mallet by plaintiff's attorney.

Form 3.12 — Request for Production from Nonparties

IN THE SIXTH JUDICIAL CIRCUIT COURT
IN AND FOR PINEAPPLE COUNTY, ATLANTIS

SCARLET ROSE,
      Plaintiff,

v.   Civil Action No.: 00-125-PDD

NICKEL & DIME, INC.,
      Defendant.

Notice of Production from Nonparties

TO: Bruce K. Franklin, Esq., attorney for Scarlet Rose.

YOU ARE NOTIFIED that after ten days from the date of service of this notice, if service is by delivery, or 15 days from the date of service, if service is by mail, and if no objection is received from any party, the undersigned will issue the attached subpoenas directed to the following individuals who are not party to the lawsuit to produce the items listed as specified in the subpoenas

NAME AND ADDRESS:

Records Custodian
Dr. Von N. Beebe

Records Custodian
Dr. Brendan Patrick

Records Custodian
Community Hospital

Records Custodian
Dr. Michael Mullan

Records Custodian
Physical Therapy Inc.

Records Custodian
Emergency EMT

CERTIFICATE OF SERVICE

I HEREBY CERTIFY that a true and correct copy of the foregoing has been mailed by U.S. Mail to Bruce K. Franklin, Esq., 616 Turner Street, Clearwater, Atlantis 34616, this 25th day of July, 2000.

Alan Richards, Esq.
515 Maple Street
Clearwater, Atlantis 34616

After Chris had filed the Notice of Intent to Subpoena Records pursuant to the rule, he could not have the subpoena served upon the person from whom he was to receive records until ten days had expired. Plaintiff's attorney could object to defendant's notice of what it intended to do. In most cases, Chris could expect to receive a request for copies from plaintiff. It is somewhat unusual for there to be an objection, unless the records to be subpoenaed were extremely sensitive, such as a rare disease or psychiatric and psychological information that may or may not be relevant.

Chris put a note in the file to do further discovery once plaintiff responded to the interrogatories and requests for production. Alan could issue Subpoenas to Nonparties for Records without having the clerk sign the subpoena. After they received the records from nonparties, such as medical providers and former employers, Alan would consider a compulsory physical examination of plaintiff, depending upon what the medical records reflected.

As far as expert witness interrogatories were concerned, Chris remembered that under Atlantis law, there is no duty on the part of any party to a lawsuit to update answers to interrogatories. He thought it might be early to discover what experts plaintiff had and was willing to reveal at this stage of the lawsuit. He decided not to prepare a set of expert witness interrogatories, but he made a note to ask Alan how Alan handled the expert witness issue.

Closing the Pleadings

When the answer finally arrived, within the 20-day timeframe, Bruce told Marlene to prepare a document called Denial of Affirmative Defenses. Marlene was unfamiliar with such a document but, with the help of Mayda, Bruce's secretary, she found the document and submitted the following for Bruce's signature.

Form 3.13 — Plaintiff's Denial of Defendant's Affirmative Defenses

IN THE SIXTH JUDICIAL CIRCUIT COURT
IN AND FOR PINEAPPLE COUNTY, ATLANTIS

SCARLET ROSE,
    Plaintiff,

v.   Civil Action No.: 00-125-PDD

NICKEL & DIME, INC.,
    Defendant.

Plaintiff's Denial of Defendant's Affirmative Defenses

Comes now, Plaintiff, Scarlet Rose, by and through undersigned counsel, and hereby denies each and every affirmative defense asserted by the defendant, Nickel & Dime, Inc., and demands strict proof of each such defense.

CERTIFICATE OF SERVICE

I HEREBY CERTIFY that a true copy of the foregoing has been furnished to the defendant, by mailing a copy to its attorney, Alan Richards, at his office address of 515 Maple Street, Clearwater, Atlantis 34616, on this 5th day of August, 2000.

Bruce K. Franklin, Esq.
616 Turner Street
Clearwater, Atlantis 34616

Bruce explained to Marlene that the pleadings stage of the case was technically over, and the case was now moving into the discovery stage.

Maintaining the File

As Chris created documents, he kept a record of all that was being done to track when documents went out and when responses from the plaintiff were due. He created an index.

Scarlet Rose v. Nickel & Dime, Inc.
Civil Action No.: 00-125-PDD

Defendant's Discovery Index

1. Complaint
2. Summons
3. Plaintiff's Interrogatories to Defendant
4. Plaintiff's Requests for Admissions
5. Plaintiff's Request for Production
6. Notice of Appearance
7. Answer
8. Defendant's Interrogatories to Plaintiff
9. Defendant's Collateral Source Interrogatories to Plaintiff
10. Defendant's Request for Production of Documents to Plaintiff
11. Defendant's Request for Admissions to Plaintiff
12. Defendant's Expert Witness Interrogatories to Plaintiff
13. Notice of Production From Nonparty and *Subpoena Duces Tecum* Without Deposition: Brendan Patrick, M.D., and others

---

Chapter Four

THE WRITTEN DISCOVERY STAGE

After the complaint was served and the defendant's responses to the discovery requests had not been received, Marlene asked Bruce what should be done. Bruce reminded Marlene that, according to the applicable rule, she had to allow five days for mailing. He added that he had received a phone call from opposing counsel a few days earlier and had agreed to a 20-day extension for the defense to respond.

Before the 45th day arrived, Chris told his supervising attorney that he had been unable to get all of the documents from Kate Frechette or Marjorie Murphy and would not be able to respond to the discovery requests in time. Alan told him not to worry, because things like that occur in every case. Almost without exception, attorneys routinely grant opposing counsel the courtesy time extension. On the other hand, he explained, if the request for more time appears to be a tactical maneuver or if it is abused, he might not always agree. In this case, Alan had spoken to Bruce, and he had no objection to extending the defendant's response time.

Defendant's Responses to Plaintiff's Discovery Requests

Marlene marked the revised date on her calendar. After adding 20 days, that the responses to the various discovery response requests from the defendant were due 65 days from the date of service of the summons and complaint.

Bruce received the defendant's responses on the 60th day. There also were various discovery documents directed to the plaintiff included in the package of materials to be answered by Scarlet Rose.

Defendant's Responses to Negligence Interrogatories

Bruce told Marlene to review and summarize the responses received from Nickel & Dime. The first document Marlene reviewed was the Answers to Interrogatories. The answers provided Marlene with some information, but not as much as she was hoping for. She learned, among other things, the names of the employees who might have knowledge of the situation.

Form 4.1 — Defendant's Answer to Plaintiff's First Interrogatories

IN THE SIXTH JUDICIAL CIRCUIT COURT
IN AND FOR PINEAPPLE COUNTY, ATLANTIS

SCARLET ROSE,
    Plaintiff,

v.   Civil Action No.: 00-125-PDD

NICKEL & DIME, INC.,
    Defendant.

Defendant's Answers to Plaintiff's First Interrogatories

1. Please state the names, addresses and job titles, and if an officer of a corporation, identify such office or position, of all persons participating in the answering of these Interrogatories.
    ANSWER: Name: Marjorie Murphy
                        Address: 2680 Woodhall Terrace, Palm Harbor, Atlantis 34685
                        Job Title: formerly selling supervisor

2. Were you aware, before the filing of the Complaint in this action, that the plaintiff, Scarlet Rose, was injured while in Nickel & Dime located in Clearwater, Atlantis, on January 31, 2000?
    ANSWER: Yes

3. State the name, address, and job titles of any and all persons who were responsible for the maintenance of the area where the incident occurred.
    ANSWER: Caitlin Palmer, a selling supervisor, and I, also a selling supervisor, were in the vicinity of where plaintiff fell. We both witnessed the fall to some extent. We would have been responsible for maintenance and/or inspection of the area at the time of the incident. We were fully aware of the situation. Carol Westwoman, salesperson, was unloading the tote.

4. Plaintiff, Scarlet Rose, alleges that the boxes placed in the customer walkway caused her to fall. Do you contend that the boxes were not located in the aisle, nor did they impede the path of the customer, or cause the plaintiff to fall and sustain injuries? If so, state the reasons for that belief and what you contend did cause injuries to the plaintiff.
    ANSWER: There was a tote, which is not a box, in the aisle. Totes are twelve inches high and approximately three feet long and two feet deep, made of heavy plastic. One of our employees, Carol Westwoman, was taking slippers from the tote and placing them on the sales racks. The tote was in plain view. Although a customer needed to use caution, the tote is not so large as to prevent a customer from using the aisle. It is my opinion that the tote did not cause the plaintiff to fall and sustain injuries. I believe that plaintiff did not exercise good judgment after seeing the tote in the aisle and, by attempting to step over it, made a mistake in judgment.

5. Did you, or anyone on your behalf, conduct a formal investigation of the facts and circumstances surrounding the incident? If so, state the date it was made, the name, address, occupation of each person who made it, and whether or not any report was made of it.
    ANSWER: No formal investigation was made. Since Caitlin Palmer and I were there and witnessed the incident, I prepared the incident report, as is standard procedure in such circumstances. No further investigation was necessary, although I did take two photographs.

6. Were any statements obtained by you, or in your behalf, from any person concerning the accident? If so, state the date and time on which it was obtained; the name, address, occupation of the person who made it; and whether it was written or oral. If written, the name and address of the person who has custody of it.
    ANSWER: Although I did speak to the plaintiff about the situation, no formal statements were taken about the accident. I heard her talk to rescue personnel who attended to her after the fall, and I spoke with her for quite some time until she was transported from the store. There is nothing in writing, except the incident report.

7. Did any person witness the accident? If so, state the name or other means of identification, address, occupation and name of employer, and the location from which she witnessed the accident.
    ANSWER: Caitlin Palmer and I witnessed the incident. Caitlin is still working at the store located in Clearwater, Atlantis. The only other person I am aware of who might have witnessed the incident, was Carol Westwoman, a store clerk, who was loading the slippers onto the shelves at the time plaintiff fell. I do not know Carol's current whereabouts.

8. Do you know of anyone who took, or claims to have taken, photographs of the scene of the accident, the persons, or objects involved? If so, state the subject matter of the photographs, the date each was taken, the

identity and address of the persons taking the photographs, and the name and address of each person who has possession or control of the photographs.

ANSWER: To the best of my knowledge, information, and belief, I took two photographs that depicted the scene, as it was when plaintiff fell on the date of the incident. I sent the original photographs to our Boston office. Our attorney has copies.

9. Are you protected by any insurance company indemnifying you against the type of risk on which plaintiff's claim is based? If so, state the name and address of each insurer, the number of each policy, and the type of coverage.

ANSWER: Nickel & Dime is responsible for all claims up to $500,000. An insurance company is involved over and above that amount. If plaintiff desires further information, please let me know.

10. Did you have an agent or employee whose duties included the cleaning, maintenance, or care of the subject area? If so, please state the name, address, job title, and a description of his or her duties.

ANSWER: There was an employee whose duties included the cleaning, maintenance, and care of the subject area after the store was closed. I do not recall the name of that individual. However, in my opinion, cleaning, maintenance, or care of the subject area had nothing to do with why the plaintiff fell.

11. List all accidents that occurred before January 31, 2000, involving the customer walkway, aisles and surrounding area. Specifically, list the date, type of accident, and the persons involved.

ANSWER: I do not recall any similar accidents. There were other people who fell in the store, but the falls were due to something other than a customer losing his or her balance by trying to step over a tote.

12. For every allegation in the plaintiff's Complaint that you will or have denied, state the specific grounds for the denial.

ANSWER: The Complaint alleges that Nickel & Dime was negligent. In my opinion, that is not true. This incident occurred because the plaintiff did not take the time to walk around the totes or to be more careful as she walked by them. She saw the open and obvious condition. It was a necessary situation since the store racks need to be replenished on a regular basis.

13. State whether or not any representative, agent, or employee of Nickel & Dime has received any complaints concerning boxes being placed in the aisles. (Yes or No)

ANSWER: Not to my knowledge.

14. If the answer to No. 13 is "Yes," list the date of the complaint, the nature of the complaint and the actions taken by Nickel & Dime, Inc., to remedy the complaint.

ANSWER: N/A.

15. Is a diary, logbook, or similar written record maintained containing the day-to-day happenings at Nickel & Dime? If the answer is in the affirmative, where and in whose custody are the above-referenced records for the months proceeding January 31, 2000?

ANSWER: There are numerous records kept of daily activities. I have no idea where they might be. Some records would include employment records, sales receipts, etc. As indicated in previous Answers to Interrogatories, the plaintiff was in the store for some time, and I, along with others, spoke to her at some length. I recall plaintiff saying to me that she saw the totes and thought she could walk over them safely. I remember her saying that she was in a hurry, and that is why she did not walk around them. She talked about her pre-existing ankle problem and how she had broken it a year ago.

16. What statements were made in your presence by plaintiff(s) or anyone else after the accident on January 31, 2000?

ANSWER: Please see answer to Interrogatory No. 15.

17. If you would do so without a motion to produce or inspect, please attach copies of such statements to your answers to these interrogatories.
    ANSWER: No such document exists, other than the incident report, which is work-product, and was not signed by plaintiff.

18. List any other persons or entities, including their addresses, which you feel are responsible for plaintiff's injuries. For each person or entity listed, specifically describe the actions, inactions, or conduct that makes them responsible.
    ANSWER: None known of other than plaintiff.

19. Please state the names of all employees who were working at Nickel & Dime on the date of the incident.
    ANSWER: Caitlin Palmer, David Fitzgerald, Christy Davidson, Annie Edwards, Andrea Jones, Ken Whittacre, Shannon Young, Courtney Johns, Annabelle Rojas, Carol Westwoman, Betsy Ross.

_____
Marjorie Murphy

STATE OF ATLANTIS
COUNTY OF PINEAPPLE

BEFORE ME, the undersigned authority, personally appeared Marjorie Murphy, who being by me first duly sworn, on oath, deposes and says that the foregoing Answers to Interrogatories are true and correct to the best of her knowledge, and that she has read the foregoing Answers to Interrogatories and knows the contents thereof.

SWORN TO AND SUBSCRIBED before me this 5th day of September, 2000.

Notary Public, State of Atlantis at Large
My Commission Expires:

_____

CERTIFICATE OF SERVICE

I HEREBY CERTIFY that a true copy of the foregoing Answers to Interrogatories has been furnished by first class U.S. mail to Bruce K. Franklin, Esq., attorney for the plaintiff, 616 Turner Street, Clearwater, Atlantis 34616 on this 20th day of September, 2000.

_____
Alan Richards, Esq.
Attorney for the Defendant

Defendant's Responses to Requests for Admissions

The next document Marlene reviewed was Defendant's Response to Plaintiff's Requests for Admission. The responses were helpful because Scarlet Rose, as plaintiff, has the burden of proof at trial and would not need to prove what was admitted, such as ownership of the property or the duty of care that was owed by Nickel & Dime. The responses were as follows:

Form 4.2 — Defendant's Responses to Plaintiff's Request for Admissions

IN THE SIXTH JUDICIAL CIRCUIT COURT
IN AND FOR PINEAPPLE COUNTY, ATLANTIS

SCARLET ROSE,
Plaintiff,

v.   Civil Action No.: 00-125-PDD

NICKEL & DIME, INC.,
    Defendant.

Defendant's Responses to Plaintiff's Requests for Admissions

Defendant, Nickel & Dime, Inc., hereby responds to the Requests for Admissions that were served upon it by plaintiff Scarlet Rose at the time the complaint was filed, to wit:

1. Jurisdiction and Venue of this matter properly lies in Pineapple County, Atlantis.
    RESPONSE: Admitted

2. The incident stated in the complaint occurred on January 31, 2000, in the slipper department of the Nickel & Dime store located in Clearwater, Atlantis.
    RESPONSE: Admitted

3. Defendant, Nickel & Dime, Inc., owned the Nickel & Dime store where plaintiff was injured in January of 2000, at the time the incident occurred.
    RESPONSE: Admitted

4. Plaintiff sustained injuries to her back as a result of the incident.
    RESPONSE: Admitted

5. Plaintiff, as a member of the general public, was an invited guest of Nickel & Dime at the time of the incident complained of and had a legal right to be in the place where she was when the incident complained of occurred.
    RESPONSE: Admitted

6. Plaintiff was within a section of the Nickel & Dime store where she had a legal right to be at the time of the incident.
    RESPONSE: Admitted

7. Boxes should not be left in an aisle where patrons of Nickel & Dime might inadvertently trip over them.
    RESPONSE: Admitted

8. Nickel & Dime knew or should have known that a box was left in an aisle within the slipper department of the Nickel & Dime store at the time plaintiff tripped and fell over the box.
    RESPONSE: Denied

9. Nickel & Dime owed a duty to plaintiff, and all other members of the general public who patronized their store, not to leave a box in an aisle where patrons such as plaintiff might fall over the box.
    RESPONSE: Admitted

10. Nickel & Dime breached the duty of care that it owed plaintiff when it allowed a condition to exist, namely a box in an aisle, which was potentially hazardous to patrons such as plaintiff.
    RESPONSE: Denied

11. Plaintiff was injured because Nickel & Dime failed to keep the aisle in the slipper department clear of a box.
    RESPONSE: Denied

12. Nickel & Dime is legally responsible for all injuries that plaintiff sustained when she tripped and fell over a box that was left in the aisle of the slipper department.
RESPONSE: Denied

CERTIFICATE OF SERVICE

I HEREBY CERTIFY that a true copy of the foregoing Responses to Requests for Admissions has been furnished by first class U.S. mail to Bruce K. Franklin, Esq., attorney for the plaintiff, 616 Turner Street, Clearwater, Atlantis 34616 on this 20th day of September, 2000.

Alan Richards, Esq.
Attorney for the Defendant

Defendant's Responses to Requests for Production

The responses to Plaintiff's Requests for Production of Documents could yield interesting information, such as whether other people had fallen in similar situations or in the same part of the store, or if other trip-and-fall lawsuits had been filed against Nickel & Dime. Such information could be invaluable. Marlene could then view the files, find out the outcome, and read depositions given in the other lawsuits by employees and corporate representatives. All this would make her job easier. Other documents requested were not for records necessary to prove the case against defendant but were more to obtain records which documented ownership of the building, to provide a copy of an insurance policy, and to obtain copies of the actual photographs taken immediately after the incident, among other things. In this case, Marlene received the following response:

Form 4.3 — Defendant's Responses to Requests for Production

IN THE SIXTH JUDICIAL CIRCUIT COURT
IN AND FOR PINEAPPLE COUNTY, ATLANTIS

SCARLET ROSE,
Plaintiff,

v.   Civil Action No.: 00-125-PDD

NICKEL & DIME, INC.,
Defendant.

Defendant's Response to Plaintiff's First Request for Production

COMES NOW the defendant, Nickel & Dime, Inc., by and through its undersigned counsel, and files this its Response to Plaintiff's First Request for Production as follows:

1. Any and all photographs both prior to and subsequent to plaintiff's injury incident that depict the area where plaintiff alleges she tripped and fell, including the area where the boxes impeded the walkway.
ANSWER: The only photographs within defendant's possession are the two photos taken immediately after the incident, which are attached.

2. Any and all documents pertaining to the inspection and warning procedures for dangerous conditions, including employee-training manuals.
ANSWER: Defendant is unable to comply with the request because there are no such documents.

3. A copy of any and all insurance policy or policies, liability, health, medical, or otherwise, that could afford the plaintiff coverage for any expenses, medical or otherwise, sustained or incurred as a result of the alleged fall that is the subject matter of the plaintiff's Complaint.

    ANSWER: Nickel & Dime, Inc., is self-insured up to $500,000. Please see Answers to Interrogatories. There is an excess insurance policy over that amount.

4. All licenses or any permit authorizing you to operate the business known as Nickel & Dime, Inc., in Clearwater, Pineapple County, Atlantis.

    ANSWER: A copy of the business permit authorizing Nickel & Dime, Inc., to operate in Clearwater, Pineapple County, Atlantis, is attached.

5. All accident or incident reports concerning any accident of persons falling at Nickel & Dime, Inc., located in Clearwater, Pineapple County, Atlantis, on or before January 31, 2000.

    ANSWER: Defendant objects to the request for production as stated, since it is overly broad. Based upon the testimony of former employees, there were no other accidents that occurred in a manner similar to the accident involving plaintiff. Further, accident incident reports are, by definition, prepared in anticipation of litigation and are therefore privileged.

CERTIFICATE OF SERVICE

I HEREBY CERTIFY that a true copy of the foregoing has been furnished by first class U.S. mail to Bruce K. Franklin, Esq., attorney for the plaintiff, 616 Turner Street, Clearwater, Atlantis 34616 on this 20th day of September, 2000.

_____
Alan Richards, Esq.
Attorney for the Defendant

After drafting a letter to Scarlet Rose informing her of the developments, Marlene wrote a memo to Bruce telling him what further action she thought was appropriate.

Memorandum

TO: Bruce Franklin
FROM: Marlene Mertz
DATE: September 20, 2000
RE: *Scarlet Rose v. Nickel & Dime, Inc.*

After reviewing defendant's responses to our discovery, I think we should do the following:

1. Depose Marjorie Murphy, who answered the interrogatories and has personal knowledge of the incident. She took two photos after the incident. She also spoke to Ms. Rose.

2. Depose Caitlin Palmer, who supposedly watched Ms. Rose attempt to walk over the box or tote, and says Ms. Rose told her (Ms. Palmer) that she (Ms. Rose) was in a hurry.

3. Depose all listed former employees, who may have important testimony about procedures, or other incidents, even if they don't have knowledge of this incident.

Please let me know if you agree and if I should start on these actions now.

Bruce responded that he agreed with her suggestions. He asked Marlene to set the depositions of the witnesses as soon as possible.

Plaintiff's Response to Discovery Requests From the Defendant

Marlene drafted the following suggested responses and answers to the discovery requests made by Nickel & Dime upon Scarlet.

Form 4.4 — Plaintiff's Answers to Defendant's First Set of Negligence Interrogatories to Plaintiff

IN THE SIXTH JUDICIAL CIRCUIT COURT
IN AND FOR PINEAPPLE COUNTY, ATLANTIS

SCARLET ROSE,
      Plaintiff,

v.   Civil Action No.: 00-125-PDD

NICKEL & DIME, INC.,
      Defendant.

Plaintiff's Answers to Defendant's First Set of Negligence Interrogatories to Plaintiff

1.   Please state the name and address of all persons answering or assisting in the answering of these interrogatories.
    ANSWER: Scarlet Rose, 1111 Pine Street, Tarpon Springs, Atlantis 34689

2.   Please state your full name, address, Social Security number, date of birth, and place of birth.
    ANSWER: Scarlet Rose; 1111 Pine Street, Tarpon Springs, Atlantis 34689; 234-34-4567; 2/8/1962; New Orleans, Louisiana
    a.   State your height, weight, color of hair, and color of eyes.
    ANSWER: 5'5"; 135 lbs; brown hair and brown eyes.

3.   Are you presently employed? If so, please state the following:
    a.   The name and address of your employer, the dates of employment and your position
    b.   The salary earned as of the date of the accident sued upon
    c.   The amount of any wages lost from work as a result of the accident sued upon
    ANSWER: Yes. Pineapple County Public Defender's Office; 1982-present; 100 Main Street, Room 400; Investigator; $36,000 per year; $6,000.

4.   Please state whether you or your attorneys, agents, servants, have obtained any statements, written or oral from any person relating to the facts of your injuries and if so, state:
    a.   Whether written or oral and the name and address of the person
    b.   Date or dates obtained
    ANSWER: Yes, from my mother, Jane Morris, but the statement was not in writing or recorded; 1/31/2000

5.   Please state whether you or your agents or attorneys have any photographs of the scene of the incident complained of and, if so, state:
    a.   The name and address of the photographer
    b.   The date or dates such photographs were taken
    c.   The name and address of the custodian thereof
    ANSWER: Yes. One photo was taken a day or two after the incident by my mother, Jane Morris. 232 Oak Street, Tarpon Springs, Atlantis, 34689.

6.   Please state whether you have obtained any expert to examine the scene of the incident in question and, if so, state the name and address of such expert.
    ANSWER: Undetermined at this time.

7. Please describe in detail your version of how the accident occurred.
   ANSWER: I was walking down a main aisle, turned left to go through the accessories department, and fell over a box that was lying in the middle of the aisle.

8. Please state, with particularity:
   a.   All injuries known to you to have been sustained at the time of the accident
   b.   Which of the foregoing injuries have you fully recovered from, giving the date of recovery
   c.   Which injuries you believe to be permanent
   d.   List any permanent scars, disfigurement or disability, if any, arising out of the accident and state, with particularity, to which portions of the body
   ANSWER: I had surgery on my lower back because of this incident, two months after the incident. That injury is permanent, and I now have two rods in my back.

9. Have you suffered from any pre-existing mental or physical infirmity, condition, disease, or injury that you allege to have been aggravated by this accident? If so, please state:
   a.   The complete name, address and specialty, if any, of each physician or other healthcare provider who examined and/or administered treatment to you prior to this accident for same
   b.   The approximate date or dates of such treatment or examination
   ANSWER: I broke my ankle in 1998. My lower back bothered me for a while. I was well until the incident at Nickel & Dime. Dr. Mullan, general practitioner, 700 Green Street, Clearwater, Atlantis, 33759, and Dr. Patrick, orthopedic specialist, 2244 Eagle Drive, Clearwater, Atlantis, 33759, treated me for the prior injury.

10. Please state the name and address of all hospitals, clinics or institutions in which you have been a patient as a result of the accident; the exact dates of such confinement; the expenses or bills paid or incurred to date from which you seek compensation in this case, specifying, with particularity, for what services or items the charges were made.
    ANSWER: I was seen at the Community Hospital emergency room, 200 Main Street, Clearwater, Atlantis, 33759, immediately following the incident. I was also admitted into the hospital for four days in March when Dr. Beebe operated on me. My bills were $44,000. I have not seen a doctor in a few months.

11. Please state the full name, address, and specialty of all doctors who have examined and/or treated you as a result of the accident along with the date or dates of such treatment, the nature of the treatment received, whether you have been discharged from such medical care, whether any doctor has given you a permanent impairment or disability, and the type of treatment received from the doctors for each visit.
    ANSWER: Dr. Von Beebe, 777 Coconut Street, Clearwater, Atlantis 33759, surgeon, 3/3/2000-7/21/2000, dual rod stabilization surgery; Dr. Brendan Patrick, 2244 Eagle Drive, Clearwater, Atlantis 33759; and Dr. Michael Mullan, 700 Green Street, Clearwater, Atlantis 33759, general practitioner.

12. List each item of expense that you claim to have incurred as a result of the injuries sued on in this action, giving for each item the date incurred, to whom owed or paid, and the goods or services for which each was incurred.
    ANSWER: $44,000 in medical expenses; $6,000 in lost wages. Please see medical bills attached to response to Request for Production.

13. Have any benefits been paid or are any payable for the expenses listed in your answers to Interrogatories 11 and 12 above? If so, which expenses are covered by insurance, what type of insurance, and who paid the premium for the insurance?
    ANSWER: Yes, $36,000 was paid by Blue Cross/Blue Shield. This was a policy provided to me by my employer.

14. Describe each injury for which you are claiming damages in this case, specifying the part of your body that was injured; the nature of the injury; any injuries you contend are permanent.

ANSWER: Several parts of my body were injured in the incident; however, my lower back is the main problem.

15. Give the complete names and present addresses of all witnesses to this accident known by you, your attorneys, agents or representatives; the names and addresses of all person whom are known to you, your attorneys, agents or representatives who have any knowledge of the facts or circumstances surrounding this accident; and whether they are eye witnesses, medical witnesses, or expert witnesses.
    ANSWER: There was at least one Nickel & Dime employee, I believe, who saw the incident. There was another employee who came up soon after the incident. There were several other employees and customers nearby. I do not have any of their names.

16. Please state the exact date and time of day or night when the accident complained of herein occurred, the conditions at the time, and give the exact location of defendant's premises.
    ANSWER: The incident occurred at approximately 12:30 p.m., in the accessories department, on January 31, 2000.

17. If you claim you were injured by any defect of any nature, please describe in detail the defect, how, in your own words, this defendant would be responsible for such a defect, and what you claim was dangerous about it.
    ANSWER: The box I tripped over should not have been there.

18. Please state in your own words why you feel that this defendant was negligent.
    ANSWER: Please see answer above.

19. Please state whether you have ever been on said premises prior to the date of the incident in question and, if so, for each such instance, please state:
    a.   The date(s) you were upon said premises
    b.   The circumstances surrounding your being upon said premises
    c.   The length of time you were upon said premises
    ANSWER: I have been in that store on dozens of occasions, far too numerous to mention, for hours and hours.

20. Do you wear glasses? If so, please state:
    a.   The name and address of the physician who prescribed said eyeglasses
    b.   The date said eyeglasses were prescribed
    c.   The date the prescription was filled and the name and address of the person or firm filling the prescription
    d.   The last time your eyes were examined and the name and address of the physician examining them.
    ANSWER: No

21. Describe in detail the type of shoes that you were wearing at the time of the accident.
    ANSWER: I was wearing tennis shoes.

22. At any time before, or subsequent to, the date of the alleged occurrence did you sustain any injury, illness, or disability other than those that you have described in response to Interrogatory No. 18?
    ANSWER: None, other than my broken ankle.

23. If your answer to the preceding interrogatory is in the affirmative, please state:
    a.   A full and detailed description of each injury, illness, or disability
    b.   Where and when you sustained each injury, illness, or disability
    c.   For what period of time, giving dates, you suffered from such injury, illness, or disability
    d.   The name and address of each medical practitioner or other person, hospital, clinic, sanitarium, rest home, or other institution visited by you or in which you were confined for the purpose of consultation, diagnosis, x-rays, treatment, or other care, specifying the dates of such visits or the period of time of such confinement.
    ANSWER: N/A

24. Please list all physicians or other healthcare providers who you saw for any medical reason or purpose for the last ten years before this accident.
    ANSWER: None other than those doctors and hospitals previously identified herein.

STATE OF ATLANTIS
COUNTY OF PINEAPPLE

BEFORE ME, the undersigned authority, personally appeared Scarlet Rose, who after first being duly sworn, deposes and says that the foregoing Answers to Interrogatories are true and correct to the best of her knowledge, and that she has read the foregoing Answers to Interrogatories and knows the contents thereof.

_____
Scarlet Rose

SWORN TO AND SUBSCRIBED before me, this 24th day of September, 2000.

NOTARY PUBLIC, STATE OF ATLANTIS
My Commission Expires:

_____

CERTIFICATE OF SERVICE

I HEREBY CERTIFY that a true and correct copy of the above was mailed this 24th day of September, 2000, to Alan Richards, Esq., attorney for defendant, 515 Maple Street, Clearwater, Atlantis 34616.

_____
Bruce K. Franklin, Esq.
616 Turner Street
Clearwater, Atlantis 34616

Plaintiff's Answers to Collateral Source Interrogatories

Form 4.5 — Plaintiff's Answers to Collateral Source Interrogatories

IN THE SIXTH JUDICIAL CIRCUIT COURT
IN AND FOR PINEAPPLE COUNTY, ATLANTIS

SCARLET ROSE,
    Plaintiff,

v.   Civil Action No.: 00-125-PDD

NICKEL & DIME, INC.,
    Defendant.

Plaintiff's Answers to Defendant's Collateral Source Interrogatories

1. Pursuant to Atlantis Statute 627-7372, please state any and all amounts of money which you have been paid, contributed, or forfeited by you to secure any rights to collateral source payments of sums that are payable from collateral sources.
   ANSWER: $36,000 was paid by Blue Cross/Blue Shield.

2. Please list all sums paid to you or which are payable to you from Social Security, disability, and any other public program providing medical expenses, disability payments or other similar benefits.
   ANSWER: None

3. Please list all sums paid to you or which are payable to you from health, sickness or income disability insurance.
    ANSWER: See answer to No. 1 above.

4. Please list all sums paid to you or which are payable to you from any auto accident insurance that provides health benefits or income disability insurance.
    ANSWER: None

5. Please list all sums paid to you or which are payable to you from any other similar insurance benefits (except life insurance) being available to you.
    ANSWER: None

6. Please list any contract or agreement with any group, organization, partnership or corporation that would provide payments for or reimbursements for costs of hospitalization, medical/dental expenses, or other healthcare services.
    ANSWER: None, other than Blue Cross/Blue Shield

7. Please list any voluntary wage, contribution plan provided by employer(s) or any other system, intended to provide wages during a period of disability.
    ANSWER: None

8. Please list any other source of collateral indemnification payments. Indicate whether these amounts have already been paid or are to be paid in the future.
    ANSWER: None

9. Please state how much money you are out of pocket for medical expenses not covered by any policy of insurance.
    ANSWER: $8,000

_____
Scarlet Rose

STATE OF ATLANTIS
COUNTY OF PINEAPPLE

BEFORE ME, the undersigned authority, personally appeared Scarlet Rose, who after first being duly sworn, deposes and says that the foregoing Answers to Interrogatories are true and correct to the best of her information, knowledge and belief.

NOTARY PUBLIC, STATE OF ATLANTIS
My Commission Expires:

_____

CERTIFICATE OF SERVICE

I HEREBY CERTIFY that the foregoing Answers to Defendant's Collateral Source Interrogatories have been furnished by first class U.S. mail, postage prepaid, to Alan Richards, Esq., attorney for the defendant, to his office address of 515 Maple Street, Atlantis 34616, on this 24th day of September, 2000.

_____
Bruce K. Franklin, Esq.
Attorney for the Plaintiff

Plaintiff's Responses to Requests for Admissions

Marlene proposed the following responses to Defendant's Requests for Admissions for Bruce's review.

Form 4.6 — Response to Requests for Admissions

IN THE SIXTH JUDICIAL CIRCUIT COURT
IN AND FOR PINEAPPLE COUNTY, ATLANTIS

SCARLET ROSE,
     Plaintiff,

v.   Civil Action No.: 00-125-PDD

NICKEL & DIME, INC.,
     Defendant.

Plaintiff's Responses to Defendant's Requests for Admissions

1. Plaintiff had sustained injuries to her back and her ankle from an incident that occurred while she was playing tennis in 1998.
   RESPONSE: Admitted

2. The total medical expenses incurred in this case, which are potentially recoverable, as of this date are $44,000.
   RESPONSE: Admitted

3. The total amount of money that plaintiff has lost due to inability to work, as of this date is $6,000.
   RESPONSE: Admitted

4. The amount of the lien from all collateral sources as of this date is $36,000.
   RESPONSE: Admitted

5. The box over which plaintiff fell was approximately three feet wide by one foot high by two foot deep.
   RESPONSE: Denied. Plaintiff is uncertain as to the exact measurements of the box and therefore does not want to guess. The box can be measured.

6. The box was visible to the plaintiff had she been looking where she was walking and paying proper attention
   RESPONSE: Denied

7. The reason this incident occurred is because the plaintiff was not paying proper attention and did not notice the boxes, which was an open and obvious condition.
   RESPONSE: Denied

CERTIFICATE OF SERVICE

I HEREBY CERTIFY that a true copy of the foregoing Responses to Defendant's Requests for Admissions has been furnished by first class U.S. mail to Alan Richards, Esq., attorney for the defendant, 515 Maple Street, Clearwater, Atlantis 34616, on this 24th day of September, 2000.

_____
Bruce K. Franklin, Esq.
Attorney for Plaintiff
616 Turner Street
Clearwater, Atlantis 34616

Plaintiff's Responses to Defendant's Requests for Production

Marlene assembled all of the documents and records that were requested by the defendant and prepared the following proposed response:

Form 4.7 — Plaintiff's Response to Requests for Production

IN THE SIXTH JUDICIAL CIRCUIT COURT
IN AND FOR PINEAPPLE COUNTY, ATLANTIS

SCARLET ROSE,
      Plaintiff,

v.   Civil Action No.: 00-125-PDD

NICKEL & DIME, INC.,
      Defendant.

Plaintiff's Responses to Defendant's Request for Production

1. Copies of federal income tax returns, W-2 withholding tax statements, any and all other business records and/or income records, and any other evidence of income for the five years prior to the subject incident or occurrence together with evidence of any other income to date.
    RESPONSE: Attached

2. Any and all photographs, graphs, charts, and other documentary evidence of the scene, parties involved in, or pertaining to the subject incident or occurrence of issues in this cause, that the plaintiff intends to use at the trial of this action, including photographs of the scene.
    RESPONSE: Attached

3. Any and all chiropractic records, osteopathic records, faith healer's records, x-ray reports, MRI scan reports, CT scan reports, nurses' notes, physical therapy records, including copies of any radiographic materials such as x-ray films, CT films, MRI films, etc., for this accident and any and all prior or subsequent accidents.
    RESPONSE: Attached

4. Any and all reports or records concerning any prior or subsequent accidents.
    RESPONSE: Attached

5. Any and all medical reports, doctors' reports, or reports rendered by experts applicable to any and all issues in this cause for which the plaintiff intends to use the author of said report as an expert witness at trial.
RESPONSE: None at this time other than the medical records from my treating physicians, which are attached

6. Any and all written or recorded statements from the defendants on any witness concerning this action or a stenographic, mechanical, electrical, or other recording or transcription of a statement that is a substantial verbatim recital or an oral statement, the date taken, and the means of recording or preserving same.
RESPONSE: None at this time

7. Any and all copies of any applications for insurance, including health, disability, casualty, automobile, hospital, business interruption or umbrella liability policies. Plaintiff may comply by providing a listing of each and every insurance policy applied for, the name of the agent who took the application if applicable, whether the policy was issued, the effective dates of the policy and a listing of any claims submitted under the policies. This request is limited to the period subsequent to 1990.
RESPONSE: Attached

8. Any and all copies of all other medical and/or disability insurance policies, including all booklets concerning any group policies, which provide or may provide medical or disability payments to plaintiff regarding damages alleged to have been incurred as a result of the subject incident, together with the relevant declarations or face sheet reflecting available coverage and deductibles.
RESPONSE: Objection. This is not calculated to lead to evidence that may be admitted at trial.
However, other than the records available from my employer, I have none.

9. Any and all medical records from all medical providers that the claimant has seen in the last five years including hospital emergency rooms and walk-in clinics.
RESPONSE: Attached

10. Any and all medication records, whether prescription or not, that the claimant is now taking on a regular basis.
RESPONSE: None, other than nonprescription aspirin or Tylenol®

11. Any and all employment records of the plaintiff whether as a regular employee or independent contractor for the last ten years.
RESPONSE: None within my possession. Please obtain any and all such records from my employer.

12. Any and all medical records from all medical providers who have rendered any care or treatment to the plaintiff as a result of the incident complained of or subsequent to the incident complained of.
RESPONSE: Attached

CERTIFICATE OF SERVICE

I HEREBY CERTIFY that a true and correct copy of the foregoing Responses to Requests for Production were mailed this 24th day of September, 2000, to Alan Richards, Esq. 515 Maple Street, Clearwater, Atlantis 34616.

Bruce K. Franklin, Esq.
616 Turner Street
Clearwater, Atlantis 34616

Plaintiff's Answers to Expert Witness Interrogatories

Marlene discussed this interrogatory with Bruce, who indicated that he had not contacted an expert. He doubted that he would, because he thought the issue was a very obvious one and that the expense would not be necessary, but he might change his mind as the case progressed. He instructed her to simply state that there was no expert witness at present, but there might be one later. She drafted the following responses.

Form 4.8 — Plaintiff's Answers to Expert Witness Interrogatories

IN THE SIXTH JUDICIAL CIRCUIT COURT
IN AND FOR PINEAPPLE COUNTY, ATLANTIS

SCARLET ROSE,
      Plaintiff,

v.   Civil Action No.: 00-125-PDD

NICKEL & DIME, INC.,
      Defendant.

Plaintiff's Answers to Defendant's Expert Witness Interrogatories

1. Please state the name and address of each person expected by you, your attorney, or any representative of yours, to testify as an expert witness during the trial of this matter.
    ANSWER: Undetermined at this time

2. Please state the following information for each expert witness listed in No. 1 above:
    a. His or her profession or occupation and the field in which he or she is allegedly an expert
    b. The name and address of each school he or she attended and a description of each degree received
    c. The name of any professional or trade association of which he or she is a member
    d. The title, subject matter, publisher and date of publication of any books, papers, or articles on subjects in his or her field and that were relied upon by the expert in determining the facts, conclusions or opinions pertinent to this litigation
    e. The number of years each has practiced or worked in this field
    f. His or her places of employment for the past ten years
    g. The subject matter on which he or she is expected to testify.
    ANSWER: N/A

3. Please state whether any of your experts listed in No. 1 have determined any facts or formed any opinions concerning any issues involved in this case. If so, please state:
    a. The name of the expert or experts, and the issue about which he or she has an opinion
    b. The fact or facts determined and the opinion or opinions formed by each expert
    c. The substance of the facts relied on by such expert in arriving at his or her opinion or opinions
    d. A summary of the grounds relied on by each expert in reaching his or her opinion.
    ANSWER: N/A

4. Please state whether any item or object relevant to this lawsuit has been tested, analyzed, examined or inspected by any of the experts listed in No. 1. Describe in detail, sufficient to identify:
    a. Each item or object that was tested, analyzed, examined or inspected, and the name of the expert
    b. The facts or information you were seeking in having these tests, examinations, or inspections made
    c. The steps used in each test, examination, or inspection of any object or item material to this lawsuit
    d. The findings resulting from each inspection, analysis, examination or test conducted
    e. The facts or opinions derived from the tests
    f. The date of each test, the name and address of the person conducting the test, and the name of each test performed.
    ANSWER: N/A

5. Did any expert listed in 4a submit a report setting forth his or her opinions or conclusions reached from any test, analysis, examination or inspection that the expert may have conducted? If so, state:
   a. The date the report was submitted and who submitted it
   b. The name or other means of identification of the person to whom this report was submitted
   c. The name and address of the person who has present custody of this report
   d. A summary of contents of the report.
   ANSWER: N/A

6. Have any experts listed in No. 1 submitted any other reports with regard to any issues relevant to this lawsuit? If so, state:
   a. The name of each such expert
   b. A description of each report that was made
   c. The date that each report was made
   d. The name, or other means of identification, of the person to whom each report was submitted
   e. The name and address of the person who has present custody of each report
   f. A summary of the contents of each report.
   ANSWER: N/A

7. If you will do so without a Request to Produce, please attach a copy of all reports, writings, memoranda, recordings, or any other material submitted to you by any expert listed in No. 1.
   ANSWER: N/A

STATE OF ATLANTIS
COUNTY OF PINEAPPLE

BEFORE ME, the undersigned authority, personally appeared Scarlet Rose, who being duly sworn, deposes and says that the above Answers to Interrogatories are true and correct to the best of her knowledge, information and belief.

SWORN TO AND SUBSCRIBED before me this 24th day of September, 2000.

NOTARY PUBLIC, STATE OF ATLANTIS
My Commission Expires:

_____

CERTIFICATE OF SERVICE

I HEREBY CERTIFY that a true copy of the foregoing Answers to Expert Witness Interrogatories has been furnished by first class U.S. mail to Alan Richards, Esq., attorney for the defendant, at his office address of 515 Maple Street, Atlantis 34616, on this 24th day of September, 2000.

_____
Bruce K. Franklin, Esq.
Attorney for the Plaintiff
616 Turner Street
Clearwater, Atlantis 34616

Plaintiff's Requests for Copies of Records Received by Defendant Pursuant to Their Notice of Production of Records from Nonparties

After Marlene received the notice of intent to subpoena records from nonparties, which had come with all of the other discovery requests that were made upon Scarlet Rose, she knew that defendant could not have the subpoenas served upon the persons from whom she wanted to receive records until ten days had expired. Plaintiff's attorney could object to the defendant's notice of what it intended to do. In this case, Marlene prepared a request for copies for Bruce's signature.

Form 4.9 — Notice of No Objection and Request for Copies

IN THE SIXTH JUDICIAL CIRCUIT COURT
IN AND FOR PINEAPPLE COUNTY, ATLANTIS

SCARLET ROSE,
        Plaintiff,

v.   Civil Action No.: 00-125-PDD

NICKEL & DIME, INC.,
        Defendant.

Notice of No Objection and Request for Copies

Plaintiff, Scarlet Rose, by and through the undersigned attorney, respectfully files Notice to this Honorable Court that it has no objection to the Defendant's Notice of Intent to Subpoena Records From Nonparties; however, plaintiff hereby requests that she be provided with copies of all documents received from all such nonparties, within ten days from the date on which such documents are received by defendant. Copies of the records received from the following persons or places by the defendant are, therefore, requested

1. Records of Community Hospital
2. Records from Dr. Brendan Patrick
3. Records from Dr. Von Beebe
4. Records from Dr. Michael Mullan
5. Records from Physical Therapists, Inc.
6. Records from Emergency Medical Technicians

CERTIFICATE OF SERVICE

I HEREBY CERTIFY that a true copy of the foregoing Request for Copies has been furnished to Alan Richards, Esq., attorney for the defendant, at his office address on this first day of August, 2000.

_____
Bruce K. Franklin, Esq.
Attorney for the Plaintiff

Evaluating the Plaintiff's Response to Defendant's Discovery Request

Chris, too, had been very anxious to learn more about Scarlet Rose and her claim. Like Marlene, he had reviewed and summarized a large pile of records that Alan had given to him.

Chris reviewed plaintiff's responses to their requests for production, which included many medical records. Like Marlene, Chris was required to digest and understand the voluminous medical records provided, and neither had any experience in doing so. Chris remembered the appendix in his civil litigation text entitled *A Miniguide for Interpreting Medical Records*. He reviewed the material and kept it by his side as he began to decipher the records and the handwriting of the doctors and nurses. The terminology was imposing, and he found it necessary to have a medical dictionary by his side when reading the terms, as well as a book called *Physician's Desk Reference* (*PDR*).
Plaintiff's responses to the Requests for Admission were not particularly helpful, but they did establish that plaintiff was not seeking any recovery for loss of income earning ability.

Chris prepared for Alan's signature a letter to Louise Mallet, the loss prevention manager at Nickel & Dime, which summarized the records, Answers to Interrogatories, and Responses to the Requests for

Admissions that he had received. Some clients did not want a summary; they preferred to receive copies of all the materials. Louise Mallet preferred a summary.

Chris had suggested many things to do. The letter referred to the earlier authorization from the company to expend the monies necessary to accomplish all of the suggested tasks.

Alan agreed with Chris's suggestions, revised the letter somewhat, signed and mailed it. There were no new medical providers identified in the Answers to Interrogatories, which meant that Chris did not have to prepare subpoenas to obtain records from any other nonparties.

Report to the Client

Sullivan and Jagger
Attorneys At Law
515 Maple Street
Clearwater, Atlantis 34616
727-462-8888

September 30, 2000

Louise Mallet, Director
Loss Prevention Department
Nickel & Dime, Inc.
P.O. Box 1000
Boston, Massachusetts 01670

RE: *Scarlet Rose v. Nickel & Dime, Inc.*
    Your Claim No.: 2000-0033-ND-01
    Date of loss: 1/31/2000
    Our File No.: (204)01160

Dear Ms. Mallet:

I write to report Plaintiff's responses to our discovery requests. Scarlet Rose was born on 2/8/1962, in New Orleans, Louisiana, which means that she is now 38 years old. Her Social Security number is 234-34-4567. She lives at 1111 Pine Street in Tarpon Springs. She is 5'5" and weighs 135 pounds. She is employed at the office of Robert Forest, who is the Public Defender for Pineapple County. She has been employed there as an investigator since 1982. She missed three months of work.

She says that she has some pictures of the scene and that they were taken shortly after the incident. As to her version of how the incident occurred, she says:

> On 1/31/2000, I was returning a Christmas present given to me by my daughter. My mother was with me. I pulled to the front of the store, parked, and exited the vehicle, leaving my mother in the car, since I only expected to be in the store for a minute or two. I entered the store and went to the cash register to make the return. I was told to go to the back of the store to exchange merchandise. I started down one of the main aisles, but was unable to continue due to tables and racks being placed in the aisle. I turned to the left to cut through the lingerie department to avoid the obstruction. As I turned to make my first step, there was a plastic merchandise box on the floor next to a rack in the path of travel. My legs hit the box and I fell forward. As I fell, I grabbed the rack to break the fall. As a result, I twisted and hurt my back. I screamed for help because I was unable to get up.

Plaintiff says she has fully recovered from the injury, but the injuries are permanent. She has scars from the back surgery.

As far as any pre-existing condition is concerned, she says she broke her ankle in a fall on a tennis court in 1998 and it affected her back for a while as well. She says the incident greatly exacerbated her back condition, which had been asymptomatic for six months before the incident.

Plaintiff says that she had been in that store on several occasions before the date of the fall but had never noticed boxes left in an aisle before, and she did not know of anyone else who had ever fallen. As far as witnesses are concerned, she says that Jane Morris, her mother; employees of Nickel & Dime, and she, the plaintiff, are the only witnesses she has knowledge of except for medical persons. She was wearing tennis shoes at the time of the incident.

As far as itemization of expenses and damages, she attached a sheet with itemized expenses that she claims to have incurred because of this incident totaling $50,000, a copy of which is attached. She received benefits from Blue Cross/Blue Shield Insurance for 80% of her medical expenses.

In conclusion, the plaintiff will argue that surgery was necessary because of the fall at Nickel & Dime, and that is the question a jury will have to decide unless we settle this case.

There is $50,000 in medical expenses and lost wages resulting from this incident. Ms. Rose says that she was immobilized for three months and experienced a great deal of pain and suffering. There is a substantial liability question, which a jury could rule in our favor, although there are no guarantees. There is no doubt that the plastic container should not have been in a walk area unless a salesperson was within three feet of the tote, but the tote was open and obvious, and the plaintiff should have paid better attention to where she was going. It is quite possible that a jury would find comparative negligence against both.

As far as the value of the claim is concerned, given $50,000, with pain and suffering, the full value of the case is clearly in the six-figure range. As to whether or not there will be any future medical costs, I simply do not know what plaintiff's doctors will say on that issue. The number should be small in any event, at this point, because a yearly check-up is all that is presently called for, but she has a life expectancy of almost four decades.

Please let me know what further information you will need to complete your continued evaluation of this case. I will report the medical records separately.

Yours very truly,

_____

Alan Richards, Esq.

Defendant's Notice of Compliance With Request for Copies

When Chris received any records pursuant to a subpoena issued to a nonparty, such as all the doctors and Ms. Rose's employer, he immediately copied all of the records and sent them to the plaintiff's attorney, together with the following document, prepared for Alan's signature.

Form 4.10 — Notice of Compliance with Request for Copies

IN THE SIXTH JUDICIAL CIRCUIT COURT
IN AND FOR PINEAPPLE COUNTY, ATLANTIS

SCARLET ROSE,
     Plaintiff,

v.   Civil Action No.: 00-125-PDD

NICKEL & DIME, INC.,
     Defendant.

Notice of Compliance with Request for Copies

Defendant, Nickel & Dime, Inc., by and through its undersigned attorney, respectfully files Notice to this Honorable Court that, pursuant to the applicable rule, it has complied with Plaintiff's Request For Copies, and it has provided the following records to the plaintiff, which defendant received, pursuant to a Subpoena Duces Tecum from a nonparty

1. Records from Community Hospital (151 pages)
2. Records from Dr. Michael Mullan (48 pages)
3. Records from Dr. Von Beebe (34 pages)
4. Records from Dr. Brendan Patrick (25 pages)
5. Records from Physical Therapists, Inc. (15 pages)
6. Records from emergency medical technicians (3 pages)

CERTIFICATE OF SERVICE

I HEREBY CERTIFY that a true copy of the foregoing Notice of Compliance with Request for Copies has been furnished to Bruce K. Franklin, Esq., attorney for the plaintiff, at his office address on this 12th day of October, 2000.

_____
Alan Richards, Esq.
Attorney for the Defendant

Tentative Closure of the Written Discovery Stage

As further investigation revealed more information, further written discovery could be conducted. More expert witness and supplemental interrogatories were likely, and more records might be subpoenaed from nonparties. At this point, however, the bulk of the written discovery between the parties was complete, and the case was ready to proceed into the deposition stage of discovery.

DEPOSITIONS

At this point in the lawsuit, Chris had met with Kate Frechette, the loss control director at the Nickel & Dime store, and two other witnesses for Nickel & Dime, but he had not met Scarlet Rose or heard the plaintiff's explanation of the incident.

After all of the records had been received, Alan told Chris to send a notice to obtain the plaintiff's deposition. Chris asked if a subpoena should be issued. Alan told Chris that it was not necessary and to look at the rule relating to discovery depositions. They checked Alan's calendar and chose a date and time for the deposition.

Scheduling the Depositions

Because it is courteous, but not mandated by the rules, to clear all dates for depositions, hearings, and meetings with opposing counsel, Chris called Bruce's office and cleared the date before Alan signed the notice. Barbara put the date and time in the computer, on her own calendar, and the calendar that Alan kept in his office. Barbara explained to Chris that this procedure is called a "double-entry system," required by the professional malpractice insurance company that insures the law firm. Chris prepared a Notice of Intent to Depose Plaintiff.

Form 5.1 — Notice of Taking Deposition of Plaintiff

IN THE SIXTH JUDICIAL CIRCUIT COURT
IN AND FOR PINEAPPLE COUNTY, ATLANTIS

SCARLET ROSE,
    Plaintiff,

v.   Civil Action No.: 00-125-PDD

NICKEL & DIME, INC.,
    Defendant.

Notice of Taking Deposition of Plaintiff

Bruce K. Franklin, Esq.
616 Turner Street
Clearwater, Atlantis 34616

Notice is hereby given that defendant will take the deposition of the plaintiff, Scarlet Rose, who is required to appear before a person authorized by law to take depositions, at 515 Maple Street, Clearwater, Atlantis, on November 15, 2000, at 10:00 a.m., for the taking of her deposition in the above-styled cause. If you fail to appear, you may be in contempt of court.

Dated on October 20, 2000.

Alan Richards, Esq.
Attorney for Defendant
515 Maple Street
Clearwater, Atlantis 34616

Following that, Chris prepared a cover letter to accompany the Notice of Taking the Deposition of Plaintiff.

Sullivan and Jagger
Attorneys At Law
515 Maple Street
Clearwater, Atlantis 34616
727-462-8888

October 20, 2000

Bruce K. Franklin, Esq.
616 Turner Street
Clearwater, Atlantis 34616

Re: *Scarlet Rose v. Nickel & Dime, Inc.*

Dear Mr. Franklin:

This letter confirms that your client will appear for deposition at my office on November 15, 2000, at 10:00 a.m. I have enclosed a formal notice for your file.

Very truly yours,

_____
Alan Richards, Esq.

Preparing the Plaintiff for the Deposition

Marlene composed a letter for Scarlet informing her of the upcoming deposition.

Bruce K. Franklin, P.A.
Attorney At Law
616 Turner Street
Clearwater, Atlantis 34616

October 23, 2000

Scarlet Rose
1111 Pine Street
Tarpon Springs, Atlantis 34689

Re: *Scarlet Rose v. Nickel & Dime, Inc.*
        Civil Action No.: 00-125-PDD

Dear Ms. Rose:

As previously discussed, you need to testify at a deposition about the incident and your injuries. Mr. Franklin and I will work to prepare you for the deposition.

The deposition is scheduled for Monday, November 15, 2000, at 10:00 a.m., at the law offices of Sullivan and Jagger, 515 Maple Street, Clearwater, Atlantis 34616. Parking is available in front of the office. Please be there by 9:30 a.m.

A deposition is an examination by the opposition, in the presence of a court reporter, of a witness under oath. The examination determines the witness' version of facts, the evidence in support of those facts, and the location of the evidence, names, and addresses of persons having information about the evidence. Depositions produce evidence that might lead to a settlement in a case, or they can be used to test the consistency and credibility of a witness at trial. The opposition will be evaluating you as a witness; therefore, good preparation on your part is important.

When preparing for the deposition, please keep in mind the following:

- Depositions are occasionally postponed and, if so, you will be informed.

- Chronologically review the facts of the case up to your current medical status. Anticipate questions on dates, times, direction, distances, speeds, weather, clothes, events, injuries, medical treatments, expenses, witnesses, statements, etc. If you do not know distances, reasonable approximations are acceptable. It might be helpful to return to the scene of the accident to verify distances, obstructions, and approximations.

- Inform your attorney on all matters regarding the incident, your honesty, and credibility. Do not surprise your attorney to your detriment.

- Expect the opponent's attorney to do most or all of the questioning. Your attorney will object when it is necessary.

- Dress neatly, be pleasant, and speak up.

- Listen to each question carefully. If you do not understand the question, do not guess at its meaning; state that you do not understand.

- Think about your answer, be cautious of questions in quick succession, and answer at your own pace.

- Tell the truth. You will be under oath, so do not guess. If you need to correct an earlier answer, indicate your desire to do so, and the attorney will assist you.

- If you are asked, "Did you speak with your attorney about testifying today?" answer "Yes." There is nothing wrong with speaking with your attorney about testifying. If the question is "Did your attorney tell you what to say?" the best answer is, "He told me to tell the truth." Other than that, your attorney will not tell you what to say. However, the other attorney can never inquire about conversations that you had with your attorney, because those are privileged communications.

- When testifying, answer the question to the best of your ability, and do not seek guidance from your attorney. If your attorney feels the question is improper, he will make an objection, and you should stop answering.

- Adverse attorneys often remain silent after your answer in the hope that you will feel compelled to add more information; therefore, resist the temptation to add information to fill the silence.

- Avoid discussing your case or your testimony with anyone other than your attorney.

- You may be asked at the deposition to sketch a diagram of the accident scene. You do not have to do this but, if your attorney thinks this might help your case, he might ask you to do so. Try some practice sketches to reduce difficulty.

- During the deposition, you may be given documents, diagrams, photographs, or other items to identify. Carefully examine each item before you agree to their accuracy.

- Be prepared to describe your injuries and medical treatment in detail. Do not exaggerate or understate.

- Be prepared to discuss any injuries you suffered or claims you made prior to the accident.

- Bring all requested documents.

- Be prepared to discuss loss of pay, property damage, and other out-of-pocket expenses.

- Do not memorize possible answers.

In summary, please allow me to offer you my assurances that, if you are well prepared, thoughtful, deliberate, and truthful, you will do a good job at your deposition.

I will contact you to set up a time when you can meet with Mr. Franklin to discuss the deposition. Meanwhile, if you have any questions or concerns, please contact Mr. Franklin or me at your earliest convenience.

Very truly yours,

_____

Marlene Mertz
Paralegal

Depositions by the Plaintiff

At the same time Chris was arranging the deposition for the plaintiff, Marlene was preparing to schedule depositions for the employees who were on duty when the incident occurred. Because Marjorie Murphy was no longer an employee at Nickel & Dime, a subpoena was prepared for her. Marlene asked if the subpoena needed to be issued by the court. Bruce explained that an attorney is permitted to issue a subpoena without first going to court. A notice was all that was necessary for Caitlin Palmer because she was still an employee, and the defendant would be required to produce her without a subpoena.

Form 5.2 — Subpoena for Deposition

IN THE SIXTH JUDICIAL CIRCUIT COURT
IN AND FOR PINEAPPLE COUNTY, ATLANTIS

SCARLET ROSE,
     Plaintiff,

v.   Civil Action No.: 00-125-PDD

NICKEL & DIME, INC.,
     Defendant.

Subpoena for Deposition

THE STATE OF ATLANTIS:

Marjorie Murphy
2680 Woodhall Terrace
Palm Harbor, Atlantis 34685

You are hereby commanded to appear before a person authorized by law to take depositions, at 616 Turner Street, Clearwater, Atlantis 34616, on November 19, 2000, at 11:00 a.m., for the taking of your deposition in the above-styled cause. If you fail to appear, you may be in contempt of court.

You are subpoenaed to appear by the following attorneys, and unless excused from this subpoena by these attorneys or the court, you shall respond to this subpoena.

Dated on October 25, 2000.

Bruce K. Franklin
Attorney for Plaintiff
616 Turner Street
Clearwater, Atlantis 34616

Form 5.3 — Notice of Taking Deposition

IN THE SIXTH JUDICIAL CIRCUIT COURT
IN AND FOR PINEAPPLE COUNTY, ATLANTIS

SCARLET ROSE,
    Plaintiff,

v.   Civil Action No.: 00-125-PDD

NICKEL & DIME, INC.,
    Defendant.

Notice of Taking Deposition

To: Alan Richards   Clerk of the Court
        515 South Maple Street   315 Court Street
        Clearwater, Atlantis 34616   Clearwater, Atlantis 34616

PLEASE TAKE NOTICE that pursuant to Rule 1.310, Atlantis R. Civ. P., the plaintiff, Scarlet Rose, through her counsel, will take the deposition by oral examination of the persons named below on the date and at the time and place stated below before Executive Reporting Service or before its duly designated representative, who is not of counsel to the parties or interested in the event of the cause. This deposition is for the purpose of discovery, use at trial, or such other purposes as are permitted under the Atlantis Rules of Civil Procedures.

Name: Marjorie Murphy
Date and Time: November 19, 2000, at 10:00 a.m.

Name: Caitlin Palmer
Date and Time: November 19, 2000, at 11:00 a.m.

Name: Andrea Jones
Date and Time: November 19, 2000, at 12:00 p.m.

Name: Christie Davidson
Date and Time: November 19, 2000, at 1:30 p.m.

Name: Annie Edwards
Date and Time: November 19, 2000, at 2:00 p.m.

Name: Shannon Young
Date and Time: November 19, 2000, at 2:30 p.m.

Name: Carol Westwoman
Date and Time: November 19, 2000, at 3:00 p.m.

Title: Record Custodian
Date and Time: November 19, 2000, at 4:00 p.m.

Name: Betsy Ross
Date and Time: November 19, 2000, at 4:30 p.m.

Place of Taking Deposition: The Law Office of Bruce K. Franklin
                                     616 Turner Street, Clearwater, Atlantis 34616

CERTIFICATE OF SERVICE

I HEREBY CERTIFY that the original of this document was filed with the Clerk of the above-mentioned Court and a true copy of the foregoing Notice of Taking Deposition has been furnished by first class U.S. mail to Alan Richards, Esq., attorney for the defendant, 515 Maple Street, Clearwater, Atlantis 34616, on this 25th day of October, 2000.

                                                        _____
                                                        Bruce K. Franklin,
                                                        Attorney for the Plaintiff
                                                        616 Turner Street
                                                        Clearwater, Atlantis 34616

cc: Executive Reporting Service

Bruce instructed Marlene to have a *subpoena duces tecum* issued for the records custodian of Nickel & Dime. He explained that he wanted to obtain the personnel records for Marjorie Murphy and Caitlin Palmer. Marlene consulted *Black's Law Dictionary* and discovered that a *subpoena duces tecum* requires the subpoenaed person to bring documents with him or her.

Marlene asked why a subpoena had to be issued to Ms. Murphy but not to Ms. Palmer. Bruce explained that Nickel & Dime was not required to produce Ms. Murphy without a subpoena because she was no longer an employee. An employee of Nickel & Dime is considered to be a representative of the defendant, but anyone who was not an employee had to be subpoenaed. Ms. Rose, Ms. Palmer, and all other current employees of Nickel & Dime were required to appear without a subpoena, pursuant to the applicable rule, because they were parties of the lawsuit.

Bruce K. Franklin, P.A.
Attorney At Law
616 Turner Street
Clearwater, Atlantis 34616

October 25, 2000

Alan Richards, Esq.
Sullivan and Jagger
515 Maple Street
Clearwater, Atlantis 34616

Re: *Scarlet Rose v. Nickel & Dime, Inc.*

Dear Mr. Richard:

This will confirm that, as discussed, all listed employees will appear for deposition at my office on November 19, 2000, at 10:00 a.m. I have enclosed a formal notice for your file. Please provide me with a list of last known addresses for any persons who are scheduled for deposition but are no longer employed by Nickel & Dime, and I will have them subpoenaed.

Very truly yours,

_____

Bruce K. Franklin, Esq.

Enclosure

Predeposition Conferences by the Defense

Alan asked Chris to arrange a predeposition conference with the witnesses who were to be deposed. The purpose of the conference was to prepare witnesses for the deposition and to give Alan a chance to hear what the witnesses were going to say before opposing counsel did. In addition, it would be necessary to explain to the witnesses exactly what to expect and how to handle the situation. Alan told Chris to attend the predeposition conference and to send a letter to the witnesses explaining what to expect.

Deposition of the Plaintiff

The court reporter asked Scarlet Rose to raise her right hand to administer an oath. She asked Ms. Rose if the testimony she was about to give would be the truth, the whole truth and nothing but the truth.

Alan asked the questions while Chris took notes and sized up the plaintiff. He found her to be a middle-aged woman who was short, neatly dressed, and nervous but cheerful. As the deposition progressed, Chris found Ms. Rose to be quite likeable and friendly.

Bruce made objections to the form of several of the questions. At depositions, attorneys are allowed to ask questions that might lead to discoverable evidence. Attorneys may ask questions during depositions that might not be admissible at trial, but to preserve an objection to the use of questions and answers, it is necessary for the opposing attorney to object. Because, however, the courts have become increasingly unhappy about problems that routinely arise during depositions, attorneys who instruct clients not to answer or who terminate a deposition without good cause, can face fines and sanctions.

After Alan had finished questioning Ms. Rose, Bruce said, "We will read and take a copy if ordered." When Ms. Rose, Marlene, and Bruce had left the room, Chris asked Alan what that meant. Alan explained that a witness has the right to read transcribed testimony and, if necessary, correct or change his or her testimony.

Chris asked why the deposition would not be transcribed at this time. Alan explained that, depending upon the length of the deposition, it could cost several hundred dollars to have the deposition transcribed. Since a trial was not scheduled and settlement discussions had not begun, he felt it was premature to spend the money at this time.

Because Alan wanted to hear how Chris felt about the plaintiff's testimony, he asked Chris to dictate a deposition summary.

Report of Plaintiff's Deposition

Sullivan and Jagger
Attorneys At Law
515 Maple Street
Clearwater, Atlantis 34616
727-462-8888

October 20, 2000

Louise Mallet, Director
Loss Prevention Department
P.O. Box 1000
Boston, Massachusetts 01670

Re: *Scarlet Rose v. Nickel & Dime, Inc.*
      Your Claim No.: 2000-0033-ND-01
      Date of loss: 1/31/2000
      Our File No.: 00-0160

Dear Ms. Mallet:

I write to report on the deposition of Scarlet Rose taken on November 15, 2000. Ms. Rose is a 38-year-old woman who stands 5'5" and weighs about 135 lbs. She says that her weight is about the same as it was the day of the incident. She was married to Bob Benjamin from 1978 to 1990. They had one child, a daughter named Sarah, who is now 13.

Ms. Rose hurt her back when she fell on a tennis court and broke her ankle in 1998; however, she claims that the fall at Nickel & Dime further aggravated her back.

Ms. Rose says she was planning to have lunch with her mother but wanted to stop at Nickel & Dime to return a Christmas present, a pair of jean shorts from her daughter. She states that the main aisle was blocked with a merchandise display table, and she made a "judgment call" to take an alternate route. She said she took one step off the main aisle and landed inside the plastic merchandise box. Although she does not know how she got inside the box, she said that both knees were inside, and she could not get herself out. When she fell into the box, she grabbed a rack to break her fall and pulled it down on top of her.

Ms. Rose's description of the incident is different from that of former employees. She says that the box was in the middle of the aisle between two racks that were about three feet apart. She decided to take an alternative route because the aisle was blocked, and she was looking up in the general direction of where she was going, not down at the floor. She says that she may have seen the box out of her peripheral vision. This would make the box an open and obvious condition and the plaintiff at least partially responsible for what happened.

A customer came to her aid, and she asked the customer to get her mother and some help. She remembers two Nickel & Dime employees coming to her aid, one of whom had a bunch of keys on her wrist. The other came from the front of the store. She did not see any salespeople near where she fell.

After the fall, EMTs took her to the Community Hospital emergency room. They conducted tests and discharged her to follow up with her treating physician, Dr. Mullan. She did not see an orthopedic doctor until several weeks after the incident. She went to see Dr. Patrick, who had treated her for her broken ankle. He told her to see a specialist for her back and referred her to Dr. Beebe, who recommended surgery.

Plaintiff missed three months of work and lost $6,000 in wages. There is no claim for loss of ability to earn future income, and no major problems are anticipated for future medical expenses.

Plaintiff's attorney is providing us with copies of lien letters from Blue Cross/Blue Shield, which paid $36,000. Scarlet had an 80/20 co-pay and a deductible, and she paid, or owes, about $8,000 for medical bills. The medical bills total $44,000.

As far as her current ailments, she says she has occasional minor discomfort that occurs when she overexerts herself or lifts heavy items. She takes over-the-counter pain pills and muscle relaxants for pain. Although she was told to see Dr. Beebe, she hasn't seen an orthopedic specialist because her back has not required medical attention. She claims that the incident at Nickel & Dime aggravated her pre-existing back condition and caused her to undergo surgery; therefore, she should receive a substantial amount of money.

Summary and Conclusion

I was impressed with Ms. Rose. Her medical problems are well documented, and we have the medical records to verify the chronology of events. She has recovered well from her diskectomy involving the insertion of dual rods in her spine. Because the fall aggravated Ms. Rose's condition, if she can establish that Nickel & Dime is liable, plaintiff's attorney will argue that she is entitled to all expenses, plus considerable pain and suffering.

There is $50,000 in special damages resulting from the incident. Ms. Rose states that she was virtually immobilized for two months and experienced a great deal of pain and suffering. The plastic container should not have been in the middle of the walkway, but it was open and obvious, and the plaintiff should have paid attention to where she was going. It is quite likely that a jury would find comparative negligence against both.

Given $50,000 special damages, when coupled with pain and suffering, the full value of the case is in the six-figure range.

I await your further instructions.

Very truly yours,

_____

Alan Richard, Esq.

Predeposition Conference with Witnesses by the Defense

To prepare them for their depositions, Chris and Alan had a conference with Marjorie Murphy, Caitlin Palmer, Kate Frechette, who would appear as the corporate representative and record custodian, and those deponents who remained current employees. For those who were no longer employees, Chris gave Marlene their last known addresses so that Marlene could issue subpoenas.

Several of the former employees had not responded; therefore, Alan asked Chris to make further efforts to contact them. If they still did not respond and cooperate, then they would be unable to meet with them to discuss their anticipated testimony at their upcoming depositions.

Depositions of Current and Former Nickel & Dime Employees

Bruce and Marlene appeared in the offices of Sullivan and Jagger on the designated day to take the depositions. Marlene had prepared a list of questions from a reference book entitled *Pattern Discovery Questions*, which suggested questions to be asked in a trip-and-fall case. The depositions were similar to the deposition of Scarlet Rose.

Report of Depositions of Former Employees

Sullivan and Jagger
515 Maple Street
Clearwater, Atlantis 34616

November 28, 2000

Louise Mallet, Director
Loss Prevention Department
Nickel & Dime Inc.
P.O. Box 1000
Boston, Mass. 01670

RE: *Scarlet Rose v. Nickel & Dime, Inc.*
     Claim No.: 2000-0033-ND-01
     Date of Loss: 1/31/2000
     Our File No.: 00-0160

Dear Ms. Mallet:

I write to report on the depositions taken of seven former Nickel & Dime employees on November 19, 2000, by plaintiff's attorney. We gave plaintiff's attorney a list of employees who were working on the date of the incident. Even though they were working that day, some of the witnesses had no knowledge of the incident. Two scheduled deponents, Carol Westwoman and Anne Edwards, did not appear. They were not served with a subpoena.

Marjorie Murphy

Ms. Murphy wrote the incident report and signed our answers to interrogatories. She is the best witness for Nickel & Dime. Ms. Murphy may be moving to South Carolina soon, so it may be necessary for us to fly her back and pay her expenses or take a videotaped deposition. Unless I hear to the contrary, I will assume that I am authorized to take a videotaped deposition.

In January 2000, Ms. Murphy was a selling supervisor in the women's department. She testified that she received over 12 years of employee training with regard to safety and stocking procedures.

Ms. Murphy described the stocking procedures and said that employees tried to restock when the store was not busy. There are two people in the department, one to wait on customers and the other to do the restocking. An employee was never allowed to be far from the restocking tote. Restocking supplies could be on rolling racks, in a cardboard box, or in a tote, which is approximately two feet long, one foot wide and one foot deep. Ms. Murphy took pictures within five to ten minutes of the incident, and it does not appear that the tote was very high. I will need you to provide me with a tote that looks like the one shown in the photograph. If necessary, I will have the photograph blown up so that the jury can see what the plaintiff attempted to step over.

Although she did not see the fall, Ms. Murphy testified that she was on the scene within minutes of the incident. She could not recall if the plaintiff was on the ground when she got there, but she remembers talking to her and preparing the incident report. The plaintiff told her she was in a hurry and thought she could step over the tote. Ms. Murphy thought she said she was on her way to the bathroom, but she wasn't certain.

Ms. Murphy testified that she saw nothing wrong with how stocking was done and did not criticize the employee, Carol Westwoman, who was doing the stocking.

Plaintiff's attorney showed Mr. Murphy photographs that were taken by his client of the main aisle and the adjacent department. By the plaintiff's account, there was a sale in progress and display tables were in the main aisle. Her photographs were taken a few days later and show the tables in the main aisles. This incident occurred in one of the cross aisles, specifically in the slipper department. As Ms. Murphy's photo depicts, there were three totes in the side aisle where the slippers were being restocked.

According to the incident report and Ms. Murphy's recollection, plaintiff said she fell and hurt her ankle and back before and may have re-injured it. In addition, she was also complaining of her left leg, which was cut from where she hit the box.

Ms. Murphy recalls that the incident occurred in the middle of the aisle.

Ms. Murphy stated that plaintiff was trying to step over the tote in order to get to the bathroom.

Caitlin Palmer

Ms. Palmer was a selling supervisor on the date of the incident. Although she was a little vague and ambiguous about the incident, she remembered the plaintiff.

Ms. Palmer remembers that Ms. Rose was in a hurry to get to the bathroom. She described watching Ms. Rose trying to climb over the tote and falling. She said that plaintiff fell forward. She did not remember the racks falling on the plaintiff, as her attorney indicated they did. Ms. Palmer said she did not complete a report or make any statements.

Plaintiff's attorney thinks it is important that Ms. Palmer did not hear plaintiff say that she saw the tote and tried to step over it. Ms. Palmer only heard Ms. Rose say that she (Ms. Rose) was in a hurry.

Andrea Jones

Ms. Jones is an unhappy former employee who now works at Walpurple. When asked if she received my letter, she indicated she did but threw it in the garbage. She worked for Nickel & Dime from January 1991 until April 2000. She said she never received training on safety procedures.

She was not working at the time the incident occurred and has no knowledge of it. She testified that putting a tote in the aisle where a customer could step over it was unsafe.

Christie Davidson

Ms. Davidson was a former employee who was employed on the day of the incident but was not in the store at that time.

Betsy Ross

Ms. Ross is a front cashier. Ms. Ross remembered that the plaintiff came back to the store a day or two after the incident and said that she wanted to talk to Ms. Murphy because she (Ms. Rose) was going to sue. Ms. Ross says that Ms. Westwoman has moved back to Montana, and she has no idea how to get in touch with Ms. Westwoman.

Shannon Young

Ms. Young was a sales supervisor in charge of the jewelry department on the date of the incident. When shown a photograph of the scene, she said that it was not done properly because there were two totes underneath two separate "A-frames" and one tote in between the two "A-frames," an area through which customers could walk. The testimony of Ms. Young may be enough to have Nickel & Dime found partly responsible for the incident in question.

Kate Frechette, Records Custodian

Ms. Frechette appeared as the records custodian for Nickel & Dime. A records custodian is the person who maintains business records that are prepared and kept in the normal course of business. Plaintiff's attorney could ask only questions that were related to the documents that Ms. Frechette had brought with her to the deposition, pursuant to the formal notice given her. The questions focused on the authenticity of the records. Plaintiff's attorney was not happy when he was told that there had never been another incident at this location, and no one had ever tripped over the boxes and been injured. Nickel & Dime had not produced the incident reports that are prepared by store employees when an incident occurs in the store. I put an objection on the record, stating incident reports are prepared in anticipation of litigation and therefore work product and not discoverable.

Summary and Conclusion

As a result of the depositions, we have a better idea of how this incident occurred and what the plaintiff's version of events will be. Plaintiff is going to say that she was walking through the department and never saw the tote. She lost her balance, grabbed hold of a rack, twisted her back and fell. On a positive note, plaintiff's attorney mentioned that since his client was doing better after surgery, he realizes the value of this case is not worth the $300,000 he had initially demanded. We had a discussion about the medical liens. He has indicated that he has written to the medical providers who have liens, or a right of subrogation, pursuant to Atlantis Statute 786.76, to find out if they will reduce their bills and how much has been paid and is owed. He is going to let me know the response. If they have not responded within the 30 days, they will have waived their right of subrogation, which would make them a collateral source because plaintiff is not allowed to recover twice.

We need to locate Ms. Westwoman and consider an independent medical examination (IME). If you have had an orthopedic IME performed for you in Pineapple County and were happy with the result, please let me know who you might want to use.

Should you have any questions or comments, please do not hesitate to contact me. I await your further instructions and thank you.

Very truly yours,

_____

Alan Richards, Esq.

Depositions of the Medical Providers

About a week after the deposition summaries were sent to Ms. Mallet, she called Alan to discuss the case. Alan was instructed to set up the depositions with Dr. Mullan, Dr. Patrick, and Dr. Beebe.

Alan instructed Chris to schedule the depositions prior to the IME because he wanted to make sure that Dr. Paul, who is the physician Alan wanted to perform the physical examination of the plaintiff, knew how the three doctors were going to testify.

When Chris mailed out the doctor's notice of taking depositions, the plaintiff cross-noticed the depositions and indicated that the depositions would be taken by video. Chris asked why plaintiff's attorney would do that. Alan explained that doctors' schedules often would not allow them to appear in court and medical emergencies routinely came up that prevented doctors from appearing. Many attorneys took video depositions of their experts.

Summarizing the Depositions of the Prior Treating Doctors

Sullivan and Jagger
515 Maple Street
Clearwater, Atlantis 34616

January 15, 2001

Louise Mallet, Director
Loss Prevention Department
Nickel & Dime, Inc.
P.O. Box 1000
Boston, Massachusetts 01670

RE: *Scarlet Rose v. Nickel & Dime, Inc.*
       Claim No.: 2000-0033-ND-01
       Date of Loss: 1/31/2000
       Our File No.: 00-0160

Dear Ms. Mallet:

I write to report that the following depositions were taken on January 14, 2001.

Dr. Michael Conor Mullan

Dr. Mullan's opinion, within a reasonable degree of medical probability, is that plaintiff's condition was made dramatically worse following the January 31, 2000, incident. He says that the surgery was a direct result of the incident and that Scarlet Rose's spine was different as a result of the incident.

Dr. Mullan is a specialist in general medicine. Dr. Mullan referred Ms. Rose to an orthopedic specialist, Dr. Patrick, for back problems that arose in connection with her 1998 ankle fracture. Dr. Mullan says that Ms. Rose had improved as a result of the back surgery in March 2000, and he had not treated her back prior to the ankle incident except for minor aches and pains relating to her playing tennis.

Dr. Brendan Patrick

Dr. Patrick is an orthopedic specialist and a surgeon. His practice concentrates on knees and ankles, not backs. He was reluctant to discuss Ms. Rose's back problems and said he treated her back because it was related to her ankle problems. He performed surgery on Ms. Rose's ankle in May 1998 and continued to treat her until July 1998. He has not treated her since then. When she went to see him after the fall at Nickel & Dime, Dr. Patrick referred her to Dr. Beebe.

Dr. Patrick testified that Ms. Rose's back was improved when he last saw her. Dr. Patrick ordered an MRI of the back in 1998 and testified that her back problems included a degenerative disk problem.

It may not be necessary for Dr. Patrick to testify at trial as long as his records are admitted into evidence. Both sides will be able to make an argument to the jury about the significance of Dr. Patrick's involvement. He is a somewhat dangerous witness for both sides because he has helpful and damaging testimony for each.

The deposition of Dr. Von Beebe is set for next week. Should you have any questions or comments, please call me.

Very truly yours,

_____
Alan Richards, Esq.

Chapter Six

VIDEO DEPOSITION
OF THE SURGEON

After receiving the defendant's notice that Alan was going to depose Dr. Beebe on January 27, 2001, Bruce cross-noticed the deposition. Because there was a change that, due to a medical emergency, Dr. Beebe would not be able to attend the trial, Bruce scheduled a video deposition.

Transcript of Videotaped Deposition

IN THE CIRCUIT COURT OF THE SIXTH
JUDICIAL CIRCUIT IN AND FOR
PINEAPPLE COUNTY, ATLANTIS

SCARLET ROSE
Plaintiff,

v.   Case No. 00-125-PDD

NICKEL & DIME, INC.,
Defendant.

Video Deposition: Von N. Beebe, M.D.

DATE: January 27, 2001
TIME: 11:00 a.m. to 12:20 p.m.
LOCATION: Office of Dr. Beebe, 777 Coconut Street, Clearwater, Atlantis 33759

TAKEN BY: Alan Richards, Counsel for defendant

BEFORE: Amy May Knott, CSR, Notary Public, State of Atlantis at Large.

APPEARANCES:
- On Behalf of the Plaintiff: Bruce K. Franklin
- On Behalf of the Defendant: Alan Richards
- Also Present: Kenneth Waldo, Videographer

EXHIBITS:
- Medical File from Dr. Beebe's Office
- Three Sets of X-Rays (copies not provided to reporter)
- 3/27/2000 Letter to Dr. Patrick
- Records from Dr. Patrick
- 7/9/1998 MRI film
- 2/16/2000 letter from Dr. Patrick
- 3/14/2000 MRI
- Records from Community Hospital regarding surgery
- Records from Carol Treschler, physical therapist.

VIDEOGRAPHER: Good morning. This is the videotape deposition of Von N. Beebe, M.D., taken in the case of Scarlet Rose, plaintiff, versus Nickel & Dime, Inc., an Atlantis corporation, defendant, in the Sixth Judicial Circuit in and for Pineapple County, Case Number 00-125-PDD. We are located at the office of Dr. Beebe, 777 Coconut Street, Clearwater, Atlantis. The date is January 27, 2001. The time is now 11:00 a.m. My name is Kenneth Waldo, and the court reporter today is Amy May Knott. Will counsel please identify themselves for the record?

MR. FRANKLIN: Bruce Franklin for the plaintiff, Scarlet Rose.

MR. RICHARDS: Alan Richards for defendant, Nickel & Dime, Inc.

VIDEOGRAPHER: Will the court reporter please swear in the witness?

Von N. Beebe, M.D., called as a witness by the plaintiff, having been first duly sworn, as hereinafter certified, was deposed.

Examination by Mr. Franklin

Q. Doctor, please state your full name for the record.
A. Von N. Beebe.

Q. What is your address?
A. 777 Coconut Street, Clearwater, Atlantis 33759.

Q. What is your occupation?
A. Neurological surgery.

Q. Please describe your educational background.
A. I received my undergraduate degree, as well as my medical degree, from Duke and did my residency training in neurosurgery in New Orleans, at the Touro Hospital. In 1979 I was recruited by the University of Miami as assistant professor of neurosurgery. I became an associate professor and a full professor of neurosurgery and neuroscience five years later. In 1985, I left the university and entered private practice.

Q. Are you licensed to practice in Atlantis?
A. Yes.

Q. Are you board certified?
A. Yes.

Q. Are you published?
A. I've published over 100 articles and papers in scientific journals and textbooks and have written two books in the field of neurosurgery and neuroscience.

Q. Are you a member of any honorary societies in your profession?
A. I am a member of most of the neurosurgical societies in North America, including the Society of Neurological Surgeons, which is limited to 100 neurosurgeons in North America.

Q. Did you have occasion to see a patient by the name of Scarlet Rose?
A. Yes.

Q. When did you first see Ms. Rose?
A. On March 12, 2000.

Q. How did you come to see Ms. Rose?
A. Dr. Brendan Patrick, a physician in Clearwater, Atlantis, referred her to me.

Q. Why did Ms. Rose come to see you in March 2000?
A. Chronic low back pain that radiated to the left buttock and leg.

Q. At the time she first presented to you, did she give you a history of her pain complaints?
A. Yes. She told me she broke her ankle after a fall on a tennis court in 1998. She received treatment and stabilized. Unfortunately, on January 31, 2000, she tripped over a box and fell, aggravating her pre-existing injuries and totally incapacitating her.

Q. Did you perform an examination in March 2000?
A. Yes.

Q. What were the results of your examination?
A. She had an unremarkable general physical examination. She walked using a four-prong cane favoring her left leg and had a restricted range of motion in her lumbar spine with pain in her left lower back and buttocks. On attempting to move her back, twist or bend, she had tenderness in the sciatic notch on the left. She has lost some sensation in the left leg. There was weakness in the hip, knee and plantar flexion. I was somewhat uncertain as to whether the weakness was from nerve injury or from pain alone.

Q. Did you have any medical records, previous MRI films, or x-rays to review when you first saw Ms. Rose?
A. I had an MRI of the lumbar spine and x-rays that were performed in July 1998; however, neither were of good quality.

Q. Did you find it necessary to order another MRI?
A. Yes.

Q. When was that MRI performed?
A. A few days after I first saw her.

Q. Did you communicate your impressions of the MRI results to Dr. Mullan?
A. Yes.

Q. What did the MRI of March 2000 reveal?
A. It demonstrated a marked collapse of the disc space at L4-L5, reactive bone formation adjacent to the disc space indicating an unstable motion segment at L4-L5, abnormal overgrowth of her facet joints at L4-L5 producing bone spurs and indicating that this was an unstable motion segment, and some development of stenosis from the bone spurs or narrowing of the nerve holes at L4-L5.

Q. Based upon the results of the MRI, did you arrive at any conclusions regarding Ms. Rose's treatment?
A. Ms. Rose had two options. One was to live with this condition, and the other was to undergo a major reconstructive procedure at L4-L5 to correct the nerve compression by decompressing the spinal nerves and to stabilize and fuse that unstable segment. Once that was healed, she would need to undergo a major rehabilitation program because of her frozen back.

Q. Did you eventually perform the back surgery on Ms. Rose?
A. Yes.

Q. In laymen's terms, what did the surgical procedure consist of?
A. An incision was made on her back and the spine was exposed. The opera microscope was brought in, and the nerve holes were drilled to take the pressure off the nerves. At this point, a short titanium rod and hooks were inserted to lock the space together. Then, a tunnel was made underneath the skin to the hip, and bone

graft shavings were taken off the hip and placed on each side of the spine to allow the area to grow together.

Q. Was this operation successful?
A. Yes.

Q. Did she respond favorably to the procedure?
A. Yes.

Q. Do you have an opinion, based upon a reasonable degree of medical probability, as to whether the surgery that you performed was related to the fall she sustained in January 2000?
A. Yes.

Q. What is your opinion?
A. Although she had a pre-existing low back condition with some degenerative changes in her spine, she appeared to be able to live reasonably well with this. The severe twist/fall injury aggravated this pre-existing condition and destabilized her spine, necessitating major spinal reconstructive surgery.

Q. Were all of the medical expenses associated with your procedure reasonable and necessary?
A. Yes.

Q. What were your fees for the treatment and surgery?
A. My fee as a surgeon was $25,000, which included all office visits and testing. There were also charges for the hospital and the anesthesiologist, but I do not know what those charges were.

Q. In your opinion, will Ms. Rose need future medical care and treatment for her back?
A. I recommend that she have yearly check-ups by an orthopedic specialist and should receive care and treatment as needed.

Q. What would you expect the annual cost of treatment to be?
A. The average yearly expense would be approximately $1,000.

MR. FRANKLIN: I have no further questions. Thank you, Doctor.

Cross-examination by Mr. Richards

Q. Good morning, Dr. Beebe. Let me begin by asking you about Ms. Rose's course of treatment following your surgery. You indicated that she responded favorably, and the operation was successful. How is Ms. Rose now in comparison to how she was before the surgery?
A. When I saw her in April 2000 she was doing well. She had some minor aches and stiffness in her back, a restricted range of motion, and needed to undergo an exercise program.

Q. Is this your complete file on this patient?
A. Yes.

MR. RICHARDS: I would ask that a copy of this be marked as Exhibit A and attached to this deposition.

Q. Does that include all of your notes and billing, or is there another file within your office?
A. No, the left-hand side is for business, and the right-hand side has my office notes, outpatient visits, operative report from the hospital, the narrative admission and history to the hospital, and the discharge summary.

Q. What hospital are you referring to?
A. Community Regional.

Q. Do you have any x-rays of Ms. Rose in your office?
A. Yes.

Q. What are the x-rays of?
A. They are preoperative and postoperative x-rays.

Q. Did you interpret them yourself?
A. Yes.

MR. RICHARDS: I will ask that those x-rays be attached as Composite Exhibit B to this deposition.

Q. Did you actually review the films, or do you rely on radiologist's interpretations?
A. I find that I disagree with the radiologist's interpretations about 50 percent of the time.

Q. You disagree with another doctor?
A. In 30 years, I've operated on thousands of spines. I correlate what I see in surgery with what I see on x-rays or MRI results. I find it difficult to accept interpretations from someone who has learned from a textbook and lecture and, in most cases, has never seen a living spine.

Q. Did you make your own interpretation of the MRI films in this case?
A. Yes.

MR. RICHARDS: I will ask that the MRI films be marked as Exhibit C to this deposition.

Q. Have you seen the report from Dr. John Arthurs, a colleague of Dr. Patrick?
A. Yes, but my interpretation is different than his.

Q. Didn't Dr. Arthurs think that the 1998 MRI revealed a generalized degenerative disease in the low back consistent with the aging process?
A. All right. Let's stop there.

Q. How did you interpret the MRI films that you took after the incident?
A. At L4-L5, there was evidence of collapsed disc space and destruction of the disc material. Adjacent to the disc is peridiscal reactive bone that occurred because of an unstable segment. The bone is reacting to the chronic grinding at the disc space level. In addition, there was some narrowing of the space between the discs.

Q. These reactive bony changes didn't exist before the incident?
A. The 1998 MRI didn't show it, but that doesn't necessarily mean that it didn't exist. I have a superior imaging machine and comparing the 1998 MRI to the 2000 MRI is complicated. For an accurate comparison, the same quality-imaging machine should be used.

Q. Are you familiar with the machine that Dr. Arthurs used?
A. No, but I can tell by the quality of the film.

Q. Please read your interpretation of the MRI that you performed on Scarlet Rose.
A. She had an MRI of her back that shows a bulging disc at L3-L4 and a laterally displaced disc at L5-S1 that seems to be compromising the L5 nerve root. Patient complains of radiating pain down into the left leg and has some occasional tingling on the medial aspect of her foot.

Q. What else did you see?
A. I saw a minor bulging disc of the degenerative process at L3-L4. It was consistent with the normal aging process. I recommended surgery because of the problem at L4-L5.

Q. Was the degenerative disc disease present at L4-L5 in the 1998 MRI films?
A. Yes.

Q. What is a lateral disc protrusion?
A. It means that there's a bulge in the disc capsule with a piece of disc pushing out to the side.

Q. Did you review any of Dr. Patrick's office notes?
A. Yes.

Q. Let me quote from his July 20 note. "She is having left leg pain and has been referred by her primary treating physician, Dr. Mullan. I have reviewed her MRI and there's evidence of a lateral disc protrusion at L4-L5 on the right and lateral protrusion of L5-S1 on the left potentially compressing the L5 nerve root. Nerve tension signs seem to be unremarkable today. No hip esthesia. Motor strengths seem to be intact. I feel that Ms. Rose could have some L5 nerve root symptoms based on her left leg pain. She has two level disc pathology, not all of which appears to be symptomatic. I have concerns that surgical intervention may not improve her symptoms." Does that analysis differ from what you saw in March 2000?
A. Yes.

Q. In what regard?
A. What I saw was severe discopathy and degenerative changes at L4-L5 that were outside anything that Dr. Patrick was discussing.

Q. Did you find a herniated disc at L4-L5?
A. I found a disc protrusion, or bulge, which becomes a herniated disc if it impinges on the nerve root. To some extent, it is a matter of semantics.

Q. Didn't Dr. Patrick suspect a possible disc herniation at L4-L5?
A. Yes, but he's not a neurosurgeon.

Q. What does the term "degenerative lumbar disc disease" mean?
A. The correct term is spondylosis. It refers to the aging of the intervertebral disc associated with the change in the two facet joints. Each motional segment has a disc in front with two other joints behind that acts as a shock absorber cushion and allow for little movement at that segment toggling on the disc. They are like a three-legged stool. If something happens to one of them, something will happen to the other two. There are consequences related to this. One is congenital predisposition. How good are your tissues? How good are the discs? Discs will age and dry out at different rates depending on their inherent biology. The second thing is the aging itself. How long has this disc aged? Twenty years is different from 60 years. And the third is trauma. Being alive and walking about is repetitive micro-trauma to the joints, and no joint in the human body lasts forever. They wear out. This is part of the wearing out, but it is largely due to the collapse and wearing out of the disc, which is a combination of those three factors.

Q. What does it mean when you say, "settling of a disc"?
A. Narrowing. collapse.

Q. Is the degenerative disc disease a progressive disease?
A. Yes, but it can be accelerated by major traumatic episodes.

Q. Would you expect some changes between the 1998 MRI and the 2000 MRI?
A. Not necessarily. In most people, there are not substantial changes over a period of a couple of years unless they have a markedly unstable motion segment.

Q. What do you mean by "markedly unstable motion segment"?

A. We develop bone spurs at a joint because of abnormal movement. If you have a lax disc space where the bones can rub back and forth, the facet joints will rub. The looser it is, the faster these changes will develop.

Q. Does that have anything to do with an unusual or abnormal gait?

A. Not that we know of. A lot of people develop abnormal gaits if they have pain or a knee or ankle problem, but no one has shown that it accelerates this process.

Q. What does the term "antalgic gait" mean?

A. It means that the patient favors one leg because the other is hurt. It can be anything from a low back disorder to a knee, ankle or hip disorder.

Q. Didn't Scarlet Rose have an ankle disorder?

A. Yes.

Q. Did she have an antalgic gait when you first saw her?

A. Yes.

Q. Did she have an antalgic gait when you last saw her?

A. Yes.

Q. Was it improved?

A. Yes.

Q. An antalgic gait and an ankle problem would make it more difficult for a person to ambulate, correct?

A. Yes.

Q. What does "chronic" mean?

A. It means long term. It is anything that lasts more than three to six months.

Q. How would you recommend managing degenerative disc disease?

A. The expression is a little broad because degenerative disc disease exists in all of us beginning around age 40, but the management is ideally walking, stretching, and exercise. On the other hand, if the patient has intractable and incapacitating pain and he or she has failed rational nonsurgical management, then surgery may be an option. There are only two problems associated with degenerative disease that surgery can correct. One is nerve compression. We can take the pressure off the nerves. Secondly, we can stabilize an unstable motion segment. If the patient has one or both problems, we can help the patient with surgery.

Q. Did Scarlet Rose have nerve compression prior to the incident at Nickel & Dime?

A. No.

Q. Dr. Patrick spoke of possible nerve compression, correct?

A. Dr. Patrick suspected possible nerve compression, which is why he ordered an MRI. I didn't see nerve compression on her original MRIs.

Q. What is L5 radiculopathy?

A. It implies sickness of the L5 nerve root.

Q. Does it necessarily imply any impingement on the nerve root?

A. That is the most common cause for L5 radiculopathy, but there are other causes.

Q. In Dr. Patrick's note that I showed you earlier, there is reference to pain radiating down the left leg, correct?

A. Yes. It says, "her leg symptoms remain about the same with radiation down her left leg."

Q. Radiation down her left leg would be an indication of nerve root compression, correct?

A. It is suggestive of nerve root compression, but you do not have to have nerve root compression to have pain radiating down your leg from a low back injury.

Q. Please explain the difference between a disc herniation and a disc bulge.

A. A disc bulge implies that the disc has protruded out of the disc space but is still encapsulated by the fibrous annulus of the disc and the surrounding ligaments. A disc herniation usually implies that there is a tear of the disc with a slit in the annulus and a hunk of disc has extruded out.

Q. Where, in relation to the nerve root, would it extrude? Could it impinge on the nerve root?

A. Yes. Depending on where the tear is and the direction the disc gets pushed, they can extrude, migrate up the canal, be at the level of the disc, or go in different directions.

Q. What does "lateral collapse of the disc" mean?

A. It means that there is narrowing on one side more than another.

Q. In your notes, you talked about collapse destruction of the disc or disc disease, correct?

A. Yes.

Q. At L4 and L5?

A. Yes.

Q. Do you know whether Scarlet Rose's condition preexisted the fall of January 2000?

A. There was pre-existing disease at L4-L5 prior to her fall.

Q. There is no question of that?

A. No.

Q. What does "collapse" mean?

A. It means that there is a narrowing of the disc space.

Q. Do you know if that was there?

A. No, I do not.

Q. You focused on the L4-L5 collapse of the disc as the reason for the surgery. Was that a dual rod stabilization procedure?

A. Yes.

Q. You attached a small titanium rod with a hook, correct?

A. Yes.

Q. To what did you attach it?

A. To the lamina.

Q. Which particular discs were we addressing?

A. L4-L5.

Q. Did you do anything to L3-L4 or L5-S1 during that procedure or find any problems that needed to be addressed?

A. No. The things I saw were unremarkable and consistent with asymptomatic degenerative disease.

Q. Asymptomatic degenerative disease?
A. Yes.

Q. For L3-L4 and L5-S1?
A. Yes.

Q. You didn't feel that the degenerative disc disease problems that you found at the L3-L4 or L5-S1 were related to the problems she was having with her back?
A. Correct. Normal people have degenerative disease, and the degenerative disease can be severe and asymptomatic.

Q. Judging by the results of the dual-rod stabilization procedure, L4-L5 was the affected area, correct?
A. As near as we can tell.

Q. Ms. Rose has dramatically improved and her prognosis is good, correct?
A. Yes.

Q. Was spinal stenosis one of the conditions that you noted in Ms. Rose when you examined her?
A. Yes.

Q. You also talked about stabilization of an unstable segment, correct?
A. Yes.

Q. What do you mean by that, Doctor?
A. The low back is complicated. It varies from asymptomatic micro-instability, which is what you see in the normal aging process and people who are asymptomatic, to gross symptomatic hypermobility of the joints, as in Ms. Rose, where there has been acute reactive bony changes. If you perform conventional x-rays, the movement is not great enough for you to see. You can only see reactive changes of the bone on an MRI.

Q. Were there bony changes seen in Ms. Rose's back when you saw her?
A. Yes, adjacent to the disc.

Q. Were the bony changes that you saw within the L4-L5 disc present before you saw her?
A. Not the same type of changes that we're talking about.

Q. How do you know that they are not the same type of changes?
A. You can see it on an MRI.

Q. Were there any options other than surgery?
A. There were three reasonable options.

Q. What were they?
A. The first one was microsurgical decompression. That's where, in the case of a single segment problem, we make a small incision on the back and operate under a microscope. The neurosurgeon gently drills out the nerve holes to make more room for the nerves.

Q. What's that called?
A. Microsurgical interlaminar decompression.

Q. Is that also called a laminectomy?
A. For coding purposes, it's called a laminectomy.

Q. You also talked about continuing conservative treatment, correct?
A. Yes.

Q. What would that consist of?

A. Walking, stretching and living with pain.

Q. What is a trigger point injection?

A. It's an injection of local anesthetic and/or cortisone into a tender place. In some patients, it relieves the pain.

Q. That's another form of conservative treatment?

A. Yes, but there is no evidence that it makes a long-term difference.

Q. Were any trigger point injections given before surgery?

A. No.

Q. Did you talk about walking and stretching?

A. Yes.

Q. Did the unstable segment in Ms. Rose's spine preexist the January 2000 incident at Nickel & Dime?

A. I have no way of knowing with certainty.

Q. What indicates that there's an unstable segment?

A. The most important indication is spinal pain. People with mechanical pain or pain they can get rid of when they lie down are likely to have an unstable segment. Because there's little stress on the spine when you're lying down, the pain generator of an unstable segment should dissipate when you lie down.

Q. That's exactly what Ms. Rose told you she did after the ankle injury caused her back to hurt, correct?

A. Yes, it is true that her back pain went away when she lay down, but that does not necessarily mean that she had an unstable back segment prior to the incident at Nickel & Dime. The bottom line is, did the fall make her worse. And I can't tell you that answer. Based on what Ms. Rose told me, it did. If Ms. Rose's history is accurate and this incident markedly decompensated her spine, then the fall was a major contributing cause of her surgery. In my opinion, the fall made her worse and precipitated her surgery, but I have no way of knowing with certainty.

Q. Is everybody a good candidate for surgery?

A. No, the majority of people with back and neck pain don't need surgery.

Q. If two people have nerve compression and an unstable segment but different medical makeup, compositions and background, is it possible that one could be a better surgical candidate than another?

A. Yes.

Q. Did Ms. Rose have any contraindications to surgery?

A. She did not have any medical problems that indicated that she was not a good candidate for surgery.

Q. You spoke about diffuse spondylosis with Mr. Franklin. What does "diffuse" mean?

A. It means that more than one segment is affected, and there are aging changes in multiple motion segments in the low back.

Q. At L3-L4, L4-L5, L5-S1?

A. L5-S1.

Q. Was that the disc where you found a bulge?

A. I saw a small disc bulge on the right side of the original MRIs, which indicates that it's an asymptomatic bulge.

Q. Having reviewed all the records, can you testify, within a reasonable degree of medical probability, what medical conditions existed prior to the incident at Nickel & Dime?

A. The disk and unstable segment were probably not there prior to the incident. Ms. Rose told me her back was worse after the fall, and the surgery made her better. That's all I can say.

MR. RICHARDS: I have no further questions. Thank you for your time and patience.

Redirect by Mr. Franklin

Q. Have any of the medical records that you reviewed or the questions that were posed by counsel led you to change the opinions you gave me on direct examination?

A. No.

MR. FRANKLIN: That's all I have. Thank you, Doctor.
MR. RICHARDS: No further questions.

VIDEOGRAPHER: The time is 12:21. End of the deposition. Off record.

Deposition of Dr. Beebe

Sullivan and Jagger
515 Maple Street
Clearwater, Atlantis 34616

January 29, 2001

Louise Mallet, Director
Loss Prevention Department
Nickel and Dime, Inc.
P.O. Box 1000
Boston, Mass. 01670

RE: *Scarlet Rose v. Nickel & Dime, Inc.*
  Claim No.: 2000-0033-ND-01
  Date of Loss: 1/31/2000
  Our File No.: 00-0160

Dear Ms. Mallet:

I write to report about Dr. Beebe's deposition on January 27, 2001.

Dr. Beebe is an extremely qualified witness. He is a neurological surgeon and was a teacher at the University of Miami for 18 years. He has published over 150 articles and papers and is one of the top neurosurgeons in North America.

Dr. Beebe first saw the plaintiff on March 12, 2000, when Dr. Patrick referred her to him. He characterized the problem as intractable low back pain with radiating pain to the right leg. He says that the plaintiff told him that she had recovered from the first accident, involving the ankle fracture, and became worse as a result of the incident at Nickel & Dime.

Dr. Beebe is an extremely self-confident man who believes that only he can accurately read MRIs and x-rays. He reviewed some medical records but interpreted the MRIs and x-rays himself. He described the 1998 MRI as being of poor quality and ordered an MRI in March 2000. He says that there was a difference between the two and felt that the difference was attributable to our incident.

Dr. Beebe inserted two rods into the L4-L5 level. He described the problem as a severe collapse and disruption due to disc disease. He did not do anything to the L3-L4 disc or the L5-Sl. After the surgery, plaintiff felt better, so Dr. Beebe made an accurate diagnosis.

Dr. Beebe did not place much emphasis on the prior medical records. He acknowledges that plaintiff had a pre-existing condition, but he could not state how those conditions changed after the incident at Nickel & Dime. He said the incident at Nickel & Dime caused Ms. Rose to undergo surgery.

In order for Dr. Beebe to conduct surgery, the patient must have a compressed nerve and instability in one of the segments. A compressed nerve would cause radiating pain, and an unstable segment existed if there was continued pain, such as Ms. Rose had, for over a month. We can argue that the surgery was necessary due to a pre-existing condition.

Very truly yours,

_____

Alan Richards, Esq.

Chapter Seven

**CONTINUED NEGOTIATIONS,
PHYSICAL EXAMINATION
OF PLAINTIFF, AND
DEPOSITION OF THE
DEFENDANT'S EXPERT**

Reassessing the Case

Since depositions had been taken of the plaintiff, most of the former and current employees of Nickel & Dime and the treating physicians, both sides had most, but not all, of the information they needed to evaluate the merits and value of the case. Bruce asked Marlene to arrange a meeting with Scarlet Rose to review the case and decide what to do next. Alan and Chris were awaiting further instructions from Louise Mallet, the loss prevention manager. Both sides needed to review strengths and weaknesses of the case. If the case didn't settle at this point, both sides would be spending more time and money, and the case would move toward a trial.

Plaintiff's Perspective

Scarlet Rose continued to claim that Nickel & Dime was negligent, and the testimony of Marjorie Murphy and Caitlin Palmer was biased because they were supporting their employer. Bruce told Ms. Rose that, while it appeared Nickel & Dime employees were negligent in placing the box unattended in the aisle, he was concerned about causation. Because Ms. Rose failed to watch where she was going, the defense could argue that she caused the incident.

A $36,000 lien for the medical bills had to be paid before Ms. Rose or Bruce received any money. In addition, since Ms. Rose's surgery was a success, the likelihood of a large recovery was reduced. Bruce was afraid that if the jury returned a $100,000 verdict and the jury found Ms. Rose to be 50% responsible, then most of the $50,000 recovery would go toward medical bills. After all costs and fees were paid, Ms. Rose would not receive very much money.

Bruce asked Ms. Rose to settle the case for a sum less than the $300,000 originally demanded. She authorized him to settle the case for $100,000.

Although only $8,000 of the $44,000 in medical bills remained unpaid, in order to convince the doctors and hospital to settle for less money, Bruce and Marlene would have to persuade them that it was wiser to receive some money than no money at all. If Nickel & Dime won, Ms. Rose would have no money to pay the bills, and although it was unlikely, she could declare bankruptcy. In similar situations, doctors and hospitals usually agree to accept less. The agreement that is reached by the plaintiff and doctors can either facilitate or prevent a settlement between a plaintiff and a defendant.

In this case, the doctors and hospital agreed to accept $4,000 from Ms. Rose's $8,000 out of pocket expenses. The insurer agreed to accept 50% of the $36,000 that it had paid.

Defendant's Perspective

The decision to settle the case was up to Louise Mallet, the loss prevention manager. As Alan had explained in his letter, the plaintiff would be able to argue that the box should not have been left in the aisle. But, even if a jury found Nickel & Dime negligent, Alan was confident that a jury would find Scarlet Rose partially responsible for the incident.

Because she lost $6,000 in wages and the medical bills were $44,000, the verdict would be $50,000 without compensation for pain and suffering. Unless Bruce told him, Alan would not know about the negotiations between Bruce and the doctors, hospital, and medical care health insurance provider.

After Ms. Mallet reviewed the deposition summaries, she called Alan and instructed him to offer $5,000 to settle the case and to file an offer of judgment, or proposal for settlement, pursuant to the applicable Atlantis statute and rules of procedure.

Proposals for Settlement and Offers of Judgment

A proposal for settlement, or offer of judgment, represents an attempt by the legislature through a duly enacted statute and the Atlantis Supreme Court through the promulgation of a rule of civil procedure to reduce the number of trials throughout the state of Atlantis. The rule reads as follows:

Rule 1.442. Proposals for Settlement

1. *Applicability.* This rule applies to all proposals for settlement authorized by Atlantis law regardless of the terms used to refer to such offers, demands, or proposals, and supersedes all other provisions of the rules and statutes that may be inconsistent with this rule.

2. *Time Requirements.* A proposal to a defendant shall be served no earlier than 90 days after service of process on that defendant; a proposal to a plaintiff shall be served no earlier than 90 days after the action has commenced. No proposal shall be served later than 45 days before the date set for trial or the first day of the docket on which the case is set for trial.

3. *Form and Content of Proposal for Settlement.*
    a. A proposal shall be in writing and shall identify the applicable Atlantis law under which it is being made.
    b. A proposal shall
        * name the party or parties making the proposal and the party or parties to whom the proposal is being made
        * identify the claim or claims the proposal is attempting to resolve
        * state with particularity any relevant conditions
        * state the total amount of the proposal and state with particularity all nonmonetary terms of the proposal
        * state with particularity the amount proposed to settle a claim for punitive damages, if any
        * state whether the proposal includes attorney fees and whether attorney fees are part of the legal claim
        * include a certificate of service in the form required by rule 1.080(f).
    c. A proposal may be made by or to any party or parties and by or to any combination of parties properly identified in the proposal. A joint proposal shall state the amount and terms attributable to each party.

4. *Service and Filing.* A proposal shall be served on the party or parties to whom it is made but shall not be filed unless necessary to enforce the provisions of this rule.

5. *Withdrawal.* A proposal may be withdrawn in writing provided the written withdrawal is delivered before a written acceptance is delivered. Once withdrawn, a proposal is void.

6. *Acceptance and Rejection.* A proposal shall be deemed rejected unless accepted by delivery of a written notice of acceptance within 30 days after service of the proposal. The provisions of Rule 1.090(e) do not apply to this subdivision. No oral communications shall constitute an acceptance, rejection, or counteroffer under the provisions of this rule.

7. *Sanctions.* Any party seeking sanctions pursuant to applicable Atlantis law, based on the failure of the proposal's recipient to accept a proposal, shall do so by service of an appropriate motion within 30 days after the entry of judgment in a nonjury action, the return of the verdict in a jury action, or the entry of a voluntary or involuntary dismissal.

8. *Costs and Fees.*
    a. If a party is entitled to costs and fees pursuant to applicable Atlantis law, the court may, in its discretion, determine that a proposal was not made in good faith. In such case, the court may disallow an award of costs and attorney fees.
    b. When determining the reasonableness of the amount of an award of attorney's fees pursuant to this section, the court shall consider, along with all other relevant criteria, the following factors:
        *   the then apparent merit or lack of merit in the claim
        *   the number and nature of proposals made by the parties
        *   the closeness of questions of fact and law at issue
        *   whether the party making the proposal had unreasonably refused to furnish information necessary to evaluate the reasonableness of the proposal
        *   whether the suit was in the nature of a test case presenting questions of far-reaching importance affecting nonparties
        *   the amount of the additional delay cost and expense that the party making the proposal reasonably would be expected to incur if the litigation were to be prolonged.

9. *Evidence of Proposal.* Evidence of a proposal or acceptance thereof is admissible only in proceedings to enforce an accepted proposal or to determine the imposition of sanctions.

10. *Effect of Mediation.* Mediation shall have no effect on the dates during which parties are permitted to make or accept a proposal for settlement under the terms of the rule.

The statute reads as follows:

768.79. Offer of judgment and demand for judgment

1. In any civil action for damages filed in the courts of this state, if a defendant files an offer of judgment that is not accepted by the plaintiff within 30 days, the defendant shall be entitled to recover reasonable costs and attorney's fees incurred by her or him or on the defendant's behalf pursuant to a policy of liability insurance or other contract from the date of filing of the offer if the judgment is one of no liability or the judgment obtained by the plaintiff is at least 25 percent less than such offer, and the court shall set off such costs and attorney's fees against the award. Where such costs and attorney's fees total more than the judgment, the court shall enter judgment for the defendant against the plaintiff for the amount of the costs and fees, less the amount of the plaintiff's award. If a plaintiff files a demand for judgment that is not accepted by the defendant within 30 days and the plaintiff recovers a judgment in an amount at least 25 percent greater than the offer, she or he shall be entitled to recover reasonable costs and attorney's fees incurred from the date of the filing of the demand. If rejected, neither an offer nor demand is admissible in subsequent litigation, except for pursuing the penalties of this section.

2. The making of an offer of settlement that is not accepted does not preclude the making of a subsequent offer. An offer must

    a.   Be in writing and state that it is being made pursuant to this section
    b.   Name the party making it and the party to whom it is being made
    c.   State with particularity the amount offered to settle a claim for punitive damages, if any
    d.   State its total amount.

3.   The offer shall be construed as including all damages that may be awarded in a final judgment.

4.   The offer shall be served upon the party to whom it is made, but it shall not be filed unless it is accepted or unless filing is necessary to enforce the provisions of this section.

5.   An offer shall be accepted by filing a written acceptance with the court within 30 days after service. Upon filing of both the offer and acceptance, the court has full jurisdiction to enforce the settlement agreement.

6.   An offer may be withdrawn in writing, which is served before the date a written acceptance is filed. Once withdrawn, an offer is void.

7.   Upon motion made by the offer or within 30 days after the entry of judgment or after voluntary or involuntary dismissal, the court shall determine the following:
    a.   If a defendant serves an offer that is not accepted by the plaintiff, and if the judgment obtained by the plaintiff is at least 25 percent less than the amount of the offer, the defendant shall be awarded reasonable costs, including investigative expenses, and attorney's fees, calculated in accordance with the guidelines promulgated by the Supreme Court, incurred from the date the offer was served, and the court shall set off such costs in attorney's fees against the award. When such costs and attorney's fees total more than the amount of the judgment, the court shall enter judgment for the defendant against the plaintiff for the amount of the costs and fees, less the amount of the award to the plaintiff.
    b.   If a plaintiff serves an offer that is not accepted by the defendant, and if the judgment obtained by the plaintiff is at least 25 percent more than the amount of the offer, the plaintiff shall be awarded reasonable costs, including investigative expenses, and attorney's fees, calculated in accordance with the guidelines promulgated by the Supreme Court, incurred from the date the offer was served.

For purposes of the determination required by paragraph (a), the term "judgment obtained" means the amount of the net judgment entered, plus any postoffer collateral source payments received or due as of the date of the judgment, plus any postoffer settlement amounts by which the verdict was reduced. For purposes of the determination required by paragraph (b), the term "judgment obtained" means the amount of the net judgment entered, plus any postoffer settlement amounts by which the verdict was reduced.

8.   If a party is entitled to costs and fees pursuant to the provisions of this section, the court may, in its discretion, determine that an offer was not made in good faith. In such case, the court may disallow an award of costs and attorney's fees.
    a.   When determining the reasonableness of an award of attorney's fees pursuant to this section, the court shall consider, along with all other relevant criteria, the following additional factors:
        • the then apparent merit or lack of merit in the claim
        • the number and nature of offers made by the parties.

As is evident, the legislature and the Supreme Court wanted to reduce the number of cases that would require a trial by jury or a trial by a judge alone, which is called a nonjury case. The effect of a proposal for settlement, or an offer of judgment, is to make the stakes a little higher.

If a proposal for settlement has been made by one side and rejected by the losing party, the party who decided to go to trial and lost is going to have to pay a substantial amount of money in attorney's fees to the opposing side. A party is determined to have lost if the verdict is either 25% higher than the amount demanded or 25 % lower than the amount offered. The court and the legislature have declared that, if the result is 25% higher than the amount demanded or 25% lower than the amount offered, the party that rejected the proposal for settlement did so unreasonably.

Proposal for Settlement by the Defendant

Chris prepared and sent by certified and regular mail to plaintiff's attorney the following proposal for settlement.

Form 7.1 — Proposal for Settlement

IN THE CIRCUIT COURT OF THE SIXTH
JUDICIAL CIRCUIT IN AND FOR
PINEAPPLE COUNTY, ATLANTIS

SCARLET ROSE,
Plaintiff,

v.   Case No. 00-125-PDD

NICKEL & DIME, INC.
Defendant.

Proposal for Settlement

COMES NOW the defendant, Nickel & Dime, Inc., by and through its undersigned counsel, and pursuant to Rule 1.442 of the A.R.C.P. and Section 768.89, Atlantis Statutes, hereby files this Proposal for Settlement as to plaintiff, Scarlet Rose, as follows:

1. The party making this Proposal for Settlement is the defendant.

2. The party against whom this Proposal for Settlement is being made is the plaintiff.

3. The total amount of this Proposal for settlement is $5,000, including attorney's fees, costs and interest. If plaintiff accepts the amount within the applicable time period, plaintiff will, upon receipt of the settlement check, execute a mutually acceptable release of all claims for personal injury and related damages, and further cause a stipulation for dismissal, with prejudice, to be filed in this action.

CERTIFICATE OF SERVICE

I HEREBY CERTIFY that a true and correct copy of the above was sent via certified mail and regular mail to Bruce K. Franklin, attorney for the plaintiff, 616 Turner Street, Clearwater, Atlantis 34616, on this 15th day of February, 2001.

_____
Alan Richards
Attorney for Defendant

Plaintiff's Proposal for Settlement

After Bruce received the Proposal for Settlement from the defendant, he instructed Marlene to prepare a Proposal for Settlement on behalf of Scarlet Rose. The plaintiff filed a Proposal for Settlement in the amount of $100,000.

Form 7.2 — Plaintiff's Proposal for Settlement

IN THE CIRCUIT COURT OF THE SIXTH
JUDICIAL CIRCUIT IN AND FOR
PINEAPPLE COUNTY, ATLANTIS

SCARLET ROSE,
Plaintiff,

v.   Case No. 00-125-PDD

NICKEL & DIME, INC.
Defendant.

Proposal for Settlement

COMES NOW the plaintiff, Scarlet Rose, by and through her undersigned counsel, and pursuant to Rule 1.442 of the A.R.C.P. and Section 768.89, Atlantis Statutes, hereby files this Proposal for Settlement to defendant, Nickel & Dime, Inc., as follows:

1. The party making this Proposal for Settlement is the plaintiff.

2. The party against whom this Proposal for Settlement is being made is the defendant.

3. The total amount of this Proposal for Settlement is $100,000, including attorney's fees, costs and interest. If defendant accepts the amount within the applicable time period, plaintiff will, upon receipt of the settlement check, execute a mutually acceptable release of all claims for personal injury and related damages, and further cause a stipulation for dismissal, with prejudice, to be filed in this action.

CERTIFICATE OF SERVICE

I HEREBY CERTIFY that a true and correct copy of the above was sent via certified mail and regular mail to Alan Richards, Esq., attorney for the defendant on this 26th day of February, 2001.

                                                              _____
                                                              Bruce K. Franklin,
                                                              Attorney for Plaintiff

Compulsory Physical Examination of the Plaintiff

At this point, it appeared that a trial was a possibility. Alan recommended to Louise Mallet that an IME, or compulsory physical examination of the plaintiff, was necessary. Chris copied all medical records and the deposition of the plaintiff and sent them to Dr. Paul.

After clearing the date through Bruce, Chris prepared a notice of compulsory physical examination. Bruce told Alan that Alan might attend the examination and bring a court reporter. Alan told Chris to inform Dr. Paul so Dr. Paul wouldn't be surprised.

Form 7.3 — Notice of Scheduling Compulsory Physical Examination of Plaintiff

IN THE CIRCUIT COURT OF THE SIXTH
JUDICIAL CIRCUIT IN AND FOR
PINEAPPLE COUNTY, ATLANTIS

SCARLET ROSE
Plaintiff,

v.   Case No. 00-125-PDD

NICKEL & DIME, INC.,
Defendant.

Notice of Scheduling Compulsory Physical Examination of Plaintiff

Defendant, Nickel & Dime, Inc., by and through its undersigned attorney, and pursuant to Rule 1.360 Atlantis Rule of Civil Procedure, hereby gives notice to this Honorable Court that it has requested that the plaintiff, Scarlet Rose, submit to a physical examination by a qualified expert concerning a condition that is in controversy herein.

The examination shall proceed at the following:

The examiner: Dr. Christopher Paul
Place of Exam: Office of Dr. Paul, 700 South Ft. Harrison Street, Clearwater, Atlantis 33759
Date of Exam: March 15, 2001

The defendant respectfully requests that plaintiff, Scarlet Rose, file any objections she might have to the compulsory physical examination. If plaintiff fails to appear at the designated time and a cancellation fee is charged, defendant will expect plaintiff to pay the fee. The plaintiff is further requested to provide the examining doctor with any medical reports that she wishes the examiner to review.

CERTIFICATE OF SERVICE

I HEREBY CERTIFY that a true copy of the foregoing Notice of Scheduling Compulsory Physical Examination of plaintiff has been furnished to Bruce K. Franklin, Esq., attorney for the plaintiff, on this 24th day of February, 2001.

_____
Alan Richards, Esq.
Attorney for the Defendant

Plaintiff's Response to Defendant's Request for a Compulsory Physical Examination

Marlene drafted the following letter to Scarlet Rose:

Bruce K. Franklin, P.A.
616 Turner Street
Clearwater, Atlantis 34616
(727) 462-1000

March 1, 2001

Scarlet Rose
1111 Pine Street
Tarpon Springs, Atlantis 34689

Dear Ms. Rose:

As you may recall, I mentioned in our initial interview that the defendant could request an examination by a doctor of its choosing to confirm the existence and extent of your injuries. Alan Richards, attorney for the defendant, has contacted us to request such an exam.

The exam is scheduled for March 15, 2001, at 10:00 a.m. The examining physician is Dr. Christopher Paul. Please make arrangements to be at Dr. Paul's office at the appointed time. I intend to have both a court reporter and a videographer there with you.

The exam will consist of a routine examination of your injuries, brief strength and movement tests, and a discussion with the doctor about your injuries and disabilities. The exam should last about an hour.

Before going to the examination, you may choose to make a list of your injuries, treatments, pain, disabilities and current status. Review your injury diary to help you.

You should cooperate fully in the exam. Do not overstate or understate the progress of your condition.

Because the exam will prove that your injuries and complaints were real and not imagined, Mr. Franklin believes the exam will be beneficial to your case. If you have any concerns, please let me know.

Very truly yours,

_____

Marlene Mertz
Paralegal

Deposition of the IME Doctor

After the examination was completed, Marlene scheduled a deposition of the doctor. Even though they received a written report prior to the deposition, Bruce felt it necessary to depose Dr. Paul. Marlene prepared the appropriate notice, and the deposition was set for March 30.

Marlene prepared a summary of the deposition for Ms. Rose so she would know what the doctor said.

Report of the Deposition of the IME Doctor by the Defense

Chris also attended Dr. Paul's deposition and prepared the following summary:

Sullivan and Jagger
515 Maple Street
Clearwater, Atlantis 34616

Louise Mallet, Claims Director
Loss Prevention Department
Nickel and Dime, Inc.
P.O. Box 1000
Boston, Massachusetts 01670

RE: *Scarlet Rose v. Nickel & Dime, Inc.*
    Your Claim No.: 2000-0033-ND-01
    Our File No.: 00-0160

Dear Ms. Mallet:

Dr. Christopher Paul's video deposition, taken on March 30, went well. My report of the deposition is as follows:

Dr. Christopher Paul

Dr. Paul is a board certified orthopedic surgeon, specializing in the back and upper extremities. Dr. Paul reviewed extensive medical records, took a history from Scarlet Rose and conducted a physical examination. He wrote a report documenting his various findings.

Dr. Paul testified, within a reasonable degree of medical probability, that 75% to 100% of plaintiff's back problems preexisted the January 31, 2000, incident at Nickel & Dime.

Although the fall at Nickel & Dime aggravated the pre-existing condition, Dr. Paul could not tell from the records how long the aggravation of the pre-existing condition existed. Plaintiff will argue that she is entitled to compensation for whatever degree of aggravation existed after the fall at Nickel & Dime.

The main issue in the case is whether surgery was necessary as a result of the fall at Nickel & Dime. The surgery was a tremendous success, but she now has two rods in her spine. The argument will be that she would not have had the surgery if she hadn't fallen at Nickel & Dime.

Should you have any questions or comments on any aspect of this case, please call me.

Very truly yours,

_____
Alan Richards

Continuing Negotiations

Chris and Marlene continued to inform their respective clients of new developments. In most cases, there is an ongoing discussion with regard to the possibility of settlement, but in this case, there was very little progress in negotiations. Plaintiff would not reduce her demand until the defendant made an offer that was more realistic than $5,000.

End of Discovery Stage of the Case

Both sides had conducted written discovery and had taken depositions to further discover how the witnesses were likely to testify. The defendant had a compulsory physical examination of the plaintiff performed. Unless a trial became necessary, there was little, if any, further discovery to be conducted.

Chapter Eight

PRETRIAL MOTIONS, ORDERS OF THE COURT AND HEARINGS BEFORE THE COURT

Pretrial Motions and Notices

Once the case was filed, a judge was assigned to the case. The assignment is made on a rotating basis because Pineapple County has more than one circuit judge presiding over civil matters.

The judge is available to hear motions, at a regularly scheduled motion calendar, that can be heard and determined within five minutes. In larger metropolitan areas, motion calendars are conducted on a daily basis. In more rural areas, the motion calendar may be a weekly event. For matters that require more than five minutes, the attorneys schedule a specific time with the judge's judicial assistant. In this case, neither the plaintiff nor the defendant had filed any motions; therefore, they had not required hearings before the court.

In an effort to speed up the litigation process and shorten the amount of time it takes to conclude a lawsuit, the court often sets hearings to determine the status of a case. The Supreme Court of the State of Atlantis has determined and ordered that every civil action be resolved within 18 months from the date the suit was originally filed. Judges who have cases on their dockets for more than 18 months are required to report to the Supreme Court the reasons for the delay in concluding those lawsuits. Because this reflects poorly on a judge's ability to control his or her docket, it is not uncommon for judges to schedule a status conference on its own motion to determine the progress of a case.

It has been ten months since *Scarlet Rose v. Nickel & Dime, Inc.* was filed, and it is at the point of either settling the case or scheduling the trial.

The plaintiff's attorney is often anxious to push the case toward trial because the plaintiff is often in dire need of money. In addition, the plaintiff's attorney usually does not receive any money until the case is settled or is resolved by trial. In personal injury cases, the attorney usually takes the case on a contingency fee basis, which is what Bruce did in this case.

The plaintiff's attorney files notice with the court that the case is ready for trial, which can be filed immediately after the defendant answers the complaint. Provided the plaintiff's attorney has properly prepared the case, the plaintiff is ready for trial once suit is filed; however, the defense must struggle to acquire information and prepare for trial.

Marlene filed the following document with the Court

Form 8.1 — Notice that Case is at Issue and Ready for Trial

IN THE CIRCUIT COURT OF THE
SIXTH JUDICIAL CIRCUIT IN AND FOR

PINEAPPLE COUNTY, ATLANTIS

SCARLET ROSE,
Plaintiff,

v.   Case No.: 00-125-PDD

NICKEL & DIME, INC.,
Defendant.

Notice that Case is at Issue and Ready for Trial

Comes now the plaintiff, Scarlet Rose, by and through her undersigned counsel, and hereby gives notice to this Honorable Court and the defendant, that this case is now at issue and ready for trial. Plaintiff requests that the court place this case on the next available jury trial docket.

CERTIFICATE OF SERVICE

I hereby certify that a true and accurate copy of the foregoing notice that case is at issue and ready for trial was sent to Alan Richards, the attorney for defendant, by regular mail, to his office address of 515 Maple Street, Clearwater, Atlantis, on this 5th day of April, 2001.

_____
Bruce K. Franklin
Attorney for Plaintiff

The plaintiff's attorney generally sends a copy of the foregoing notice directly to the judge assigned to the case and the original to the clerk's office for filing in the court file. Within a week after the judge assigned to this case, Judge Patrick D. Doherty, received the notice from Bruce that the case was at issue, the court issued an order setting the case for trial and an order directing the parties to schedule a mediation conference. Those two orders were issued simultaneously.

Form 8.2 — Trial Order

IN THE CIRCUIT COURT OF THE
SIXTH JUDICIAL CIRCUIT IN AND FOR
PINEAPPLE COUNTY, ATLANTIS

SCARLET ROSE,
Plaintiff,

v.   Case No.: 00-125-PDD

NICKEL & DIME, INC.,
Defendant.

Uniform Order Setting Trial and Pretrial Conference (Jury Trial)

This cause being at issue and the court being otherwise fully advised in the premises, it is hereby ordered and adjudged as follows:

1. That the above-entitled cause is hereby set for jury trial during the two-week trial period commencing July 6, 2001, at 8:30 a.m., or as soon thereafter as counsel may be heard.

2. That a pretrial conference shall be held in chambers before the Honorable Patrick D. Doherty, Circuit Judge, Atlantis County Courthouse, 419 Pierce Street, Room 31, Clearwater, Atlantis, 33602, on June 19, 2001, at 2:15 p.m., pursuant to Rule 1.200, Atlantis Rules of Civil Procedure, to consider all matters suggested therein and to simplify the issues to expedite the trial of this cause.

3. At least 45 days before the pretrial conference, counsel for the plaintiff shall furnish to counsel for the defendant and file directly with the clerk a list of the names and addresses of all witnesses who are expected to testify at the trial of this cause, including experts. At least 30 days before the pretrial conference, counsel for the defendant shall furnish to counsel for plaintiff and file directly with the clerk a list of names and addresses of all witnesses that are expected to testify at the trial of this cause, including experts. The witness lists shall specifically designate all expert witnesses.

4. That the attorneys for all parties are directed to meet together by agreement, initiated by counsel for the plaintiff, no later than seven days before the pretrial conference, to
   a. mark all exhibits for identification
   b. prepare an exhibit list for use of clerk and court (actual exhibits and documentation evidence shall be available for inspection at this time)
   c. stipulate to the admission into evidence or list specific objections, if any, to each proposed exhibit
   d. stipulate, as to any matter of fact and law, that there is no issue to avoid unnecessary proof
   e. review all depositions that are to be offered for any purpose other than impeachment to resolve objections to the portions to be offered in evidence
   f. discuss the possibility of settlement
   g. submit an itemized statement of special damages plaintiff expects to prove
   h. discuss and complete any other matters that may simplify the issues or aid in the speedy disposition of this action, the pretrial conference or trial
   i. draft one pretrial order (using the form attached) signed by all participating counsel that shall be submitted directly to the court at least three days prior to the pretrial conference. in the event the parties are unable to agree on any matter in the pretrial conference order, they shall leave the matter blank and it will be resolved at the pretrial conference.

5. All motions shall be filed prior to the pretrial conference. All motions, except motions *in limine*, not heard by the pretrial conference shall be deemed abandoned.

6. Counsel are urged to complete all discovery, including independent medical examinations, at least 30 days prior to the pretrial conference. No discovery shall be permitted after the pretrial conference except on the order of the court for good cause shown and will not delay the trial of this cause.

7. The case shall be mediated or arbitrated prior to the pretrial conference unless waived by the court.

8. No later than the last business day of the week prior to trial week, each party shall submit to the court, with a copy to opposing counsel, written jury instructions and proposed verdict forms. Each jury instruction shall be on a separate sheet of paper; shall be plainly marked with the name and number of the case; shall contain citations of supporting authorities, if any; shall designate the party submitting the instructions; and shall be numbered in sequence. Counsel should confer prior to trial and attempt to agree as to the jury instructions and verdict forms. This paragraph shall not foreclose the right of each party to modify instructions up to and including the instruction conference at the close of evidence. Any party who intends to request that the court provide a set of written jury instructions for the jury's consideration during deliberations shall be responsible for providing a clear copy of the full jury instructions to the court.

9. Counsel shall be prepared to negotiate settlement at the pretrial conference and have full authority to settle the case or have available at the conference a party or representative who does have full authority to settle.

10. That in order for the full purpose of the pretrial procedures to be accomplished, it is directed that each party be represented at all meetings and hearings herein provided for by an attorney and parties or agent who will participate in the trial of the cause and a person who is vested with full authority to make admissions and disclosures of fact and to bind his or her clients by agreements in respect to all matters pertaining to the trial of the cause and the pretrial conference.

11. Failure to comply with the requirements of this order shall subject counsel and the parties to such sanctions as the court shall determine just and proper under the circumstances.

12. The parties shall do all things reasonable and necessary to assure the availability of their witnesses for the entire trial period or to otherwise preserve their testimony for trial as provided by the Rules of Civil Procedure.

13. Counsel shall immediately notify this court in the event of settlement and submit a stipulation for Order of Dismissal and a Final Disposition form.

14. All provisions of this order that require compliance by counsel is likewise applicable to any party appear *pro se*.

Done and ordered in chambers at Clearwater, Pineapple County, Atlantis, this 10th day of April, 2001.

Patrick D. Doherty
Circuit Court Judge

Copies furnished to: Alan Richards, Esq.; Bruce K. Franklin, Esq.

Form 8.3 — Order for Referral to Mediation

IN THE CIRCUIT COURT OF THE
SIXTH JUDICIAL CIRCUIT IN AND FOR
PINEAPPLE COUNTY, ATLANTIS

SCARLET ROSE,
Plaintiff,

v.   Case No. 00-125-PDD

NICKEL & DIME INC.,
Defendant.

Order for Referral to Mediation

This court, having set this case for trial, does hereby determine that the cause is appropriate for mediation.

Whereupon, in accordance with Atlantis Rule of Civil Procedure 1.700-1.830, *et seq.*, and upon the court's own motion and/or upon stipulation of the parties, it is ordered

1. The above-styled cause is hereby referred to mediation.

2. Within ten days of the date of service of this order, the parties may agree upon a mediator and a date and time for mediation. The mediation conference must be held within 60 days of this order unless otherwise ordered by the court.

3. Plaintiff's counsel is responsible for contacting the Arbitration and Mediation Program (Program), 315 Court Street, Room 427, Clearwater, Atlantis 33756, 727-464-4943, with the mediator and date selection. If the Program is not contacted within the ten-day period, the Program will select a certified mediator by rotation as well as the date and time for mediation. The Program appointments will not be changed absent good cause shown.

4. Each party shall personally appear at the mediation conferences. Pursuant to Atlantis Rule of Civil Procedure 1.720(b), if a party to mediation is a public entity required to conduct its business pursuant to Chapter 286, Atlantis Statutes, that party shall be deemed to appear at a mediation conference by the physical presence of a representative with full authority to negotiate on behalf of the entity and to recommend settlement to the appropriate decision making body of the entity. Otherwise, unless stipulated by the parties or changed by order of the court, a party is deemed to appear at a mediation conference if the following persons are physically present:
    a. The party or its representative having full authority to settle without further consultation;
    b. The party's counsel of record, if any;
    c. A representative of the insurance carrier for any insured party who is not such carrier's outside counsel and who has full authority to settle up to the amount of the plaintiff's last demand or policy limits, whichever is less, without further consultation.

5. The mediator shall be compensated as follows:
    a. If the parties select the mediator, the mediator shall be compensated at the rate agreed to by the mediator and the parties.
    b. If the Program selects the mediator by rotation, the mediator shall be compensated at the rate of not more than $200 per hour.
    c. The mediator's fee shall be divided equally among all the parties.

6. Any party ordered to pay as described in paragraph 4 above, shall bring sufficient funds to the scheduled mediation conference to pay the mediator. Payment is due at the conclusion of each scheduled conference, payable directly to the assigned mediator. Pursuant to Atlantis Rule of Civil Procedure 1.720(g), parties may object to the rate of the mediator's compensation within 15 days of the date of this order by serving an objection on all other parties, the mediator, and the Program. The referring/presiding judge shall hear such objection.

7. Unless stipulated by the parties or ordered by the court, the mediation process shall not suspend discovery.

8. During its pendency, any matter pertaining to this referral shall be heard by the presiding judge. Time for completion of mediation shall be tolled where mediation is interrupted pending resolution of such matters.

9. The presiding judge may hear interim or emergency relief not specifically pertaining to this referral. However, mediation shall continue while such relief is pending unless otherwise ordered.

10. Pursuant to Atlantis Rule of Civil Procedure 1.700(c), any party may move to have this case deferred from mediation within 15 days of the date of this order. The presiding judge shall hear such motion.

11. If you are a person with a disability who needs any accommodations in order to participate in this proceeding, you are entitled, at no cost to you, the provision of certain assistance if your mediation conference will be conducted in a Pineapple County Court facility. Within two working days of your receipt of this order of Referral to Mediation, please contact the Human Rights Office, 400 South Fort Harrison Avenue, Suite 300, Clearwater, Atlantis 33756, 727-464-4062 (Voice/TDD).

Done and entered this 10th day of April, 2001

Patrick D. Doherty
Circuit Court Judge

Status of the Case

Although over 96% of all lawsuits filed are settled, it appeared that this case was going to require a trial.

The plaintiff had requested in the complaint, at the time the case was filed, a trial by jury. A trial by jury made a trial more difficult to prepare for than a trial before the judge. Bruce had asked for a trial by jury because a jury was more likely to award a larger sum of money for pain and suffering than a judge would.

Defense Perspective

Alan had received authorization from Ms. Mallet to do everything necessary to prepare for trial. He dictated a letter summarizing exactly what he intended to do and told Chris that there were numerous things that needed to be done in preparation for trial.

1. *Expert Witness Interrogatories.* Alan wanted to know if plaintiff had retained an expert regarding the store's restocking procedures and whether the expert would testify that Nickel & Dime was negligent. Chris prepared and mailed a set of expert witness interrogatories to the plaintiff.

2. *Locate Expert Witness for Nickel & Dime on Negligence Issue.* In the event that plaintiff had an expert, Alan wanted to have someone whom he could call as a witness. He asked Chris to find the names of experts used by the firm in the past. Because he could not retain an expert without Ms. Mallet's approval, he wanted to send a résumé and statement of fees to her and ask her if she had a preference. Chris contacted three potential experts and sent the résumé and statement of fees to Louise Mallet.

3. *Further Depositions.* Alan instructed Chris to contact the witnesses who the defense intended to call at the time of trial to see if the plaintiff had subpoenaed them and to make sure that the witnesses were available for trial. If the witnesses were not available, it would be necessary to take a videotape deposition.

4. *Further Investigation.* Alan told Chris to keep trying to locate Carol Westwoman, the store clerk who was restocking the shelves at the time of the incident. He told Chris to hire an investigator. The investigator would need a full name, date of birth, Social Security number, last known address, and any other information they had.

5. *List of Witnesses and Exhibits.* As required by the trial order, Alan asked Chris to prepare the necessary list of witnesses and exhibits and to make sure the date for compliance was on all calendars.

Defendant's Witness List

Chris prepared the following list of witnesses.

Form 8.4 — Witness List

IN THE CIRCUIT COURT OF THE SIXTH
JUDICIAL CIRCUIT IN AND FOR
PINEAPPLE COUNTY, ATLANTIS

SCARLET ROSE,
Plaintiff,

v.   Case No.: 00-125-PDD

NICKEL & DIME, INC.
Defendant.

Defendant Nickel & Dime, Inc., List of Witnesses

COMES NOW the defendant, Nickel & Dime, Inc., by and through the undersigned counsel and, pursuant to this court's uniform order setting trial and pretrial conference, hereby files this its list of witnesses expected to testify at trial:

- Scarlet Rose - Plaintiff
- Kate Frechette
- Michael Mullan, M.D. - Treating Physician
- Von N. Beebe, M.D. - Neurosurgeon
- Marjorie Murphy - Store Manager
- Caitlin Palmer - Department Supervisor
- Christopher Paul, M.D. - Defendant's IME doctor
- Brendan Patrick, M.D. - Treating Physician
- Records Custodians

RESPECTFULLY SUBMITTED this 5th day of May, 2001.

CERTIFICATE OF SERVICE

I HEREBY CERTIFY that a copy of the foregoing List of Witnesses has been furnished to Bruce Franklin, Esq., attorney for the plaintiff, 616 Turner Street, Clearwater, Atlantis, 34616 on this 5th day of May, 2001.

Alan Richards, Esq.
Attorney for the Defendant
515 Maple Street
Clearwater, Atlantis 34616
727-462-8888

Defendant's Exhibit List

Form 8.5 — Defendant's Exhibit List

IN THE CIRCUIT COURT OF THE SIXTH
JUDICIAL CIRCUIT IN AND FOR
PINEAPPLE COUNTY, ATLANTIS

SCARLET ROSE,
Plaintiff,

v.   Case No.: 00-125-PDD

NICKEL & DIME, INC.
Defendant.

Defendant Nickel & Dime, Inc., Exhibit List

COMES NOW the defendant, Nickel & Dime, Inc., by and through the undersigned counsel, and files this its
List of Exhibits as follows:

LIST OF EXHIBITS

Any and all exhibits listed by the parties, without waiving objections thereto

1. Community Hospital Emergency Room Records (January 2000)
2. Community Hospital records; 3/17/2000-3/20/2000; back surgery
3. Michael Mullan, M.D., office records, including x-rays and other tests
4. Brendan Patrick, M.D., office records, including MRI results, etc.
5. Von N. Beebe, M.D., office records, including MRI results, etc.
6. EMT records
7. All medical bills for the above
8. Blue Cross/Blue Shield and Core Source medical insurance policies
9. Blue Cross/Blue Shield and Core Source medical insurance statements and paid bills
10. Public Defender employment records of plaintiff
11. IME report of Christopher Paul, M.D., (expert)
12. Procedure manuals relating to inspection and safety procedures, including employee training manuals
13. Plastic merchandise tote
14. Photographs of accident scene
15. Diagram of incident scene.

CERTIFICATE OF SERVICE

I HEREBY CERTIFY that a copy of the foregoing List of Exhibits has been furnished to Bruce K. Franklin,
Esq., attorney for the plaintiff, 616 Turner Street, Clearwater, Atlantis 34616, on this 5th day of May, 2001.

_____
Alan Richards, Esq.
Attorney for the Defendant
515 Maple Street
Clearwater, Atlantis 34616
727-462-8888

Trial Interrogatories and Requests for Production

Since there is no duty, under Atlantis law, to update answers to discovery requests, Alan instructed Chris to prepare discovery requests seeking updated information.

Plaintiff's Perspective

Like Chris, Marlene was busy making final preparations for trial. It was not necessary for the plaintiff's attorney to take more discovery depositions. They could talk to the physicians who treated Ms. Rose, but they had to pay for the conferences. Marlene was instructed to do the following:

1. Arrange a conference with the doctor(s) to be called to the witness stand at trial: Bruce said he intended to call Dr. Mullan at the time of trial. Dr. Beebe would be presented by video.

2. Prepare Trial Witness and Exhibit List.

3. Prepare Proposed Jury Instructions.

4. Prepare Updated Trial Interrogatories: Marlene prepared discovery requests, including expert witness interrogatories.

5. Prepare Proposed Verdict Form.

6. Assemble a Trial Notebook.

7. Prepare Witness and Exhibit List.

Form 8.6 — Plaintiff's Witness List

IN THE CIRCUIT COURT OF THE SIXTH
JUDICIAL CIRCUIT IN AND FOR
PINEAPPLE COUNTY, ATLANTIS

SCARLET ROSE,
Plaintiff,

v.   Case No. 00-125-PDD

NICKEL & DIME INC.,
Defendant.

Plaintiff's List of Witnesses

COMES NOW the plaintiff, Scarlet Rose, by and through the undersigned counsel and, pursuant to this court's uniform order setting trial and pretrial conference, hereby files this its List of Witnesses expected to testify at trial:

- Scarlet Rose - Plaintiff
- Jane Morris - Plaintiff's Mother
- Brendan Patrick, M.D. - Treating Physician
- Michael Mullan, M.D. - Treating Physician

- Von N. Beebe, M.D. - Plaintiff's Neurosurgeon
- Marjorie Murphy - Store Manager
- Caitlin Palmer - Department Supervisor
- Andrea Jones - Former Store Employee
- Christie Davidson - Former Employee
- Betsy Ross - Former Employee
- Shannon Young - Former Employee
- Carol Treschler - Physical Therapist

CERTIFICATE OF SERVICE

I HEREBY CERTIFY that a copy of the foregoing List of Witnesses has been furnished to Alan Richards, Esq., attorney for the defendant, 515 Maple Street, Clearwater, Atlantis 34616, on this 15th day of May, 2001.

Bruce K. Franklin, Esq.
Attorney for the Plaintiff
616 Turner Street
Clearwater, Atlantis 34616
727-462-1000

Form 8.7 — Plaintiff's Exhibit List

IN THE CIRCUIT COURT OF THE SIXTH
JUDICIAL CIRCUIT IN AND FOR
PINEAPPLE COUNTY, ATLANTIS

SCARLET ROSE,
Plaintiff,

v.   Case No. 00-125-PDD

Nickel & Dime, Inc.
Defendant.

Plaintiff's Exhibit List

COMES NOW the plaintiff, Scarlet Rose, by and through the undersigned counsel, and files this her List of Exhibits as follows:

LIST OF EXHIBITS

- Community Hospital Emergency Room Records (January 2000)
- Community Hospital records; 3/12/00-3/16/00; back surgery
- Dr. Michael Mullan, M.D., office records, including x-rays and other tests
- Dr. Brendan Patrick, M.D., office records, including MRI results, etc.
- Dr. Von N. Beebe, M.D., office records, including MRI results, etc.
- Emergency medical technician (EMT) records
- All medical bills for the above
- Blue Cross/Blue Shield and Core Source medical insurance policies
- Blue Cross/Blue Shield and Core Source medical insurance statements and paid bills
- Public Defender employment records of plaintiff
- Records from Carol Treschler, physical therapist
- Procedure manuals relating to inspection and safety procedures, including employee training manuals
- Photographs of accident scene

- Diagram of incident scene
- Demonstrative aids.

CERTIFICATE OF SERVICE

I HEREBY CERTIFY that a copy of the foregoing List of Exhibits has been furnished to Alan Richards, Esq., attorney for the defendant, 515 Maple Street, Clearwater, Atlantis 34616, on this 15th day of May, 2001.

Bruce K. Franklin, Esq.
Attorney for the Plaintiff
616 Turner Street
Clearwater, Atlantis 34616
727-462-1000

Pretrial Motions

Even though a Motion for Summary Judgment was unlikely to be successful, Chris drafted one because Alan thought it was important to let the court know the facts of the case. There was a small chance that the court might grant the motion on the grounds that the fall was caused by an open and obvious condition. Chris prepared the following motion:

Form 8.8 — Defendant's Motion for Summary Judgment

IN THE CIRCUIT COURT OF THE SIXTH
JUDICIAL CIRCUIT IN AND FOR
PINEAPPLE COUNTY, ATLANTIS

SCARLET ROSE,
Plaintiff,

v.   Case No.: 00-125-PDD

Nickel & Dime, Inc.
Defendant.

Motion for Summary Judgment

The defendant, Nickel & Dime, Inc., by its attorney and pursuant to Rule 1.510 of the Atlantis Rules of Civil Procedure, moves the court to enter a summary judgment for the defendant on the ground that there is no genuine issue as to any material fact, and the defendant is entitled to judgment as a matter of law.

The undisputed material facts are as follows:

1. The defendant in the above-styled case owned and controlled the premises on which the plaintiff, Scarlet Rose, fell on January 31, 2000.

2. On January 31, 2000, the plaintiff slipped and fell over a merchandise tote while walking through the customer aisles located within the premises owned by defendant.

3. The merchandise tote was an open and obvious condition on the premises.

4. The plaintiff either saw or she should have seen, by the exercise of due diligence and paying proper attention, the merchandise tote, and defendant suggests that she deliberately attempted to step over the tote.

5. The undisputed material facts clearly establish that plaintiff, and solely the plaintiff, was responsible for this incident, and that defendant is entitled to the entry of summary judgment in its favor.

6. To support these undisputed material facts, the defendant has filed various documents, including the pleadings, interrogatories, depositions, and responses to requests for admissions.

Memorandum of Law in Support of Motion for Summary Judgment

The plaintiff's complaint alleges that the plaintiff fell as a result of the defendant's negligence and lack of due care in maintaining a safe walkway. A long-standing precedent in the state of Atlantis is the case of *Dixie Inc. v. Peters*, 291 A.2d 66 (1974). The facts of the *Dixie* case are similar to the facts of our case in that a patron of a store fell, injured himself and claimed that the store was negligent in the manner that it maintained the store. The Second District Court of Appeal of Atlantis reversed a judgment entered for the plaintiff by the Circuit Court in Escambia County, who found that the store was negligent and liable to the plaintiff for all damages proven by the plaintiff. The *Dixie* case established that, although business owners have a duty to exercise ordinary or reasonable care to see that their premises are reasonably safe, the customer is obligated to exercise a reasonable degree of care for his or her own safety, including observing the obvious and apparent condition of the premises. Momentarily forgetting the existence of a hazard or failing to pay attention to what he or she is doing is no excuse for his or her failure to observe the hazard.

To recover injuries sustained in a trip-and-fall case, the plaintiff must show that the proprietor had actual notice of the condition or that the dangerous condition existed for such a length of time that the occupant should have known and taken action to remedy it or guard the plaintiff from harm.

In this case, slippers were being unloaded from a merchandise tote. The merchandise tote was located in plain view. A store employee was taking the slippers out of the tote, and Ms. Rose tripped over the tote.

The courts have held that a storekeeper is not an insurer of the safety of all those who come upon the premises. He or she need only exercise reasonable care to protect the patrons from harm that might result from a dangerous condition that he or she has actual or constructive notice of. Defendant submits that this Honorable Court should find and determine that Ms. Rose had a duty to observe the open and obvious condition, and her failure to do so bars her claim for recovery.

WHEREFORE, the defendant, Nickel & Dime, Inc., prays that this Honorable Court enter an order granting defendant's Motion for Summary Judgment and ultimately enter judgment in favor of the defendant.

CERTIFICATE OF SERVICE

I HEREBY CERTIFY that a true copy of the foregoing Motion for Summary Judgment has been furnished by first class U.S. mail to Bruce K. Franklin, Esq., attorney for the plaintiff, 616 Turner Street, Clearwater, Atlantis 34616 on this 15th day of May, 2001.

Alan Richards, Esq.
Attorney for the Defendant
515 Maple Street
Clearwater, Atlantis 34616

Because the Motion for Summary Judgment was based upon the facts of the case, Chris needed to submit those facts. He prepared the following document.

Form 8.9 — Notice of Filing for Consideration by the Court
of Defendant's Motion for Summary Judgment

IN THE CIRCUIT COURT OF THE SIXTH
JUDICIAL CIRCUIT IN AND FOR
PINEAPPLE COUNTY, ATLANTIS
SCARLET ROSE,
Plaintiff,

v.   Case No.: 00-125-PDD

Nickel & Dime, Inc.
Defendant.

Notice of Filing for Consideration by the Court of Defendant's Motion for Summary Judgment

Comes now defendant, Nickel & Dime, Inc., by and through undersigned counsel, and hereby submits the following documents for the court to review and consider at the time it hears and determines the Motion for Summary Judgment that has been filed by defendant, to wit:

- Transcript of deposition of Scarlet Rose
- Transcript of deposition of Marjorie Murphy
- Transcript of deposition of Caitlin Palmer
- Transcript of deposition of Andrea Jones
- Plaintiff's Answers to Interrogatories
- Plaintiff's Responses to Requests for Admissions.

CERTIFICATE OF SERVICE

I HEREBY CERTIFY that a true copy of the foregoing Motion for Summary Judgment has been furnished by first class U.S. mail to Bruce K. Franklin, Esq., attorney for the plaintiff, 616 Turner Street, Clearwater, Atlantis 34616, on this 15th day of May, 2001.

_____
Alan Richards, Esq.
Attorney for the Defendant
515 Maple Street
Clearwater, Atlantis 34616

Motion in Limine

Chris prepared a Motion *in Limine* to keep out some employees' testimony that Carol Westwoman violated an unwritten store policy.

Form 8.10 — Motion *in Limine*

IN THE CIRCUIT COURT OF THE SIXTH
JUDICIAL CIRCUIT IN AND FOR
PINEAPPLE COUNTY, ATLANTIS

SCARLET ROSE,
Plaintiff,

v.   Case No.: 00-125-PDD

Nickel & Dime, Inc.
Defendant.

Motion *in Limine*

COMES NOW the defendant, Nickel & Dime, Inc., by and through undersigned counsel, and respectfully moves this Honorable Court limit and prevent the plaintiff from introducing any testimony into evidence which suggests that Nickel & Dime, Inc., violated its own internal procedures with regard to cleaning the area where the incident in question occurred and, therefore, violated its own internal policies, and such fact(s) is/are evidence of negligence. The issue before the court is whether the defendant committed any acts of negligence, and defendant submits it is irrelevant as to whether Nickel & Dime, Inc., violated its own internal procedures.

In support of this motion, defendant offers the case of *May v. Supermarkets, Inc.*, 686 So.2nd 801, (Atlantis 4th DCA 1997). In that case, the District Court held that a party's internal rule does not itself fix the legal standard of care in a negligence action. In so ruling, the court cited *Mart Corp. v. Kitchen*, 662 So.2nd 977 (Atlantis 4th DCA 1995), which held that it would be improper for the trial court to instruct the jury that a violation of the internal policy or procedure of a party was evidence of negligence.

WHEREFORE, defendant prays that this Honorable Court grants the subject Motion *in Limine* and prevents plaintiff from introducing any evidence of whether Nickel & Dime, Inc.'s internal procedures were violated.

CERTIFICATE OF SERVICE

I HEREBY CERTIFY that a true and correct copy of the above was mailed this 15th day of May, 2001, to Bruce K. Franklin, Esq., attorney for the plaintiff, 616 Turner Street, Clearwater, Atlantis 34616.

_____
Alan Richards, Esq.
Attorney for the Defendant
515 Maple Street
Clearwater, Atlantis 34616
727-462-8888

Preparation for the Hearing on Behalf of the Plaintiff

Marlene found a case that discussed the issue of a store's policy and procedure and gave three copies to Bruce to take to the hearing with him. One copy was for the court, one copy for opposing counsel, and one was for Bruce. The case read as follows:

DEPARTMENT STORE INC.,
Appellant,

v.   Case No. 98-3731

KELLIE CLOSET,
Appellee.

District Court of Appeal of Atlantis,
Fourth District.

October 18, 1998

Kellie Closet brought action against store for negligence in selling a firearm to her intoxicated ex-boyfriend who shot and severely injured her. The Circuit Court, Pineapple County, awarded woman $1,580,768 in damages. Store appealed. The District Court of Appeal, held that: (1) store could not be held liable to woman for selling firearm to intoxicated customer, and (2) store's internal policy did not fix store's standard of care.

Reversed and remanded; question certified.

Issue: Store could not be held liable to third party for negligence in selling firearm to intoxicated customer who shot third party, because there was no evidence that customer engaged in erratic behavior, making it foreseeable that someone would be injured as a result of the sale. Imposing common law liability on a vendor under such circumstances would extend law in an area that the legislature had entered a field by regulating sale of firearms.

A business's internal rule does not itself fix the standard of care in negligence action against the business.

Thomas West, after a daylong drinking spree, purchased a .22 caliber rifle at a department store and shot his ex-girlfriend, leaving her a quadriplegic. A jury found Department Store, Inc. guilty of common law negligence and returned a verdict in the amount of $1,580,768. We reverse because we conclude that, where there is no statutory prohibition against the sale of a firearm to a person who is intoxicated, the seller is not responsible to a third person for the improper use of the firearm. We do certify the question as one of great public importance.

The facts, in a light most favorable to plaintiff, reflect that West, by his own estimate, had consumed a fifth of whiskey and a case of beer on the morning of December 14, 1987, until he left a bar around 8:30 p.m. After becoming angry with plaintiff, his ex-girlfriend, West drove to the department store and purchased a .22 caliber bolt-action rifle and a box of bullets at approximately 9:45 p.m. West then drove back to the bar and, after observing that plaintiff left in an automobile with friends, followed them in his truck and rammed them from behind when they were stopped at a light. He then forced them off the road and shot plaintiff, rendering her a permanent quadriplegic.

West, who pled guilty to attempted murder and is serving a 55-year sentence, had no recollection of what occurred in the department store. The clerk who sold the rifle testified that the handwriting on the federal form required for a firearm purchase was not legible, and he filled out another form for West and had him initial the "yes/no" answers and sign his name at the end. The clerk testified that West did not appear to be intoxicated, and the store has a policy against selling firearms to intoxicated people. There was no direct evidence regarding West's behavior in the store besides the testimony of the clerk. Plaintiff presented experts who testified that, if West had consumed as much alcohol during the day as West had indicated, it would have been apparent to the clerk that West was intoxicated.

Plaintiff's complaint alleged both common law negligence and violations of section 790.17, Atlantis Statutes (1987) (prohibiting sale to minors or persons of unsound mind), and the Federal Gun Control Act, 18 U.S.C. § 922 (prohibiting sale to minors, felons, unlawful drug users, adjudicated mental defectives, et cetera); however, the trial court directed a verdict for the store on the statutory claims and submitted the case to the jury only on the theory of common law negligence. The court instructed the jury that store's violation of its own internal rule against selling firearms to intoxicated persons was evidence of negligence. We conclude that the jury should not have been so instructed, and the trial court should have directed a verdict in favor of the store.

In the Atlantis case *Angel v. Lumber Co.*, 363 So.2d 571 (Atlantis 2d DCA 1978), the seller of a firearm had been held subject to liability for common law negligence. In that case, however, the customer was engaging in bizarre behavior in the store, and after observing that behavior, the store's employee called the sheriff's office and told one of the officers that a woman wanted to buy a rifle but was acting strangely. The officer advised him that he did not have to sell the rifle, but he, nevertheless, sold her the rifle, along with ammunition, and shortly thereafter she shot and killed another person. The court held that the complaint stated a cause of action because the customer's erratic behavior made it foreseeable that someone would be injured as a result of the sale. In the present case, there was no evidence that West engaged in any type of erratic behavior.

In all of the other Atlantis cases relied on by plaintiff it was undisputed that the vendors violated the Federal Gun Control Act. See also *Coke v. Market*, 642 A.2d 774 (lst DCA 1994). Although we do not favor the indiscriminate sale of firearms, we are persuaded by decisions of the Atlantis Supreme Court involving analogous factual situations that we cannot extend the common law liability of a vendor under the circumstances of this case. In *Bank v. Brent*, 74 507 A.2d 1385, 1387 (1987), the Supreme Court rejected common law liability of a social host who furnished alcoholic beverages to a minor who then drove while drunk and injured the plaintiff. After concluding that there was no violation of a statute, the court stated:

> Petitioner's final argument is that we should recognize a common law cause of action in favor of similarly situated plaintiffs. We decline. We do not hold that we lack the power to do so, but we do hold that when the legislature has actively entered a particular field and has clearly indicated its ability to deal with such a policy question, the more prudent course is for this court to defer to the legislative branch.

We cannot distinguish the present case from *Bank*. As it has with alcohol, our legislature has also entered the field of regulating the sale of firearms. Section 790.17, Atlantis Statutes (1987), which provides:

> Whoever sells, hires, barters, lends, or gives any minor under 18 years of age any pistol, dirk, electric weapon or device, or other arm or weapon, other than an ordinary pocketknife, without permission of the parent of such minor, or the person having charge of such minor, or sells, hires, barters, lends, or gives to any person of unsound mind an electric weapon or device or any dangerous weapon, other then an ordinary pocketknife, is guilty of a misdemeanor of the first degree, punishable as provided in s. 775.082 or s. 775.083 or s. 775.084.

In 1991, several years after this incident, the legislature passed section 790.151, Atlantis Statutes (1991), which makes it unlawful for a person to use a firearm while under the influence of alcohol or a controlled substance. The legislature has not, however, gone so far as to prohibit the sale of a firearm to a person who is known to be intoxicated. See Miss. Code Ann., § 97-37-13 (1972).

Since our legislature has not extended vendor liability for the sale of a firearm under the circumstances of this case, our imposition of liability on the store would be taking a step that our Supreme Court declined to take in *Bank*. We therefore conclude that the trial court should have directed a verdict in favor of the defendant.

Because we anticipate plaintiff will seek review of our decision in the Supreme Court, we address another issue raised by appellant that would, if we were not reversing for entry of a directed verdict, require a new trial. The evidence showed that the store had an internal policy to not sell a firearm to a visibly intoxicated person, and over the store's objection, the trial court instructed the jury that a violation of the internal policy or procedure was evidence of negligence. While we recognize that defendant's rules of conduct are relevant, it would be improper to instruct the jury that a violation of such a rule is evidence of negligence. See also *Horn v. Plenty, Inc.*, 533 A.2d 261 (1988), in which an automobile salesman sold and delivered a vehicle to a purchaser whom the salesman knew was an incompetent driver. In holding that the plaintiff, whom the customer struck shortly after leaving the dealership, had no cause of action against the dealer, the Supreme Court, citing *Bank*, said that expansion of the liability of a vendor was for the legislature.

Although we rest our conclusion that the store cannot be held liable entirely on Atlantis law, we would note that plaintiff has not cited any cases from other jurisdictions in which the seller of a firearm was held liable in a similar factual situation.

The court quoted from Professor Wigmore, who explained: "To take the (defendant's) conduct as furnishing a sufficient legal standard of negligence would be to abandon the standard set by the substantive law, and would be improper. . . The proper method is to receive it, with an express caution that it is merely evidential and is not to serve as a legal standard." 2 J. Wigmore, *Evidence* § 461, at 593.

In *Bucs v. McKay*, 441 Mch. 96, 490 N.W.2d 330 (1992), the Michigan Supreme Court disapproved the same type of jury instruction.

Imposition of a legal duty on a retailer on the basis of its internal policies is actually contrary to public policy. Such a rule would encourage retailers to abandon all policies enacted for the protection of others in an effort to avoid future liability. See the concurring opinion in *Stein v. Glass*, 531 A.2d at 201: "Rather than instructing this jury that the violation of the internal rule was negligence, the Court should have instructed that an internal rule does not itself fix the standard of care." *Stein*, 531 So.2d at 200; Wigmore.

We therefore reverse and remand for entry of a judgment in favor of Appellant, but certify the following question as one of great public importance:

Can a seller of a firearm to a purchaser known to the seller to be intoxicated be held liable to a third person injured by the purchaser?

BENNETT, J., concurs. MOONEY, J., concurs in part and dissents in part with opinion.

I agree with certification of the question and with reversal because the jury was instructed over appellant's objection that violation of the store's internal policy was evidence of negligence. However, I disagree with the majority's reliance upon *Bank* and *Horn*, and I believe the issue of foreseeability here was properly submitted to the jury.

The court in *Bank* concluded that it could not consider common law liability because the legislature had considered and limited the scope of civil liability. *Horn*, too, involved judicial reluctance to tread on legislative turf. Neither situation exists here.

Accordingly, I view the door of common law liability as being wide open and regret its being shut.

Form 8.11 — Notice of Hearing

IN THE CIRCUIT COURT OF THE SIXTH
JUDICIAL CIRCUIT COURT IN AND FOR
PINEAPPLE COUNTY, ATLANTIS

SCARLET ROSE,
Plaintiff,

v.   Case No. 00-125-PDD

Nickel & Dime, Inc.
Defendant.

Notice of Hearing

TO: Bruce K. Franklin, Attorney at Law
      616 Turner Street
      Clearwater, Atlantis 34616

PLEASE TAKE NOTICE that on Monday, the 15th day of June, 2001, at 1:30 p.m. or as soon thereafter as counsel may be heard, the undersigned will bring on to be heard, pursuant to the Atlantis Rules of Civil Procedure, defendant's Motion for Summary Judgment and defendant's Motion *in Limine* before the Honorable

Patrick D. Doherty, one of the judges of the above Court in Chambers in Room 529 of the Pineapple County Courthouse, 315 Court Street, Clearwater, Atlantis 33756. The time allotted is 45 minutes.

PLEASE GOVERN YOURSELF ACCORDINGLY.

CERTIFICATE OF SERVICE

I HEREBY CERTIFY that a true copy of the foregoing Notice of Hearing has been furnished by first class U.S. mail to Bruce K. Franklin, Esq., attorney for the plaintiff, 616 Turner Street, Clearwater, Atlantis 34616 on this 15th day of May, 2001.

Alan Richards, Esq.
Attorney for the Defendant
515 Maple Street
Clearwater, Atlantis 34617
727-462-8888

Hearing on Defendant's Motion *in Limine* and Motion for Summary Judgment

On the designated day, the lawyers, Marlene, Chris, and Ms. Rose appeared before the court to argue the motions filed by Nickel & Dime. Because Chris had ordered one, a court reporter was present. The following is a transcript of the hearing.

IN THE CIRCUIT COURT OF THE SIXTH
JUDICIAL CIRCUIT IN AND FOR
PINEAPPLE COUNTY, ATLANTIS

SCARLET ROSE,
Plaintiff,

v.   Case No. 00-125-PDD

NICKEL & DIME INC.,
Defendant.

JUDGE: Honorable Patrick D. Doherty, Circuit Court Judge

TAKEN ON: June 15, 2001
TAKEN AT: Pineapple County Courthouse, Clearwater, Atlantis

APPEARANCES: Bruce K. Franklin, Esq., on behalf of plaintiff
Alan Richards, Esq., on behalf of defendant

REPORTED BY: Susan Sullivan, Court Reporter

THE COURT: We are here today to consider a Defense Motion *in Limine* and a Defense Motion for Summary Judgment, correct?

MR. RICHARDS: Yes, Your Honor. I have a Motion *in Limine*. I'm requesting that the court prohibit the plaintiff from making reference to or admitting any testimony from any current or former Nickel & Dime employees, whom the plaintiff is going to ask what the policy and procedure of Nickel & Dime was, at the time of the incident, with regards to placement of a tote.

There is case law that says that the internal procedures of a store, like Nickel & Dime, is not admissible because of the fact that it would allow the jury to decide that the standard of care for negligence is the store's internal policy and procedure.

The question is, did they commit negligence by failing to do what a reasonable store would do as far as restocking shelves and tote placement. The issue that I am raising by this motion is that these former employees cannot testify as to whether the placement of the totes in this particular location was a violation of the internal procedure of Nickel & Dime.

MR. FRANKLIN: Although the violation of internal policies is not evidence of negligence, the issue of admissibility of one's internal procedures, safety procedures and violation thereof is relevant to the standard of care. The case of *May v. Supermarket* states that the court has recognized that safety rules and procedures, established by a party to govern the conduct of the employees, are relevant to the evidence of the standard of care.

A party's own internal operating manuals are admissible if relevant to the issues raised. *Mart v. Kitchen* established that a party's internal rule does not itself fix the legal standard of care in a negligence action and the party is entitled to an appropriate jury instruction to that effect. The court said that the store's internal policy that said that no employee should sell firearms to a visibly intoxicated person was admissible, and despite Mart's objection, the trial court instructed the jury that a violation of the internal policies and procedures was evidence of negligence. The appellate court ruled that was inappropriate. The Supreme Court of Atlantis overruled the appellate court and reinstated the ruling of the trial court. It held that the admission of those policies and procedures does not establish a higher standard of care or evidence of negligence, but it is relevant to the standard of care.

The court said that the proper method is to allow the testimony into evidence, but the court should caution the jury that the evidence is merely evidence of negligence. The evidence did not establish, as a matter of law, that Mart was negligent in that case, and it should not serve as a legal standard of care. The rule of law is that an internal rule does not itself fix the standard of care. So, the question of whether it comes in is clearly established by these cases, but the court needs to caution the jury that it is not conclusive proof of negligence.

MR. RICHARDS: The case that Mr. Franklin is reading is dicta. It is not the holding in the case. In the *May* case, the Supreme Court found that there was a manual and a policy that was violated. In this case, there are no manuals or written internal procedures that say employees cannot stock the shelves this way. The plaintiff wants three disgruntled former employee to come in here and say, "This is the way we were supposed to do it." These are their opinions, and they are not experts.

THE COURT: Mr. Franklin, are you calling three former employees as witnesses in order to have them testify about the policy of Nickel & Dime at the time of the incident?

MR. FRANKLIN: They are going to testify that they were trained not to put totes in the walkway of the store. That's the issue in this case. These totes were in a walkway where my client tripped over them. A policy doesn't have to be in written form or in a written manual. It can be the way these employees were trained. I'm not going to ask these employees to render an opinion.

THE COURT: The *May* case states that internal operating manuals are admissible if relevant.

MR. FRANKLIN: In the *Closet* case, your Honor, the court found those policies and procedures to be relevant and admissible. The evidence in that case showed that Mart had an internal policy not to sell a firearm to a visibly intoxicated person. A policy can be instructions to employees on how to conduct themselves within the store. We're trying to show that it was the policy not to place totes on the floor in areas where customers could trip over them. I'm not going to ask these employees what their opinion is regarding whether this was negligence.

THE COURT: I deny defendant's Motion *in Limine* at this time. If the witnesses are asked inappropriate questions during the trial, I will consider the matter at that time.

As far as the Motion for Summary Judgment is concerned, I have read the motion, the memorandum of law offered in support of the motion, the cases cited in the motion and the memorandum, and I have decided to deny the motion at this time, without prejudice and without the necessity of an argument. I believe the issue is a factual one and that the jury must decide the factual issues raised by the pleadings and the depositions taken in the case.

Form 8.12 — Entry of Order Denying Motions

IN THE CIRCUIT COURT OF THE SIXTH
JUDICIAL CIRCUIT IN AND FOR
PINEAPPLE COUNTY, ATLANTIS

SCARLET ROSE,
Plaintiff,

v.   Case No. 00-125-PDD

NICKEL & DIME INC.,
Defendant.

Order Denying Defendant's Motion for Summary Judgment and Defendant's Motion *in Limine*

This cause came before the court on the 15th day of June, 2001, upon defendant's Motion for Summary Judgment and defendant's Motion *in Limine*. Appearing before the court were attorney Bruce K. Franklin, on behalf of the plaintiff, and attorney Alan Richards, on behalf of the defendant. Upon due consideration of the matter presented, it is hereby

ORDERED AND ADJUDGED that defendant's motions are hereby denied, without prejudice to the defendant to further argue the matters during trial of this cause should that become necessary.

DONE AND ENTERED, in chambers, this 15th day of June, 2001.

_____
Patrick D. Doherty
Circuit Court Judge

Pretrial Stipulation

As required by the pretrial order, Marlene and Chris worked on preparing a pretrial stipulation. They prepared the following for the approval of the attorneys.

IN THE CIRCUIT COURT OF THE SIXTH
JUDICIAL CIRCUIT IN AND FOR
PINEAPPLE COUNTY, ATLANTIS

SCARLET ROSE,
Plaintiff,

v.   Case No. 00-125-PDD

NICKEL & DIME INC.,
Defendant.

Pretrial Stipulation

COME NOW the parties, by and through their respective undersigned attorneys and pursuant to the applicable Rules of Civil Procedure and this court's order setting trial and file the following stipulation:

Statement of Case

1. This case involves an incident on January 31, 2000, wherein the plaintiff, Scarlet Rose, tripped and fell in a Nickel & Dime store located in Clearwater, Atlantis.

2. The plaintiff, Scarlet Rose, contends that the defendant was negligent and created a dangerous condition by placing a box on the floor that the plaintiff fell over and was injured.

3. The defendant, Nickel & Dime, Inc., denies that it was negligent and claims that the plaintiff was negligent in causing the incident by failing to observe the box and not paying proper attention.

Pleadings Upon Which the Case Will be Tried

This case will be tried on the plaintiff's Complaint and the defendant's Answer and Affirmative Defenses.

Facts Admitted

1. The incident occurred in Pineapple County, Atlantis, on January 31, 2000.

2. The defendant, Nickel & Dime, Inc., is the owner and/or entity in possession of the premise in which the incident occurred.

3. All other facts admitted in the pleadings.

Matter Requiring Action by the Court

Defendant's Motions *in Limine* and defendant's Motion for Summary Judgment were denied, without prejudice. No other matters are pending.

Legal and Evidentiary Issues

Admissibility of testimony from former employees of defendant regarding the actions of defendant in placing a box on floors and in walkways.

Special Jury Instructions

The parties anticipate that some special instructions will be requested. Special instructions shall be made available to the parties and the court prior to the close of evidence.

Witness Lists

The parties have filed witness lists with the court.

Exhibit Lists

The parties have each filed an exhibit list with the court. It is anticipated that both parties will utilize demonstrative aids during their presentation. These aids will likely be enlargements of the documentary evidence previously identified on the exhibit lists. The parties have stipulated to the admissibility of all medical records regarding to the plaintiff's medical condition both prior to January 31, 2000, and thereafter.

The plaintiff will secure the court reporter.

SUBMITTED this 15th day of June, 2001.

Bruce K. Franklin   Alan Richards
616 Turner Street   515 Maple Street
Clearwater, Atlantis   Clearwater, Atlantis
727-462-1000   727-462-8888

Mediation

Mediation is one way to resolve a lawsuit. The court order required the attorneys to choose a mediator within ten days. The attorneys exchanged a list of attorneys who would be acceptable and agreed on one. If they had not agreed, the court would have appointed a mediator.

A date, time and place was agreed upon and cleared by the attorneys, mediator, Scarlet Rose, and the adjuster. The court order made it clear that the person who attended mediation on behalf of the insurance company must have complete authority to settle the case.

Other than the adjuster, the court order did not require anyone to be at mediation on behalf of Nickel & Dime, but Chris informed Kate Frechette of the mediation and told her that she was welcome to attend.

The parties agreed on a retired judge, Henderson Dale Miller, who had been a personal injury lawyer before the Governor of the State of Atlantis appointed him to the bench.

Both Chris and Marlene were directed by their respective attorneys to prepare mediation statements to be submitted to the mediator at least seven days before mediation. Chris prepared the following letter:

Report Letter Before Mediation

Sullivan and Jagger
Attorneys At Law
515 Maple Street
Clearwater, Atlantis 34616
727-462-8888

June 16, 2001

Louise Mallet, Director
Loss Prevention Department
Nickel & Dime, Inc.
P. O. Box 1000
Boston, Massachusetts 01670

RE: *Scarlet Rose v. Nickel & Dime, Inc.*
    Your Claim No.: 2000-0033-ND-01
    Date of Loss: 1/31/2000
    Our File No. 00-0160

Dear Ms. Mallet:

I understand that the nuisance value of $5,000 is all that will be offered at mediation and have shared this position with the plaintiff's attorney. He indicates that he is going to file an Offer of Judgment for $50,000 in special damages plus pain and suffering. He hopes that a jury will find that his client was 50% comparatively negligent and award her the expenses that she incurred. If he does this, you should consider paying that amount because there are former Nickel & Dime employees who are going to testify that it was negligence, in their opinion, to leave totes in the aisles.

In addition, we cannot find Carol Westwoman, who was supposed to have been within a few feet of the totes. I believe that the plaintiff is primarily responsible for the incident, but with $50,000 in special damages combined with the adverse testimony from former employees, I cannot guarantee that I can achieve better results.

I think we would be wise to consider filing a proposal for settlement in the largest amount that you would be willing to pay, so we would have an opportunity to recover our attorney's fees if we prevail at trial. Furthermore, I think we should announce that we will be offering no more than $5,000 at mediation in hopes that the plaintiff will file a Proposal for Settlement as he has indicated. Because there is $50,000 in special damages and the fact that a jury might be sympathetic, this could be a dangerous situation.

After giving full consideration to all of the issues, you may decide to stay with your $5,000 offer. The decision is entirely up to you, but I wanted to make certain that you were aware of the foregoing in making that decision.

Please be reminded that mediation is set for Monday, June 19 at 1 p.m.

I await your further instructions.

Very truly yours,

———————————
Alan Richards, Esq.

Defendant's Mediation Summary

Sullivan and Jagger
Attorneys At Law
515 Maple Street
Clearwater, Atlantis 34616
727-462-8888

June 22, 2001

Judge Henderson Dale Miller, retired
10124 Weatherington Road
P. 0. Box 800
Mount Vernon, Atlantis 33333

RE: *Scarlet Rose v. Nickel & Dime, Inc.*
     Claim No.: 2000-0033-ND-01
     Date of Loss: 1/31/2000
     Our File No.: 00-0160

Dear Judge Miller:

I write to provide you with the defendant's mediation summary in the above-referenced case. Mediation is scheduled for Monday, June 19, 2001, at 1 p.m. This case involves a trip-and-fall incident at the Nickel & Dime store in Clearwater, Atlantis.

Liability Issues

Ms. Rose states that she had driven with her mother to Nickel & Dime to return a pair of jean shorts. She claims that the main aisle was blocked with a display table, and she decided to take an alternative route to the customer service department. She took one step off of the main aisle and landed inside a plastic box used to restock shelves. She has no idea how she got inside the box, but she said that both knees were inside the box, and she could not get out by herself. She said the box was open, and she landed inside it. As she was falling into the box, she grabbed a rack and pulled it down on top of her.

Former employees describe the event differently. Ms. Rose said that the box was in the middle of the aisle between two racks that were about three feet apart. She was looking in the general direction of where she was going, not at the floor. The employees said she was in a hurry and deliberately tried to walk over the box. This makes the box an open and obvious condition and plaintiff partially responsible for what happened.

Damages

After the fall, EMTs took Ms. Rose to the emergency room of Community Hospital. They conducted tests and discharged her to follow up with her treating physician, Dr. Mullan. She went to see a neurological surgeon, Dr. Von Beebe, within weeks after the incident.

Ms. Rose says she was unable to work for two months and was unable to drive for about eight weeks. Ms. Rose is 39 years old, divorced, and the mother of a 14-year-old girl. There is no loss-of-consortium claim.

Ms. Rose is an investigator for the county public defender's office. She receives $640 per week as salary. There is a loss of income claim for $6,000.

She has a pre-existing physical condition. The plaintiff fell on a tennis court and broke her ankle in 1998. Her back was affected, and she received treatment for her back. A difference of opinion exists as to whether the fall at Nickel & Dime caused the injury requiring the surgery that was performed by Dr. Beebe in March 2000.

Mr. Franklin estimates that the plaintiff has paid $8,000 out of her own pocket. She had 80/20 co-pay through Blue Cross/Blue Shield, her group health insurer. Blue Cross/Blue Shield paid approximately $36,000.

As far as her current ailments are concerned, she says she is doing well. She continues to have occasional back problems after exercise and has not been able to play tennis. She was told that she should see an orthopedic specialist every year.

Dr. Christopher Paul, who performed the IME for Nickel & Dime, has indicated that, unless there is further injury, her medical condition should not cause her too many problems in the future.

Ms. Rose claims that the incident at Nickel & Dime aggravated her pre-existing condition. At present, she has only occasional back problems. She has not seen Dr. Beebe since April 2000 and has no plans to see him.

Settlement Possibilities

The plaintiff originally demanded $300,000. Because the surgery improved her condition, her proposal for settlement is $100,000. The defendant offered a $5,000 judgment. I am not certain how much Nickel & Dime is willing to pay given the questionable liability of the case. We will come to mediation with an open mind and a genuine desire to settle the case if possible.

PLEASE DO NOT SHARE ANY OF THE ABOVE WITH PLAINTIFF'S ATTORNEY WITHOUT THE EXPRESSED CONSENT OF THE UNDERSIGNED.

Very truly yours,

_____

Alan Richards, Esq.

Plaintiff's Mediation Summary

Marlene prepared a similar mediation summary on behalf of the plaintiff. Bruce emphasized that the tote should not have been there and that the employees admitted that the tote should not have been left unattended. Ms. Rose has $50,000 in special damages, two rods in her back, two fused disks, and an uncertain medical future. As far as the plaintiff was concerned, her position is that this was a case of clear liability and serious damages, with a potential recovery in the mid six-figure range.

Mediation Day

The mediator explained that the purpose of mediation was to bring an end to the lawsuit. A bad settlement was better than a good trial, the mediator said, and it was better for them to resolve the case between themselves than it would be to let six strangers decide the case for them. No one, the mediator pointed out, could predict what a jury would do with any case.

The mediator was to act as a go-between for the parties. The mediator would not take sides or offer advice to either party. Anything said at mediation could not be repeated after mediation was concluded. The attorneys would make brief opening statements. The mediator would meet privately with each side, going back and forth between the sides until the case either settled or was at an impasse. The mediator has no interest in the outcome of the case and would be paid $150 for each hour spent at mediation. The fee was to be split evenly between the parties.

Once the mediator completed his initial presentation, he asked Bruce to make a brief opening statement on behalf of the plaintiff. The mediator had already read the mediation summary and he knew Alan was unlikely to waiver. Thus the only person to convince was the adjuster, because the adjuster had the checkbook and would write the settlement check.

Everything Bruce said was calculated to influence the adjuster. He poignantly stated that the case would be expensive to take to trial. He claimed that the plaintiff came to mediation with the intention of settling, but because the plaintiff's injuries were real and not imagined, she could not settle for less than $100,000. Bruce emphasized that Nickel & Dime was negligent, and employees had broken the internal policy and procedure of the store by leaving the box out in an area where customers would be walking. Bruce referred to the former employees who would testify to these facts. Because there was no question that a jury would find against Nickel & Dime on the liability issue, Bruce noted, the only thing to be decided by the jury would be the amount of damages to which Ms. Rose was entitled. Since the medical bills and wage loss totaled $50,000, the demand of $100,000 was reasonable.

For the defense, Alan spoke directly to Ms. Rose, since it was she who would decide whether to accept the settlement offer. He told Ms. Rose that Nickel & Dime would argue to a jury that she wasn't paying attention to where she was going. He said that store employees were standing next to the box and did not violate their internal store policies. He also told her that a jury would be unreceptive to her position because every member of the jury would know that a store restocked its shelves on a regular basis and that restocking occurred during regular business hours. He concluded by saying that Nickel & Dime would not make a further offer at that time, but the matter would be discussed with the mediator.

The mediator met with Alan, Chris, and Paul Larson, who was present on behalf of Louise Mallet. Mr. Larson made it clear to the mediator that Nickel & Dime was of the opinion that this was a no-liability case, and Nickel & Dime did not intend to pay anywhere near the $100,000 demanded by the plaintiff. He agreed to increase the offer by $1,000.

The mediator then met with Bruce, Marlene, and Scarlet Rose to convey the offer of $6,000. Scarlet was greatly offended and wanted to end the mediation. The mediator tried to convince them to be as realistic and to continue to negotiate. At his request, the plaintiff reduced her demand to $75,000.

Judge Miller tried to convince the adjuster that the costs of going to trial would exceed the $6,000 offered and the least he could do was offer the amount of money that it would cost to defend the case. Mr. Larson increased the offer to $6,500.

Judge Miller met with the plaintiff's side and told them of the increased offer. Scarlet Rose was outraged, but Bruce convinced her that the costs of trial would be substantial. She agreed to reduce her demand to $60,000.

Mr. Larson was convinced that Scarlet Rose was responsible for the incident, and the jury would not find Nickel & Dime legally responsible. His final settlement offer was $7,500.

After lengthy discussion and debate, Ms. Rose agreed to settle the case for $50,000, which was little more than the cost of her medical bills. Bruce told her that he was confident that he could get the bills reduced, he would reduce his fee, and she would receive approximately $10,000, so Ms. Rose agreed.

An impasse was declared because Mr. Larson would not budge from his position. The mediation process had taken three hours. Within a few days, the plaintiff served a proposal for settlement in the amount of $50,000, and the defendant served a proposal for settlement in the amount of $7,500. The mediator filed the Notice of Impasse with the court.

Form 8.13 — Notice of Impasse

IN THE CIRCUIT COURT OF THE SIXTH
JUDICIAL CIRCUIT IN AND FOR
PINEAPPLE COUNTY, ATLANTIS

SCARLET ROSE,
Plaintiff,

v.   Case No. 00-125-PDD

NICKEL & DIME INC.,
Defendant.

Notice of Impasse

This cause was referred to the office of Arbitration and Mediation by Order of the Court, Circuit Judge Patrick D. Doherty. This matter was mediated before the Honorable Henderson Dale Miller, retired judge, pursuant to said Order. The court is hereby notified that the parties were unable to resolve and settle the matter and that the mediator has declared an impasse.

Dated this 22nd day of June 2001.

Respectfully submitted,

_____

Henderson D. Miller, retired judge

c: Bruce K. Franklin, Esq.
Alan Richards, Esq.

Report on Mediation

Sullivan and Jagger
Attorneys At Law
515 Maple Street
Clearwater, Atlantis 34616
727-462-8888

June 25, 2001

Louise Mallet
Director Loss Prevention Department
Nickel & Dime, Inc.
P.O. Box 1000
Boston, Massachusetts 01670

RE: *Scarlet Rose v. Nickel & Dime, Inc.*
     Your Claim No.: 2000-0033-ND-01
     Date of Loss: 1/31/2000
     Our File No.: 00-0160

Dear Ms. Mallet:

I write to report the mediation took place at the office of the plaintiff's attorney, Bruce Franklin, on Monday, June 19, 2001. The mediator was Henderson Dale Miller, a former partner in the law firm of Bowler and Black. As you know, Paul Larson, a regional manager, attended on behalf of Nickel & Dime, since you were unable to attend.

During opening statements, the plaintiff's attorney acknowledged that the plaintiff was in better physical condition than she was before the fall. He also acknowledged that a percentage of fault could be found against his client. The plaintiff demanded $100,000, which was the amount offered a month ago in the proposal for settlement.

During my opening statement, I made it clear that it was Nickel & Dime's position that, because the totes were in an open and obvious position, the plaintiff was entirely responsible for the incident. We cannot, however, overlook the fact that a former employee testified that it was negligent to put the tote between the racks. Whether the jury chooses to find some degree of negligence against Nickel & Dime for that reason is entirely up to the jury.

Given Dr. Beebe's testimony that surgery was necessary because of the incident, it is possible that a jury could find that all medical expenses are directly related to our incident. To counter, we have an expert who will testify that the plaintiff had similar complaints prior to the incident and that surgery would have been necessary at some time in the future any way.

Mediation ended with plaintiff at $50,000 and Nickel & Dime at $7,500. The mediator thought this case could be settled for $25,000 to $40,000. If you want to continue negotiations, please let me know. Trial is less than a month away.

I await your further instructions.

Very truly yours,

_____
Alan Richards, Esq.

Chapter Nine

**FINAL TRIAL
PREPARATION**

Status of the Case

It appeared that the chances of settling this case were slim. Final trial preparations began.

Defense's Perspective

Alan told Chris that there were many things that had to be done to prepare for trial, some of which had to be done immediately.

1. *Expert Witnesses.* It appeared that the plaintiff would not be calling an expert for the store maintenance and procedures issue; therefore, Alan was not going to call an expert either.

2. *Further Depositions.* All witnesses were available, and no further depositions were necessary.

3. *Further Investigation.* Chris informed Alan that Carol Westwoman, the store clerk who was restocking the shelves at the time of the incident, could not be located. The investigators told her that she is believed to have moved out of the country and did not leave a forwarding address.

4. *Order of Proof.* Alan asked Chris to prepare an order of proof, which is a list of expected witnesses to be called by the plaintiff and the defendant at trial in the order they are expected to testify. Chris prepared the following:

   a. Plaintiff's case in chief
      - Scarlet Rose
      - Dr. Michael Mullan - treating physician
      - Dr. Von N. Beebe - neurosurgeon
      - Shannon Young - former employee
      - Andrea Jones - former employee
      - Christy Davidson - former employee
      - Betsy Ross - former employee
      - Dr. Brendan Patrick - surgeon
      - Records custodian, if necessary
      - Jane Morris - mother of Scarlet Rose

   b. Defendant's case in chief
      - Marjorie Murphy
      - Caitlin Palmer
      - Dr. Christopher Paul - IME doctor

5. *Trial Subpoenas.* Alan directed Chris to prepare subpoenas for all of their witnesses. If the witness failed to attend trial after being subpoenaed, the court would ask the witness for an explanation and not penalize the defense. Judges have been known to send police officers out to locate a witness who does not appear, after being subpoenaed, and bring the witness to court immediately.

6. *Trial Demonstrative Aids.* Alan liked to have portions of medical records, testimony from depositions, photographs, or relevant jury instructions put on poster board to display before a jury. In this case, the photo Marjorie Murphy took should be enlarged to 24 inches by 36 inches. Alan told Chris to locate a box exactly like the box on which Scarlet Rose had tripped.

7. *Getting Depositions Transcribed.* Alan directed Chris to call the court reporter and ask her to transcribe all of the depositions as soon as possible but not on an expedited basis. Regular service, he explained, is normally 7 to 10 days, and expedited service is overnight or within a few days. Expedited service costs more than regular service. He also instructed Chris to ask for an ASCII disk and a mini version of the deposition. An ASCII disc, formatted in Word Perfect®, could be put in a laptop to be used at trial. The mini-version of the deposition would reduce the amount of paper carried to court and save time.

8. *Trial Interrogatories and Requests for Production.* Responses from the plaintiff to the updated discovery requests provided no new information.

9. *Trial Depositions.* Doctors are often unable to attend trials because of their schedules. Alan wanted to take a video deposition of Dr. Paul, the doctor who performed the compulsory physical examination of the plaintiff. Then, if the doctor was unable to attend trial, Alan could play the videotape of his deposition. However, he would prefer to have Dr. Paul attend in person.

10. *Court Exhibits.* Alan told Chris to copy and label all medical records and depositions so that a complete set of exhibits could be given to the clerk in compliance with the court order.

11. *Create an Appellate Notebook.* Since the court had denied defendant's Motion *in Limine*, Alan told Chris to record that item in the appeals notebook as possible grounds for appeal. Likewise, since the court allowed the defendant's special jury instructions, despite Bruce's argument that standard jury instructions were sufficient for this particular case, Marlene would record that issue in her book for appeal.

12. *Court Reporter at Trial.* Alan instructed Chris to make certain that a court reporter would be present when the trial began.

13. *Standard Jury Instructions.* Alan instructed Chris to assemble and prepare a set of jury instructions. He told Chris to locate the reference book on jury instructions in the law library and to look at it for reference. He found the following on the office computer:

Form 9.1 — Notice of Filing Requested Jury Instructions

IN THE CIRCUIT COURT OF THE
SIXTH JUDICIAL CIRCUIT IN AND FOR
PINEAPPLE COUNTY, ATLANTIS

SCARLET ROSE,
Plaintiff,

v.   Case No.: 00-125-PDD

NICKEL & DIME, INC.,
Defendant.

Notice of Filing Requested Jury Instructions

COMES NOW the defendant, Nickel & Dime, Inc., by and through its attorney and, pursuant to this court's pretrial order, does hereby file the following proposed jury instructions:

1.0	Preliminary Voir Dire Instruction
1.1	Preliminary Instruction
1.3	Deposition Testimony
1.3	Video Deposition Testimony
2.1	Introductory Instruction
2.2a	Believability of Witness
2.2b	Expert Witness
3.1	Preemptive Charge
3.5	Negligence Issues
3.5f	Negligence Issues
3.6	Issues as to Legal Cause and Damage
3.7	Greater Weight of Evidence and Burden of Proof Defense Issues
3.8a	Contributory Negligence
3.9	Greater Weight of Evidence Defined
4.1	Negligence
5.1	Legal Cause
6.1	Comparative Negligence in Issue
6.2	Damages: Pain and Suffering
6.2b	Damages: Aggravation of Pre-Existing Condition
6.2c	Damages: Medical Expenses
6.3	Damages: Permanency
6.10	Reduction of Damages to Present Value
6.13a	Collateral Source
7.1	Prejudice and Sympathy
7.2	Election of Foreperson
7.3	Jury Deadlock

I hereby certify that a true copy of the foregoing requested Jury Instructions has been furnished by first class U.S. mail to Bruce K. Franklin, Esq., attorney for the plaintiff, 616 Turner Street, Clearwater, Atlantis 34616, on this 20th day of June, 2001.

_____

Alan Richards, Esq.
Attorney for the Defendant
515 Maple Street
Clearwater, Atlantis 34616
727-462-8888

Specially Requested Jury Instructions

Special jurisdictions are instructions that are not included, as the standard jury instructions lawyers will create a set of "special" instructions, which are usually taken from an appellate opinion, and are directed to the specific issues of the case being tried. In this case, Alan wanted the jury to be instructed about an "open and obvious" condition.

Form 9.2 — Specially Requested Jury Instructions

IN THE CIRCUIT COURT OF THE
SIXTH JUDICIAL CIRCUIT IN AND FOR
PINEAPPLE COUNTY, ATLANTIS

SCARLET ROSE,
Plaintiff,

v.   Case No.: 00-125-PDD

NICKEL & DIME, INC.,
Defendant.

Notice of Filing Specially Requested Jury Instruction Number One

COMES NOW the defendant, Nickel & Dime, Inc., by and through its attorney and this court's pretrial order and files the following:

Special Jury Instruction Number One

There is no duty to warn a patron such as Scarlet Rose against blatant or obvious conditions that are not dangerous *per se*. A patron is under a corresponding duty to exercise reasonable care for his or her own safety and to observe that which is obvious and may be seen by one exercising such care.

To constitute a hidden danger, it must be hidden from the knowledge as well as from the sight and must be one that could not be discovered by the exercise of reasonable care. *Dixie Inc. v. Peters*. 291 App 2d 66 (1974).

Granted   ___
Modified   ___
Denied   ___

CERTIFICATE OF SERVICE

I HEREBY CERTIFY that a true copy of the foregoing Specially Requested Jury Instruction has been furnished by first class U.S. mail to Bruce K. Franklin, Esq., attorney for the plaintiff, 616 Turner Street, Clearwater, Atlantis 34616 on this 11th day of July, 2001.

Alan Richards, Esq.
Attorney for the Defendant
515 Maple Street
Clearwater, Atlantis 34616
727-462-8888

Identify Evidentiary Issues, Prepare Motions and Memoranda of Law

Because there were issues regarding the admissibility of evidence, Alan wanted a Motion *in Limine* and a Memorandum of Law for each issue. He wanted to be prepared to argue for or against a Motion for Summary Judgment or Directed Verdict on liability.

Courtroom Readiness

It was necessary to make sure that the courtroom had the props and equipment necessary to display the medical records, x-rays and MRI results. Due to increasing computer use, it was necessary to locate electrical outlets and decide where to put a projector screen, and make sure a television for displaying a video deposition was available.

Create a Trial Notebook

Chris prepared a trial notebook to help Alan keep track of the witnesses, exhibits, jury selection, possible appellate issues, his draft opening statements, and his draft closing arguments. In the notebook, Chris would record all things that occurred during the trial.

Mock Trial

Chris asked about a possible mock jury trial or hiring a jury consultant, but Alan did not feel that this case was large enough to justify the expense.

Plaintiff's Perspective

Like Chris, Marlene was preparing for trial. It was not necessary for the plaintiff's attorney to take any more discovery depositions, and they could talk to the physicians who treated Scarlet Rose without subpoenas, but they had to pay for conferences. Marlene was instructed to do the same things Chris was asked to do, including the following:

1. Prepare demonstrative aids
2. Prepare Offer of Proof
3. Make sure depositions are transcribed
4. Get trial subpoenas out to all witnesses
5. Assemble a trial notebook

6. Arrange for a court reporter to be at trial
7. Prepare a proposed verdict form.

Maintaining the File

Marlene kept the correspondence file, pleadings and court file documents current.

Scarlet Rose v. Nickel & Dime, Inc.

Pleadings Index

- Complaint
- Summons
- Civil Cover Sheet
- Notice of Service of Plaintiff's Interrogatories to Defendant
- Notice of Service of Plaintiff's Request for Production of Documents
- Notice of Service of Plaintiff's Request for Admissions
- Notice of Service of Plaintiff's Expert Witness Interrogatories
- Notice of Taking Deposition: Marjorie Murphy
- Notice of Taking Deposition: Caitlin Palmer
- Notice of Taking Deposition: Andrea Jones
- Notice of Plaintiff's Request for Copy of Report of Physical Examination
- Notice of Service of Plaintiff's Response to Interrogatories
- Notice of Service of Plaintiff's Response to Defendant's Request for Production
- Notice of Service of Plaintiff's Response to Defendant's Request for Admissions
- Notice of Service of Plaintiff's Response to Defendant's Second Set of Interrogatories
- Notice of Service of Plaintiff's Response to Collateral Source Interrogatories
- Notice of Service of Plaintiff's Response to Defendant's Expert Witness Interrogatories
- Notice of Service of Plaintiff's Update Interrogatories to Defendant
- Order Directing Mediation
- Order Setting Pretrial Conference and Jury Trial
- Motion for Summary Judgment
- List of Witnesses
- List of Exhibits
- Notice for Trial
- Joint Pretrial Stipulation
- Pretrial Order
- Plaintiff's Motion *in Limine*
- Notice of Hearing for Plaintiff's Motion *in Limine*
- Defendant's Specially Requested Jury Instructions
- Standard Jury Instructions
- Verdict
- Final Judgment

Continuing Negotiations

Chris and Marlene kept their clients updated on all developments. Settlement discussions had not progressed. Two weeks before trial, Louise Mallet called Alan and told him to increase the settlement offer to $10,000, but it was rejected. Chris asked Alan if he should serve a Proposal for

Settlement, but he told Chris that the proposals had to be filed within 30 days of trial. The trial was now fewer than 30 days away.

Pretrial Conference

On July 19, pursuant to the pretrial order previously issued by the court, the attorneys were required to appear before Judge Doherty for a pretrial conference. Counsel were required to appear with their clients to label all exhibits that were going to be admitted into evidence and to stipulate as many facts as possible.

After the plaintiff's attorney went through the records and deleted references to insurance, the attorneys stipulated that all medical records and bills could be admitted into evidence without calling a record custodian. Although Alan could require Bruce to bring a witness in to testify to the amount and the reasonableness of the bills, he allowed Bruce to prepare a summary of medical bills because Alan did not challenge the bills.

Further stipulations included the amount of time each attorney had to make opening statements and closing arguments. They agreed on most but not all of the jury instructions and agreed that the trial should conclude within three days.

The court inquired about any pending motions and depositions that were to be read at trial. If there were objections, unless the attorneys agreed beforehand, they would be dealt with at that time. Because the Motion *in Limine* regarding testimony about the internal procedures at Nickel & Dime, and the Motion for Summary Judgment filed by the defense had been denied without prejudice, there were no pending motions.

All the exhibits were marked, and a copy was given to the clerk and both attorneys. To eliminate surprises, the attorneys were required to show the photographs and records they would use as demonstrative aids. Both sides knew what physical evidence would be presented at trial and who was likely to testify.

The court told the attorneys that they were the number one case for the two-week trial calendar and should have their clients appear in courtroom A at 9 a.m. The attorneys were to meet in chambers at 8 a.m. to resolve any last-minute motions and jury instructions that could not be agreed upon.

The court reviewed the stipulation that was submitted by the parties and discussed the results of mediation. Since it appeared that there was no further movement in the negotiations, the court determined that a trial would be necessary, and entered the following order:

Form 9.3 — Pretrial Conference Order

IN THE CIRCUIT COURT OF THE
SIXTH JUDICIAL CIRCUIT IN AND FOR
PINEAPPLE COUNTY, ATLANTIS

SCARLET ROSE,
Plaintiff,

v.   Case No.: 00-125-PDD

NICKEL & DIME, INC.,
Defendant.

Pretrial Conference Order

THIS MATTER having come before the Court for pretrial conference on July 19, 2001. Present at the hearing were the attorney of record for the plaintiff, Bruce K. Franklin, and the attorney for the defendant, Alan Richards. After reviewing the stipulation filed by the parties and otherwise being apprised of the status of the case by counsel, it is therefore;

ORDERED AND ADJUDGED as follows:

This matter is scheduled for a three-day jury trial beginning on July 29, 2001. Jury selection shall begin on Monday morning, July 29, 2001, at 9 a.m. with the presentation of evidence to begin on Tuesday, July 30, 2001, at 9 a.m.

Present: for plaintiff: Bruce K. Franklin
Present: for defendant: Alan Richards

1. Statement of Case: A personal injury negligence case involving a trip-and-fall incident in a department store
2. Amendments to pleadings: None
3. Issues: Negligence of defendant, if any, and comparative negligence of plaintiff, if any
4. Number of peremptory challenges: Three per side
5. Admissions to avoid unnecessary proof: The defendant owned the store, the defendant owed a duty of care to the plaintiff, jurisdiction and venue
6. List of witnesses with address attached
7. Any problems with attendance of witnesses: None known
8. Limitations on the number of witnesses (*e.g.*, expert witness, "before and after" witnesses, etc., to prevent cumulative testimony): No problems anticipated
9. List of special damages attached with stipulation as to relevance, materiality, reasonableness and/or necessity: Admitted by agreement of counsel
10. Other than routine matters of law, evidence or procedures that may arise, with attached memoranda when anticipated to be necessary: No problem anticipated
11. Time allowed for each opening statement: 30 minutes per side
12. Time allowed for each closing argument: 45 minutes per side
13. Stipulations (checked)
    a. Fewer than six jurors if one becomes incapacitated: Will be addressed during trial, if necessary.
    b. Use of expert testimony anytime: Agreed
    c. Waive x-ray technicians: Yes
    d. Waive records custodians: Yes
    e. Waive photographers: Yes
    f. Copies of ordinances or foreign laws: Not applicable
    g. Other: None known of at present
14. Necessity of taking judicial notice: N/A
15. Estimated length of trial: Three days
16. Resolution of any objections to depositions to be read into evidence: Yes
17. View of scene necessary: No
18. Any elements of surprise or surveillance: No

19. All discovery complete: Yes
20. List of pending motions: None
21. List of all photographs, documents and exhibits attached (Counsel shall confer before trial and initial those agreed to be admitted in evidence.)

Failure to comply with the requirements of this Order will subject the party and/or counsel to appropriate sanctions.

DONE AND ORDERED in Chambers, at Clearwater, Pineapple County, Atlantis this 19th day of July, 2000.

Patrick D. Doherty
Circuit Court Judge

Copies furnished to:
Bruce K. Franklin, Esq.
Alan Richards, Esq.

Final Report Before Trial

As the trial approached, Alan instructed Chris to send a final letter to Louise Mallet and let her know what final trial preparations had been made and what was likely to take place at trial.

Sullivan and Jagger
Attorneys At Law
515 Maple Street
Clearwater, Atlantis 34616
727-462-8888

July 19, 2001

Louise Mallet, Director
Loss Prevention Department
Nickel & Dime, Inc.
P.O. Box 1000
Boston, Massachusetts 01670

RE: *Scarlet Rose v. Nickel & Dime, Inc.*
    Your Claim No.: 2000-0033-ND-01
    Our File No.: (204) 00-160

Dear Ms. Mallet:

I write to let you know what witnesses I expect to be called at trial. I expect that the plaintiff will call the following witnesses:

- Scarlet Rose
- Plaintiff's mother, Jane Morris
- Andrea Jones
- Shannon Young
- Betsy Ross
- Von Beebe, M.D. (by video)
- Michael Mullan, M.D.

The plaintiff may also call Dr. Brendan Patrick as a witness. Mr. Franklin, the plaintiff's attorney, does not have a video deposition of Dr. Patrick and may have decided that his testimony is unnecessary. I think the expense outweighs the possible benefit that his testimony may offer. In addition, he may call a physical therapist and other former employees as witnesses.

I expect to call as witnesses:

- Marjorie Murphy
- Caitlin Palmer
- Christopher Paul, M.D.

I expect the plaintiff to present her entire case in two days. We can present our entire case in half a day. We could be finished by Wednesday afternoon, but my guess is that we will be finished Thursday morning.

Should you have any questions or comments, please do not hesitate to contact me.

_____

Alan Richards, Esq.

Chapter Ten

VOIR DIRE AND
OPENING STATEMENTS

On the morning of the trial, the lawyers went into courtroom A and began to arrange the desks where they would be sitting, referred to as "counsel tables." Scarlet Rose and Bruce were at one table, and Alan sat with Louise Mallet at the other table. Chris and Marlene sat behind the counsel table because it might be necessary for them to do research, locate a file, or talk to witnesses. Each of the witnesses for plaintiff had been called and told when they could expect to be called to the witness stand. Witnesses would not arrive until the next day. The purpose of the first day of trial was to select a jury.

Commencement of the Trial

At 8 a.m., approximately 150 people with a piece of paper called a "juror summons" appeared at the courthouse and were taken to a room labeled "Jury Assembly Room."

Form 10.1 — Juror Summons

IN THE CIRCUIT COURT OF THE
SIXTH JUDICIAL CIRCUIT IN AND FOR
PINEAPPLE COUNTY, ATLANTIS

Juror Summons

By order of the Pineapple County Administrative Judge, you are hereby summoned to appear for jury service at the place, date, and time shown below:

July 29, 2001, at 8 a.m.

The right to trial by jury is one of the fundamental American rights guaranteed by the State and Federal Constitutions. It is the duty of every citizen to help preserve this right by serving as a juror when called upon to do so. YOU MUST APPEAR OR YOU MAY BE IN CONTEMPT OF COURT IF YOU FAIL TO DO SO, AND YOU MAY BE FINED UP TO $100 PER DAY AS WELL.

Please dress conservatively. Do not wear shorts, tank tops, flip-flops, etc. Pocket knives, scissors, or other sharp instruments are not permitted in the Courthouse.

In an effort to make jury service as convenient as possible for its citizens, Atlantis law provides for a one day/one trial term of service.

If on the first day of service you are not selected, you will be released from further attendance unless otherwise instructed by the court. You should not be resummoned for jury duty for at least one year.

In accordance with the Americans with Disabilities Act, if you have a disability and need a special accommodation to participate in jury duty, you should contact the Jury Manager at 386-6567. Hearing impaired (TDD) 1-800-955-8771 or voice (V) 1-800-955-8770.

Please fill out the "Questionnaire" OR the "Excusal Form" and return it in the envelope provided within five working days. PLEASE NOTE: DO NOT FILL OUT BOTH FORMS.

It is imperative that you arrive on time.

I trust you will find your juror service to be a pleasant and rewarding experience.

If you should have any questions concerning your juror service, please contact the Jury Manager at 386-6567 or 386-6566.

Juror Excusal Form

If you claim an optional exemption or mandatory disqualification listed below, you will be excused unless otherwise notified.

ANY OTHER REQUEST TO BE EXCUSED MUST BE SUBMITTED IN WRITING ON THIS FORM AS SOON AS POSSIBLE BUT NO LATER THAN FIVE WORKING DAYS PRIOR TO YOUR REPORTING DATE.

OPTIONAL – Exemption
- Served within one year
- Expectant mother OR parent not employed full-time who has custody of a child under 6 years of age
- Person 70 years of age or older
- Full-time Law Enforcement or Investigative Personnel; Practicing Attorney or Physician (at discretion of court); Medical impairment (attach doctor's statement).

SPECIAL REQUEST: You will be excused unless otherwise notified.

I request to be excused because:

MANDATORY - Disqualified
- Under prosecution (felony)
- Convicted felon, civil rights not restored
- No longer reside in county
- Declared incompetent by Court of Law.

The statements above are true to the best of my knowledge and belief.

Signature:
Home Phone:
Work Phone:

After prospective jurors were seated, they were asked to fill out the following questionnaire:

Form 10.2 — Prospective Juror Questionnaire

1. Name:
2. Address:
3. Home Phone:
4. Years of residence in Atlantis:
5. Marital Status:
6. Your occupation:
7. Employer:

8. Employer's Address:
9. If not employed, give last occupation and employer:
10. If married, give spouse's name, occupation and work phone number:
11. Have you served as a juror before? If yes, when?
12. Have you or any member of your immediate family been a victim of a crime? If yes, what crime?
13. Have you or any member of your family been a party to a lawsuit? If yes, what type of case? When? Where?
14. Have you or any member of your immediate family been a witness in a criminal case? If yes, who and when?
15. Are you or is any member of your immediate family related to a law enforcement officer?
16. Have you or any member of your immediate family ever made a claim for personal injuries?

I CERTIFY THAT I HAVE READ AND UNDERSTAND THE ABOVE INFORMATION. I FURTHER DECLARE THAT THE FOLLOWING STATEMENT APPLIES TO ME: (check one only.)

_____ I am unemployed or not regularly employed and wish to be paid for my service as a juror.
_____ I am regularly employed but my employer does not pay my regular wages while I am serving as a juror; therefore, I wish to be compensated.
_____ I am retired and wish to be compensated.
_____ I DO NOT wish to be compensated.

NOTE: Section 837.06, Atlantis Statutes, makes it a misdemeanor of the second degree to knowingly make a false statement in writing with the court.

Pursuant to Chapter 40.24, Atlantis Statutes, jurors who are regularly employed and who continue to receive regular wages while serving as a juror are not entitled to receive compensation from the State for the first three days of juror service. Jurors who are not regularly employed or who do not continue to receive regular wages while serving as a juror are entitled to receive $15 per day for the first three days of juror service. Each juror who serves more than three days will be paid $30 per day for the fourth day of service and each day thereafter, regardless of employment status.

Signature of Juror:
Date:

Each prospective juror had been randomly selected using records from the Department of Motor Vehicles.

At 8:45 a.m., a bailiff led 20 people into the courtroom and had them sit in a long row of seats. This group was referred to as the jury venire. After all the potential jurors were seated, the bailiff left the room.

The clerk of court entered the room with a stack of papers and handed out several sheets to the attorneys. She had all the exhibits and the court file. The sheets of paper contained the name, address and personal information about each of the prospective jurors.

At 9 a.m., the bailiff reentered the room and said: "All rise, the Circuit Court of the Sixth Judicial circuit in and for Pineapple County, Atlantis, is now in session, the Honorable Patrick Doherty presiding."

Once the judge sat down, the bailiff said, "Please be seated."

Introductory Remarks by the Court

Judge Doherty spoke to the assembled group and said the following:

THE COURT: Good morning, ladies and gentlemen. Welcome to jury duty in Pineapple County. The case for your consideration today is a civil case. The style of this case is *Scarlet Rose v. Nickel & Dime, Inc.* Ms. Rose, please rise so the panel knows who you are. This is Ms. Rose, and she is represented by Bruce Franklin. Thank you.

Representing Nickel & Dime is Alan Richards. Mr. Richards, you have a representative from Nickel & Dime with you. Would you introduce her?

MR. RICHARDS: Your Honor, this is Louise Mallet.

THE COURT: Our court reporter, who is keeping a record of our proceedings, is Jocelyn Frederick of the official Court Reporter's office. Our clerk, who is keeping up with the paperwork and evidence, is Kimberly Kowal of Robert David's office. Our bailiff is Deputy Sheriff Gregg Golding of the Pineapple County Sheriff's Office.

This civil case involves an incident that occurred on January 31, 2000. The plaintiff, Ms. Rose, tripped and fell in a Nickel & Dime store, and she has brought this suit for damages. Nickel & Dime has denied any responsibility.

Selection of Persons from the Jury Venire for Questioning by the Court and the Attorneys as to their Qualifications to be a Juror in the Case

THE COURT: I will ask you some preliminary questions, and the attorneys will have a chance to ask you some questions. Our questions are not intended to embarrass or to pry into your private affairs. Our questions are intended to assist the attorneys in selecting the fairest and the most impartial jurors. After the attorneys question you, they will approach the bench, and we will have what is known as a bench conference. At that time, some of you may be excused from the jury box. If for any reason you happen to be excused, please do not be offended. It is not because we don't think that you would make a good juror, but another person might be a better juror for this particular case.

The clerk will call the first jurors to the jury box. If you are not seated in the jury box, then you can have a seat in the chairs that have been placed in front of the jury box.

The clerk of the court called out the names of 13 people and asked them to sit in the jury box in the order that their names were called. There were exactly 13 seats in the box. The remaining seven remained in their seats and were available if a panel of six was not selected from the 13 names called.

Both attorneys were putting the names in the order that they were seated on their sheet of paper. The last name of each prospective juror was in large letters and highlighted.

THE CLERK: Juror number 169, Megan Snark. Juror number 170, John Flynnsky. Juror number 173, Michael Pumpernickel. Juror 180, Tiffany Barnetti. Juror 198, Erica Metz. Juror 210, Lindsley Bardsley. Juror 212, Mark Davis. Juror 215, Erica Christian. Juror 219,

Benjamin Keilor. Juror 222, Billie Elizabeth. Juror 234, Jared Walker. Juror 213, Melissa Robertson. Juror 248, Curtis Ashley.

As the clerk called out the names, the bailiff showed people to their seats in the order that their names were called.

Selecting the Jurors to Hear and Decide the Case

When the lawyers had finished questioning the jurors, the judge told the jurors that they could take a ten-minute recess while the court and the lawyers determined the six people and one alternate who would be sworn as jurors. The bailiff escorted them from the courtroom.

The judge gave the attorneys a few minutes to confer with their clients. Then, he asked the attorneys whom they wanted to excuse as jurors. Each side had three peremptory challenges and an unlimited number of challenges for cause. The court began with the plaintiff and then asked the defendant about each prospective juror. He would permit "backstriking," which meant that a lawyer could accept juror number one at the beginning of the process, but at the conclusion of all 12 prospective jurors, go back and strike juror number one.

Ms. Rose wanted a juror who understood and could sympathize with what had happened to her. Nickel & Dime wanted a juror who would say, "How could she not have seen the box?"

The judge then asked if either attorney had any challenges for cause.

Challenges for Cause

The jury selection process can be very complicated. Appeals often result because a juror was excused for an improper reason, or the court made a mistake in failing to excuse a prospective juror for "cause." "Cause" means that a particular person could not, in all probability, be a fair and impartial juror. In this case, the potential juror whose wife had been a client of Bruce's firm and a juror who had worked as an insurance adjuster were excused for cause. There is no limit to the number of challenges for cause that an attorney can make.

Peremptory Challenges

In the state of Atlantis, each state has three peremptory challenges. A peremptory challenge allows an attorney to excuse a juror for any reason or for no reason at all; however, in recent years, courts have required attorneys to state the reason for using a peremptory challenge when it is suspected that a juror was excused for racial reasons.

> THE COURT: The plaintiff goes first, and the defendant goes second. Announce one at a time, and let me know now if you have any other challenges for cause as we go through the peremptory challenges.

The judge asked the attorneys which prospective jurors they wished to excuse using their peremptory challenges.

Selection of an Alternate

Although six jurors had been selected from the 13, they still needed an alternate juror in case one of the six became ill and was not able to complete jury duty. The court indicated that each side would have one challenge as to the alternate. The next juror was Mr. Ashley. Neither side exercised a challenge to Mr. Ashley, and the court said that Mr. Ashley would be the alternate juror.

Swearing in the Jury

After the jury was selected, they were required to raise their right hands and swear or affirm that they would properly perform their duties as jurors. Following that, the case was recessed for the day.

Day Two of Trial

Preliminary Instructions to the Jury

THE COURT: Ladies and gentlemen of the jury, I'm going to give you some preliminary instructions. You have been sworn as the jury to try this case. This is a civil case involving a disputed claim between the parties. Those claims and other matters will be explained to you at a later time. By your verdict, you will decide the disputed issues of fact. I will decide the questions of law that arise during the trial. Before you retire to deliberate your verdict at the close of the trial, I will instruct you on the law that you are to follow and apply in reaching your verdict.

Before proceeding further, it will be helpful if you understand how a trial is conducted. In a few moments, the attorneys will have the opportunity to make an opening statement. They will explain to you the issues in the case and summarize the facts. Following their opening statements, witnesses will be called to testify under oath. They will be examined and cross-examined by the attorneys, documents and/or other tangible exhibits may also be produced and received into evidence.

After all of the evidence has been received, the attorneys will again have an opportunity to address you and to make their final arguments. The statements that the attorneys now make and the arguments that they will make are not to be considered by you as evidence in the case or as instructions on the law. Nevertheless, these statements and arguments are intended to assist you in properly understanding the issues, the evidence and the applicable law, so you should give them your close attention.

Following the final arguments by the attorneys, I will instruct you on the law. You should give careful attention to the testimony and other evidence as it is received and presented for your consideration, but you should not form or express an opinion about the case until you have received all of the evidence, the arguments of the attorneys and the instructions on the law from me. The case must be tried on the evidence presented during the trial. Accordingly, you must not visit any of the places described in the evidence or the scene of the occurrence that is the subject of the trial unless I so direct you to view the scene. Also, you must avoid reading any articles or newspaper headlines relating to this case and trial. You must avoid seeing, listening or hearing any reports or comments about this trial while it is in progress.

The attorneys are trained in the rules of evidence and in trial procedure. It is their duty and responsibility to make all objections they feel are necessary and proper. When an attorney makes an objection, I will either overrule or sustain the objection. If I overrule an objection to a question, the witness will answer the question. When I sustain or uphold an objection, the witness cannot answer the question. If I sustain an objection, you must not speculate on what might have happened or what the witness might have said had I permitted the witness to answer. You should not draw any inference from the question itself.

During the trial it may be necessary for me to confer with the attorneys outside of your hearing about matters of law. When these conferences occur, they will consume as little of your time as necessary for a fair and orderly trial. During the trial, we will take recesses. During these recesses, you shall not discuss the case among yourselves or with anyone else or permit anyone to say anything to you or in your presence about the case. Furthermore, you must not speak with the attorneys, witnesses or the parties about anything until your deliberations are completed. If during a recess you see one of the attorneys and he does not speak to you or pay attention to you, please understand that the attorney is not being discourteous but is avoiding improper contact with you. If anyone tries to say anything to you or in your presence about this case, tell that person that you are on the jury trying the case and ask them to stop. If that person persists, then leave that person at once, return to the courtroom and report the matter to the bailiff, who will then report it to the court.

At this time, the attorneys for the parties will have the opportunity to make their opening statements, so they can explain to you the issues in the case and give you a summary of the facts that they expect the evidence to show.

Opening Statements on the Plaintiff's Behalf

MR. FRANKLIN: Thank you, Your Honor. May it please the court. Good morning, ladies and gentlemen. The plaintiff, Scarlet Rose, filed this lawsuit, so we present our case to you first.

On January 31, 2000, Scarlet Rose fell in the Nickel & Dime store. She went to Nickel & Dime to exchange some shorts that her daughter had given her for Christmas. Ms. Rose was walking to the customer service area when she encountered a display table that blocked the aisle and her path. The evidence will show through photographs and testimony that the table blocked the majority of the aisle. Ms. Rose decided that she couldn't get around the table and went to a side aisle to get to the customer service area. As she turned left to walk through the lingerie department, she walked between two slipper display racks and immediately hit her leg on a box that had been placed on the floor in the walkway between the two display racks. She tripped and fell forward into the box. As she was falling, she grabbed a display rack and brought it on top of her. Her body twisted as she fell into the box. She was in excruciating pain and yelled out for help. A customer came over and helped her. After a minute or two, a Nickel & Dime employee responded and helped her move into a position on the floor that was less painful.

The evidence will show that Ms. Rose's mother, Ms. Jane Morris, was then summoned from the parking lot to come in. She saw her daughter lying on the floor and noticed an abrasion on her left shin where she hit the box. The EMS, emergency medical service, was called. They rendered assistance, and a half-hour after the incident occurred, she was taken to the emergency room. Ms. Rose was treated at the hospital, x-rays were taken, drugs and medicines were applied, and, after three or four hours, she was released. The evidence will show that, as a result of the fall, Ms. Rose was in bed for a month or so, and her mother had to do her laundry, dress her, and cook for her. Shortly after the fall, Ms. Rose went to see her physician, Dr. Mullan, because the pain in her back was not getting better. A week later, she started treatment for her back problem. The evidence will show that Dr. Mullan referred Ms. Rose to Dr. Patrick, an orthopedic physician. Dr. Patrick had treated Ms. Rose for an ankle and back related injury in 1998. He used physical therapy medications and other noninvasive procedures. She responded well to therapy, and he hadn't seen her for over six months prior to the incident.

When Dr. Patrick saw her after the fall at Nickel & Dime, he referred her to a neurosurgeon named Dr. Beebe. Dr. Beebe ordered an MRI of Ms. Rose's back, reviewed her previous medical records and concluded that she needed back surgery, which was performed in March 2000 and was successful. Although she is better now, she had a difficult year as a result of the fall at Nickel & Dime.

You will hear evidence that Ms. Rose fell playing tennis in May 1998 and broke her left ankle. She was immobile for quite some time and could not function normally. In addition, she had some back problems related to her ankle, and Dr. Mullan treated her until July 1998. When he discharged her, she had fully recovered, but after the fall at Nickel & Dime, Ms. Rose's condition severely deteriorated. Dr. Mullan will testify about Ms. Rose's condition prior to and after the fall at Nickel & Dime, and he will explain the reasons why he and Dr. Patrick referred her to a neurosurgeon.

As a result of the March 2000 surgery and additional treatments, Ms. Rose incurred medical bills that are approximately $44,000 She also lost $6,000 in wages because she was unable to work for three months.

This case has basically two issues. The first is who is responsible for the fall, and the second is what damages did Ms. Rose incur as a result of the fall. The defense will say that the incident occurred because Ms. Rose was in a hurry that day and tried to climb over the box. Ms. Rose will tell you that she didn't see the box. Several former Nickel & Dime employees will testify that the box should not have been left in the aisle unattended. You are going to decide who is responsible, or liable, for this incident. The second issue relates to damages or how badly was Ms. Rose hurt as a result of this incident. The evidence will show that, prior to January 31, 2000, Ms. Rose had almost fully recovered from her ankle injury. The defense will suggest that Ms. Rose had a pre-existing back problem and that the surgery was not caused by the fall at Nickel & Dime. Scarlet Rose and Dr. Beebe, the surgeon who operated on her back, will tell you that the fall at Nickel & Dime resulted in surgery. When you listen to the evidence and see the medical records, ask yourself what is more reasonable. What does the evidence show by a preponderance of the evidence?

At the close of the evidence, I will have an opportunity to address you again and will ask you to return a verdict for the plaintiff, Scarlet Rose, for the full amount of pain, suffering, loss and injury that Scarlet experienced as a result of this incident. Thank you.

Opening Statements on the Defendant's Behalf

THE COURT: Mr. Richards.

MR. RICHARDS: May it please the court. Good morning, ladies and gentlemen of the jury. The purpose of opening statements is to give you an idea of what you're going to hear from the witness stand so you understand the significance of the testimony and how it fits into the case.

Liability and damages are the two issues in this case. Ms. Rose will testify that both of her knees got stuck in a box, called a tote, but she didn't fall to the floor. People immediately came and helped her out of the box and placed her on her back until the paramedics arrived. The issue of liability is whether or not Nickel & Dime, by putting that tote in that position, is responsible for Ms. Rose's injuries and damages.

Nickel & Dime will present evidence that retail stores place the totes in the store to restock shelves, racks, and display counters. You will hear testimony from witnesses that the box was out in the open and Ms. Rose failed to see something that was open and obvious. If you find that Nickel & Dime is not responsible for this incident, then that's the end of the case. Nickel & Dime believes that it is not responsible for this incident because the tote was in the middle of the aisle where patrons, such as Ms. Rose, could see it.

In regard to damages, Ms. Rose fell and twisted her ankle in 1998. For the next two years, she saw numerous doctors and had a number of tests. These tests revealed a problem with her back involving a degenerative disease and spondylosis. In other words, she had problems with her back prior to the fall at Nickel & Dime. A big issue in this case is going to be whether the surgery she had in March 2000 was a result of the fall at Nickel & Dime or was related to her 1998 ankle injury. It is Nickel & Dime's position that it is not responsible for most of the damages that Scarlet Rose incurred and that the surgery was not caused by the fall but resulted from her pre-existing back condition.

We ask that you listen carefully to all evidence and that you do not make up your mind until you have heard all the testimony, closing arguments, and the instructions on applicable law from Judge Doherty. Thank you for your time and attention.

THE COURT: Call your first witness, Mr. Franklin.

Chapter Eleven

PLAINTIFF'S CASE
IN CHIEF

Bruce would call Scarlet Rose as his first and most important witness. He would end with his most sympathetic witness, her mother, Jane Morris. He did not expect any surprises in the testimony. The witnesses were expected to testify the same as they did at their depositions.

Testimony of the Plaintiff

MR. FRANKLIN: Your Honor, we call Scarlet Rose.

MR. FRANKLIN: State your full name for the record, please.
A: Scarlet Rose.

Q. What is your address?
A. 1111 Pine Street, Tarpon Springs, Atlantis 34689.

Q. What is your occupation?
A. I work for Robert Forest, the Public Defender for Pineapple County.

Q. What are your duties in that job?
A. It consists of locating witnesses, obtaining criminal records, contacting clients, doing research, and whatever is needed by our attorneys, who are preparing for trial or getting people out of jail.

Q. Did you fall and injure yourself in January 1998?
A. Yes, I did.

Q. Describe to the jury what happened.
A. I was playing tennis, and I slipped on a wet spot at the edge of the court. My feet went out from under me. I wound up on my back with my left knee underneath me, and I broke my ankle.

Q. What kind of pain did you have at the time of this fall?
A. My left ankle was in excruciating pain.

Q. How did the doctors treat your injury?
A. Because my leg was swollen, they didn't put a cast on my ankle. They x-rayed my ankle, knees, and left leg, examined me, and sent me home with some medications. I was to return to the emergency room in two days. When I returned to the emergency room, my ankle was even more swollen, and they gave me crutches. They suggested I see an orthopedic specialist for my ankle, so I went to see Dr. Patrick, who specializes in knees and ankles.

Q. How did Dr. Patrick treat your injury?

A. After the swelling went down, he put a cast on my leg to hold my ankle securely in place. I couldn't put any weight on it, and I was still on the crutches. He gave me medication and arranged for me to return later.

Q. Did you received additional medical treatment for the pain you had as a result of the 1998 fall?

A. After I had gone through months of physical therapy, I had surgery to repair a torn ligament in my ankle. It was several months before I was off crutches and able to walk.

Q. Did you have problems with your back at that time?

A. Yes, my back started to bother me because I was inactive, and it was hard for me to move with those crutches. But my back problems were worse after the fall at Nickel & Dime.

Q. Were you referred to a neurosurgeon by Dr. Patrick?

A. Yes, after the incident at Nickel & Dime.

Q. Had you recovered from your ankle injury before the fall at Nickel & Dime?

A. Yes. I was fully recovered and had not seen a doctor for at least six months prior to the fall at Nickel & Dime.

Q. How did Dr. Patrick treat your back?

A. He treated my back with heat, sonic waves, massage, and whirlpool baths.

Q. You responded positively to that?

A. Yes. In fact, when I first started going to him, I was in a wheelchair, then a walker, and finally a cane. I stopped using the cane about a month from the last time I saw him in 1998.

Q. Were you concerned in 1998 that you might require surgery for your back?

A. Yes. My back was aching because of the way I was walking.

Q. Didn't Dr. Patrick order an MRI for your back in 1998 and told you that if it wasn't favorable you might require back surgery?

A. Yes. Dr. Patrick said that, if the MRI showed a herniated disc, surgery might be necessary, but the MRI was negative.

Q. Did you see Dr. Patrick after the fall at Nickel & Dime?

A. Yes. He referred me to Dr. Beebe. I talked with Dr. Beebe about the surgery he recommended and asked him if he thought it would help me. He told me he thought surgery was necessary because the fall at Nickel & Dime had made my back worse.

Q. Did you discuss the possibility of surgery with Dr. Patrick as well?

A. I took my x-rays and MRI results to Dr. Patrick. He performed a physical examination of my back, and we talked about my becoming a surgical candidate. After I discussed surgery with Dr. Patrick and Dr. Beebe, I decided, because I was in unbearable pain, it was worth the risk.

Q. Was your mother assisting you as of January 2000?

A. No. She did after my ankle injury, but at that time, I was fully recovered and doing everything for myself.

Q. What things did she do for you while you were recovering from your ankle injury?
A. At first, everything.

Q. After the fall at Nickel & Dime, did your mother help you again?
A. Yes, it was just like 1998 all over again.

Q. On January 31, 2000, why were you at Nickel & Dime?
A. My daughter had given me jean shorts for Christmas, but they were not the right style for me. I wanted to pick out a style that was more comfortable. My mother and I drove to Nickel & Dime, and she waited in the car while I went in and made the exchange. I went to the women's department and picked out the pair of shorts that I wanted. When I went to the cash register, I was told that I would have to go to customer service to exchange the shorts. I walked, at my regular speed, down the main aisle towards customer service.

Q. In your opinion, was there anything unusual about the store in regards to decorations or displays?
A. Display tables were blocking the main aisle. I went about half way down the main aisle and saw a table with purses piled on it. It had racks on both sides, and some people were standing around them, so I decided to take the side aisle. I cut through the lingerie department to get to the other main aisle, and when I turned, there was a box on the floor, in the middle of the aisle, between two racks. I didn't see the box. I was looking at the table in front of me. My shin hit the box, and I fell into the box. When I fell, I grabbed the rack that was beside me, and it fell on top of me, which is how I twisted my back. One knee was in the box, and my other knee was bleeding. I did not fall on the floor. I was twisted up in the box. I could not get out of the box without hurting myself more than I already was.

Q. Did you have an immediate sensation of pain or injury at that time?
A. I felt my back twist as I went down.

MR. RICHARDS: Objection, leading.

THE COURT: Overruled.

Q. What happened after you became entangled in the box?
A. I could not move, and I screamed for someone to help me. A customer ran over to me and got an employee of Nickel & Dime. At that time, another employee came over, and they lifted me out of the box and laid me flat on the floor.

Q. Did you tell the employees of Nickel & Dime what part of your body was hurt?
A. I told them my back, arm, and leg hurt.

Q. Did you receive any medical treatment after the fall?
A. They called an ambulance.

Q. Where did they take you?
A. To the emergency room at the local community hospital.

Q. Did your mother follow you?
A. Yes.

Q. What treatment did you receive at the hospital?

A. I had x-rays and pills. After about four hours, they sent me home with my mother and told me to see my doctor if I wasn't better in the next few days.

Q. How was your condition over the next few days?

A. It was a nightmare. I was back in the bed and taking my pain medication. My mother had to bring me meals again. My back and leg pain were excruciating.

Q. Who treated you after the fall?

A. I went to see Dr. Mullan a couple of days after the incident.

Q. Did you continue to see Dr. Mullan?

A. Yes, I did, but he sent me back to see Dr. Patrick, who sent me to see Dr. Beebe.

Q. What happened when you went to see Dr. Beebe?

A. He performed an MRI and told me that he believed surgery was the best answer.

Q. How were you feeling when you first went to see Dr. Beebe?

A. I was in a lot of pain.

Q. Did he perform surgery on you?

A. Yes. In March 2000, he performed the surgery.

Q. Did surgery help you?

A. Tremendously.

Q. Are you better off now than you were before January 31, 2000?

MR. RICHARDS: Objection. Calls for speculation.

THE COURT: Overruled.

A. I feel pretty good, and I think I am ready to start playing tennis again.

Q. Are you better than you were in July 1998 when you last saw Dr. Patrick after the ankle surgery?

A. Yes. However, I have two rods in my back, and I will never be the same as I was before the incident. I have a permanent injury and will need periodic chiropractic adjustments and someone to check my back every year. It will cost me about $500 per year.

Q. Did you receive any other injuries in the January 2000 fall?

A. I hurt my knee and my shin, but my back was the real problem. When I took the rack down, I did something to this arm. At different times, I have numbness and pain. At times, I can't use my hand for a minute or two.

Q. Are you currently receiving any treatment for any parts of your body?

A. Not right now.

Q. What was the total amount of medical expenses you incurred as a direct result of your fall at the Nickel & Dime store in January 2000?
A. The total is $44,000.

Q. How much time did you lose from work?
A. I couldn't work for three months.

Q. How much do you earn as an investigator for the Public Defender's Office?
A. About $36,000 per year.

Q. How much money did you lose because of all the work you missed?
A. I lost $6,000 in salary, which is approximately two months of work. The rest of the time I missed from work was paid for by my vacation and sick leave benefits.

MR. FRANKLIN: That's all the questions I have, Your Honor.

Cross Examination of the Plaintiff by Mr. Richards

THE COURT: Cross examination, Mr. Richards?

MR. RICHARDS: Yes, Your Honor. May it please the court.

Q. Good morning, Ms. Rose.
A. Good morning.

Q. Let me begin by asking you if that photograph that I put up there is a fair and accurate depiction of the scene as it existed within the Nickel & Dime store on January 31, 2000, when you walked down that aisle in the store?
A. No, sir, it's not.

Q. It's not?
A. No.

Q. How is it different?
A. There were two racks on both sides and only the box that I fell in was in between.

Q. Was the box that you fell into like the tote shown in the photograph?
A. I can't be sure.

Q. Was it a box of slippers that you fell into?
A. I honestly don't know what was in the box.

Q. Do you recognize this box?
A. That type of box, yes, but not that particular box.

Q. Is that the type of box you fell into?
A. Yes.

Q. That tote was sitting in the aisle just like it is shown in this picture, correct?
A. To the best of my knowledge, yes.

Q. Can you tell if this is the rack, as you have described it, in this other picture?
A. It appears to be.

MR. RICHARDS: I'm going to ask the clerk to mark defense exhibit number 1 for identification purposes only.

THE COURT: Mark it as defense exhibit number 1 for identification.

Q. Can you identify that photograph?
A. Yes. That is a picture of the area where I fell, but I remember two racks there, and I only see one.

MR. RICHARDS: I'll ask the clerk to mark this as defense exhibit number 2 for identification purposes only.

Q. Does it appear to you to be a picture of the aisle that you were walking down immediately prior to the incident?
A. Yes, it does appear to be one of the two main aisles.

Q. Does it appear to be on the aisle that you were walking down seconds before this incident occurred on January 31, 2000?
A. Yes.

Q. Do you see what appears to be slippers?
A. Yes.

Q. Approximately how wide was that aisle that you were walking down immediately prior to the time that you encountered the two racks and the tote?
A. I think the aisle was about three feet wide.

Q. Can you see in the picture that there were tiles on the floor?
A. Yes.

Q. Do you remember if these were the standard one-foot by one-foot tiles?
A. I think that is correct.

Q. If they were one-foot by one-foot tiles, as they appear to be in that photo, was the aisle more like six feet wide?
A. If the tiles were one-foot by one-foot, then, yes, the aisle was six feet wide, but it seemed smaller to me.

Q. How big is this tote over here?
A. It is about two and one-half feet wide by one foot deep by about one foot high.

Q. Please tell the jury how you did not see this tote, which was in the middle of the aisle, when you turned off the main aisle.

A. I was looking up to find the shortest route to the customer service area, and my vision may have been partially blocked by the racks.

Q. Would you agree with me, Ms. Rose, that if you had looked at the floor you would have seen this tote?

A. Yes, I would have seen the tote if I had looked at the floor, but when I walk, I don't look at the floor, I look ahead to where I'm going. I also look at the items on display, which is what a store like Nickel & Dime wants customers to do, isn't it?

Q. You don't look to see where you place your feet when you walk down a sidewalk or down an aisle of a store like Nickel & Dime?

A. Sometimes I do, but I didn't think I had to worry about something being placed in my path while walking in Nickel & Dime.

Q. Did you tell Caitlin Palmer, one of the Nickel & Dime employees, that you were in a hurry?

A. No.

Q. Did you try to step over that tote?

A. No, I didn't see it.

Q. Did you tell Marjorie Murphy or Caitlin Palmer that you were in a hurry because you had to go to the bathroom?

A. I did not.

Q. Ms. Rose, let's talk about the injuries you sustained in this incident. Do you know what the L5 is?

A. I believe it's a disk in your back.

Q. In the lumbar area of your spine?

A. Yes. That is where Dr. Beebe performed his dual-rod stabilization process in March 2000 on my L4-L5 nerve root.

Q. Do you know what the term "radiculopathy" means?

A. It means radiating pain.

Q. In July 1998, when you were seeing Drs. Patrick and Mullan for ankle problems, you were also having left leg radiculopathy that was coming from the lumbar L5, correct?

A. I was having pain in my left side and leg from a sciatic nerve. The sciatic nerve is at the very bottom of the spinal column, and the L5 is further up the spinal column.

Q. From February to July 1998, you were having problems with your lower back, correct?

A. Yes.

Q. Prior to your ankle surgery, did you have radiating pain in your left leg that came from the lumbar area of your back?

A. I remember the pain in my back and leg was worse after the ankle surgery, but it might have bothered me before the surgery.

Q. In May 1998, Dr. Patrick wrote to Dr. Mullan and said that you had pain in your back after the fall on the tennis court and since that time have had pain in your back and left buttock radiating down to the left leg. Is this accurate?

A. Yes. I had some pain in my back and radiating pain in the left leg, but it was different than the pain I felt after the fall at Nickel & Dime.

Q. Do you remember him telling you that the MRI scan of your back showed a bulging disk at L3-L4 and at L5-S1 that may be compromising the nerve root at L5?

A. Yes.

Q. Did he attempt various forms of conservative treatment on your back?

A. Yes.

Q. Was surgery considered for your back in 1998?

A. I was asking them if it was necessary or not.

Q. In other words, if they would have permitted you to have surgery, you wanted to have surgery.

A. No. I wanted to know if anything could be done for me at that particular time.

Q. After you saw Dr. Patrick in May 1998, did you know that you had some degenerative back problems?

A. He said I had some problems, but they would go away if I improved the strength and mobility of my ankle.

Q. Did Dr. Patrick tell you that he wanted the MRI performed in order to consider possible surgical options?

A. Yes, but the disc was not herniated at that time, and I was not a surgical candidate.

Q. Did Dr. Patrick tell you that it was his opinion that surgery was not appropriate for you because he did not feel that the potential benefit would be worth the risk?

A. Yes.

Q. Would you agree that your back problems in 1998 were bad enough to discuss surgery?

A. Right, but my back improved when my ankle improved.

Q. In 1998, you had various tests performed on your back, right?

A. I had an MRI and x-rays done.

Q. You had conservative treatments such as medications, whirlpool, massage, and hot packs, correct?

A. Yes sir.

Q. Did Dr. Patrick provide similar treatment after the Nickel & Dime incident as he did before the incident?

A. No, he sent me straight to Dr. Beebe.

Q. Did he say that there was nothing more he could do for your back?
A. When I last saw him in July 1998, my back had improved, and he said I didn't need to see him anymore unless it got worse. After the Nickel & Dime incident, he sent me to Dr. Beebe. Although I still couldn't play tennis, my back was pain-free.

Q. Do you remember going to the hospital emergency room after the incident at Nickel & Dime?
A. Yes.

Q. Were you told that you had sustained a lumber spine sprain and should take a muscle relaxant and see your doctor in the morning if you weren't better?
A. Yes.

Q. After leaving the emergency room, who was the first doctor you saw?
A. I went to see Dr. Mullan, but he wasn't in, and I saw one of his colleagues, who gave me some pain medication until I could see Dr. Mullan.

Q. You went to see Dr. Patrick about two weeks after the incident, right?
A. Yes.

Q. Before you saw Dr. Patrick, how did you treat your injuries?
A. I went to bed and took pain medication.

Q. Did Dr. Patrick prescribe physical therapy for rehabilitation?
A. No. Dr. Patrick only saw me one time after the fall at Nickel & Dime, and he sent me to see Dr. Beebe.

Q. After evaluating you and reviewing your films, did Dr. Beebe say that you suffered from chronic lumbar sprain syndrome and frozen back syndrome, and he recommended surgery?
A. In March, yes.

Q. Are you, physically and mentally, back to where you were prior to the incident at Nickel & Dime?
A. Yes, but I still have two rods in my back that I didn't have before, and no one knows for certain what the future holds.

MR. RICHARDS. Thank you, Ms. Rose. I have no further questions.

THE COURT: Redirect?

MR. FRANKLIN: Just a couple, Your Honor.

Redirect Examination by Mr. Franklin

Q. Ms. Rose, have you started playing tennis again?
A. No.

Q. Do you know if you will be able to play tennis again?
A. I'm not sure. It might hurt my back too much.

Q. Would your life be as enjoyable if you couldn't play tennis anymore?
A. No.

MR. FRANKLIN: That's all the questions I have, Your Honor. Thank you.

THE COURT: Any re-cross?

MR. RICHARDS: No, Your Honor.

THE COURT: Call your next witness.

Testimony from a Treating Physician

MR. FRANKLIN: Dr. Brendan Mullan.

Direct Examination by Mr. Franklin

Q. Good afternoon.
A. Good afternoon.

MR. FRANKLIN: May it please the Court.

THE COURT: You may proceed, counsel.

Q. State your full name for the record.
A. Brendan Conor Mullan.

Q. What's your professional address?
A. 700 Green Street, Clearwater, Atlantis 33759.

Q. What is your occupation?
A. I'm a doctor practicing in general medicine.

Q. Please describe your educational background as it relates to the field of medicine.
A. I graduated from the University of Miami School of Medicine. I did my internship in straight internal medicine at the Jackson Memorial Hospital and my fellowship in general medicine.

Q. How long have you been practicing as a doctor?
A. Since 1975.

Q. How long have you been in Pineapple County?
A. Since 1979.

Q. And are you licensed to practice in Atlantis?
A. I am.

Q. Is general medicine considered to be a specialty?
A. Yes. It's a subspecialty intended to deal with common, day-to-day problems.

Q. Do you treat people with orthopedic problems?
A. Yes. I treat people with pain, but for surgical procedures, I refer my patients to an orthopedic specialist.

Q. Do you ever have an occasion to review MRIs and x-rays of joints?
A. Yes.

Q. Do you consider yourself qualified to review those x-rays and MRIs?
A. Yes.

Q. Do you have occasions where you refer patients to other doctors for problems that might be related to the symptoms that you're treating the patient for?
A. Yes.

Q. What other kind of doctors do you typically refer your patients to?
A. Orthopedic surgeons, neurosurgeons, physical therapy experts, and sometimes neurologists.

MR. FRANKLIN: Your Honor, I would tender this witness as an expert to give opinions on medical issues.

MR. RICHARDS: I so stipulate, Your Honor.

THE COURT: Then he is so declared.

Q. Do you know Scarlet Rose?
A. I do.

Q. How long have you known her?
A. Since June 1989.

Q. You've known her in a doctor/patient relationship only, is that correct?
A. Yes.

Q. Prior to November 1997, what did you see Ms. Rose for?
A. I saw her mostly for yearly check-ups, colds, the flu, and the usual aches and pains. Nothing out of the ordinary.

Q. Do you recall that she fell in January 1998?
A. Yes.

Q. Did you treat her for the fall?
A. I did.

Q. What treatment did you provide?
A. Anti-inflammatory medications, braces, and steroid injections into the ankle.

Q. Did you refer Ms. Rose to any other doctor for her ankle treatment?
A. I did.

Q. Who did you refer her to?
A. Dr. Patrick, an orthopedic specialist, who eventually operated on her ankle.

Q. Did Dr. Patrick keep you informed about her treatments?
A. Yes.

Q. Please describe Ms. Rose's ankle progress up to the time you referred her to Dr. Patrick.
A. She continued to have chronic pain in the ankle and left foot, which did not respond to conservative treatment and eventually led to surgery involving reattaching some ligaments to the bones in her ankle. Also, as a result of her ankle problems, she developed some low back problems. Diagnostic tests were performed on her back, and she underwent physical therapy. It was hoped that her back would improve as her ankle improved.

Q. What is chronic pain?
A. Pain on a daily basis.

Q. In February 2000, were you aware that Ms. Rose had another fall?
A. Yes.

Q. Did you continue treating her after the January 2000 incident up to the present time?
A. I did.

Q. Prior to the January 2000 incident, did Dr. Patrick involve you in the decision not to operate on Ms. Rose's back?
A. Yes.

Q. In late July 1998, Ms. Rose was discharged from Dr. Patrick's care. Did she continue to treat with you on a regular basis up until the present?
A. Yes.

Q. How would you characterize her back condition from July 1998 up to the January incident at Nickel & Dime?
A. Prior to the January fall, her back problem was related to her ankle. She had chronic ankle pain that required medication and periodic injections of steroids. After ankle surgery and therapy, Ms. Rose improved. She used a cane for a while, and she still had some problems, but her back complaints were reduced by August 1998, when I saw her for unrelated problems.

Q. Have you discussed Ms. Rose's back problem with either Dr. Patrick or Dr. Beebe from February 2000 to the present?
A. Not really.

Q. Do you recall how soon after the fall she saw you?
A. I saw her two weeks after her fall, but she came to the office a week earlier.

Q. You continued to treat her after the fall in January up to the present time, correct?
A. Yes.

Q. Did you ever feel the need to refer her to Dr. Patrick to review her back condition?
A. Yes.

Q. When did you do that?

A. On the first visit after the fall, I referred her to Dr. Patrick.

Q. In February 2000, after you referred Ms. Rose to see Dr. Patrick, were you aware that she was referred to Dr. Beebe?

A. Yes.

Q. Were you aware of Dr. Beebe's recommendations?

A. Yes.

Q. What were those recommendations?

A. After his examination and MRI, he recommended that she have back surgery.

Q. How had her symptomatology changed after the fall at Nickel & Dime?

A. She had more severe pain localized in the sacroiliac and buttocks area. Her ankle and leg pain were not as pronounced, and her functioning level had decreased.

Q. Had her back condition worsened prior to Dr. Beebe recommending surgery?

A. The pain seemed more intense, constant, and localized.

Q. Do you have an opinion, based upon a reasonable degree of medical probability, as to whether the injuries Ms. Rose received in the January 2000 fall were different from the medical problems she had before the fall?

A. I do.

Q. What is your opinion?

A. The instability that was noted on Dr. Beebe's MRI had not been noted earlier and seemed to account for her increased pain and decreased functional abilities.

Q. When you say "instability," is that of the spine?

A. Yes, the lower lumbar spine.

Q. In your opinion, was the March 2000 neurosurgical referral related to the fall on January 31, 2000?

A. I believe it was.

Q. Do you believe that the surgery Dr. Beebe performed on Ms. Rose was related to the fall at Nickel & Dime?

A. I believe it was.

MR. FRANKLIN: No further questions, Your Honor.

THE COURT: Cross examination.

Cross Examination of the Treating Physician by Mr. Richards

MR. RICHARDS: Thank you, Your Honor.

Q. Good morning, doctor.
A. Good morning.

Q. Did you treat Scarlet Rose for any of her orthopedic problems?
A. I treated her for pain and routine general health problems, which included her various ankle and back problems.

Q. Do you have your file on Scarlet Rose in front of you?
A. Yes.

Q. I found a letter in there from 2000 where you wrote, "I have at no time cared for the consequences of Ms. Rose's ankle or back." Is that correct?
A. Correct.

Q. She was being cared for by Dr. Patrick for her orthopedic problems, correct?
A. Correct.

Q. Do you defer to their assessments with regard to their care and treatment of Ms. Rose's orthopedic problems?
A. I do.

Q. Was it your opinion or Dr. Patrick's opinion that the surgery was caused by the incident at Nickel & Dime?
A. That is my opinion, based on what they have told me and how her symptomatology changed after the incident at Nickel & Dime.

Q. When you say "symptomatology," is that her subjective complaints to you?
A. Yes.

Q. Did you do any testing to measure that?
A. You cannot measure symptomatic complaints.

Q. Didn't she complain about back discomfort and difficulty with walking both before and after the incident at Nickel & Dime?
A. Yes, but the level of her discomfort increased.

Q. But you cannot quantify that, can you? Those are Ms. Rose's subjective complaints, correct?
A. Yes.

Q. You said instability of the spine became apparent on MRI after the fall?
A. Yes. When Dr. Beebe read the MRI, he mentioned the instability of the lumbar vertebrae.

Q. What does "instability" mean?
A. It means the spine is not stable, that it moves inappropriately.

Q. Do you know if the spine was unstable prior to January 31, 2000?
A. I would have to rely on Dr. Beebe for that opinion.

Q. Dr. Beebe? He would be the one that you would defer to on that point?

A. Yes.

Q. If Dr. Beebe were to say, in his opinion, he found some objective evidence of a pre-existing degenerative disease in Ms. Rose's lower back, would you agree with that?

A. Yes, I would.

Q. So, it's only her subjective complaints of pain and discomfort that you can relate to this jury, and all opinions with regard to the orthopedic care and treatment you would defer to Dr. Patrick and Dr. Beebe, is that correct?

A. Yes.

Q. Please follow Ms. Rose's medical records with me. The first time you saw her as a patient was on June 9, 1989, correct?

A. Correct.

Q. Did you see where she had an elbow that became painful?

A. Yes.

Q. Do you remember what that was about?

A. Yes. At that point, we thought she might have a problem with tendonitis.

Q. Was it the left or right elbow?

A. It was her right elbow.

Q. Did you determine whether or not it was tendonitis?

A. It was a mild case of "tennis elbow," which is an inflammation of the tendon.

Q. On March 13, 1991, you injected the right elbow this time?

A. That's for a specific acute inflammation of the right elbow. She liked to play tennis and had some further problems with tendonitis. I gave her some cortisone.

Q. On February 1992, do you see a note regarding left leg pain?

A. Yes.

Q. What did you attribute that to?

A. She had injured herself playing tennis, and I was afraid she damaged a ligament.

Q. The June 1992 note says that her left leg was very painful, and she had a burning sensation from the calf to the foot.

A. Yes, another tennis related injury.

Q. In January 1993, you injected the left knee?

A. I injected the left knee because of some pain and swelling.

Q. This is all prior to the fall in November 1998?

A. Yes.

Q. What's a venogram for?
A. To diagnose phlebitis.

Q. What's phlebitis?
A. An inflammation of the veins.

Q. Why were you concerned about phlebitis?
A. She kept complaining about problems with her calves and pulling calf muscles, so I wanted to keep an eye on it.

Q. You have her current medicine there on the right-hand side. Why was she on any medication?
A. For relief of muscular pain.

Q. Valium®.
A. Valium was a muscle relaxant and an anti-anxiety agent. She was taking five milligrams as needed for stress and general muscular problems.

Q. This is all prior to the fall in 2000, right?
A. Yes.

Q. Please look at November 1996. Do you see where it says sacroiliac is tender?
A. Yes.

Q. Sacroiliac, we talked about that earlier.
A. Yes.

Q. So, the sacroiliac pain was present prior to the fall, right?
A. Yes. It was related to over-exertion and not considered to be a chronic problem.

Q. After the fall in 2000, I do not see any further notes that reflect the care and treatment of the ankles, knees, or back, is that correct?
A. That is correct. At that point, her orthopedic problems were beyond my area of expertise and I had referred her to other physicians. I continued to be available to her for other types of medical problems, but I no longer even made notations in the file regarding her orthopedic problems.

MR. RICHARDS: Doctor, thank you for your patience with me. And I have no further questions.

THE COURT: Redirect?

Redirect Examination by Mr. Franklin

MR. FRANKLIN: Just one question.

Q. Doctor, have any of the documents that Mr. Richards made you review changed the opinion that you gave on direct examination?
A. No.

MR. FRANKLIN: That's all I have, Your Honor.

MR. RICHARDS: No further questions, Your Honor.

THE COURT: May the witness be excused?

MR. FRANKLIN: Yes, Your Honor.

THE COURT: You're excused and free to leave.

THE COURT: Call your next witness.

Testimony of Store Employees

MR. FRANKLIN: Betsy Ross.

THE COURT: Please have a seat.

Q. State your full name.
A. Betsy Caroline Ross.

Q. And your address.
A. 321 East Lake Road, Apartment 23, Palm Harbor, Atlantis.

Q. Ms. Ross, were you an employee of Nickel & Dime department store in January 2000?
A. Yes.

Q. What department did you work in?
A. Retail sales and various other departments.

Q. Have you received any training, as an employee of Nickel & Dime, on how to restock shelves?
A. Our supervisors told us how to restock shelves. We were told not to place the totes where a customer could fall and never to leave a tote on the floor unless we were standing right next to it.

Q. Who told you that?
A. Maureen Brown.

Q. Was this policy given to all the employees?
A. Yes, and it was in writing.

Q. Where was it in writing?
A. It was either in the original papers that I received from Nickel & Dime or it was posted by the time clock.

Q. Did that policy apply to all of the individual departments in the store, such as the lingerie department?
A. Yes. In fact, sometimes the lingerie department became busy when they were in the middle of unloading their tote, they were supposed to take the tote to the back of the store. But they didn't always do that.

Q. Were the areas around the display racks considered customer walkways?
A. Yes.

Q. Were you instructed about safety procedures for customer walkways?
A. Yes, we were instructed to be especially careful in areas that were used heavily by customers, and the lingerie and slippers department were two of our most popular areas.

MR. FRANKLIN: That's all I have, Your Honor, no further questions of this witness.

THE COURT: Mr. Richards, do you have questions of this witness?

Cross Examination by Mr. Richards

MR. RICHARDS: Yes, Your Honor, if I may.

Q. Ms. Ross, in January 2000, what department were you working in?
A. I worked mostly in ladies ready-to-wear, and sometimes as a cashier.

Q. As far as restocking shelves is concerned, do you know the difference between a policy that has to be followed and a procedure that is recommended?
A. Yes, policy is the way they wanted things done and procedure is how things are done.

Q. Do you know if it was Nickel & Dime's store policy or the procedure of the department manager?
A. The paper said policy on it.

Q. What did the paper say?
A. It said that we could not have the totes out on the floor where customers could trip over them.

Q. Did it say anything about how many totes you could have out at one time?
A. We could have out as many totes as we could handle.

Q. Were the totes supposed to be where people could see them, or were you supposed to hide them?
A. We were supposed to push them up against the wall at our station, so they were out of the way, but they were not hidden.

Q. In what department were ladies' slippers sold?
A. Lingerie.

Q. Did you ever work in the lingerie department?
A. Yes.

Q. When you had to restock shelves in the lingerie department, where would you put the totes?
A. They were stored between the racks.

Q. Between the racks?
A. Yes.

Q. Were they out in the open where people could see them?
A. Yes.

Q. You said that you had to stay close to the tote, right?
A. Yes. If you were called away from your area, you were supposed to put it somewhere where no one could fall over it.

Q. They told you not to put the totes where people could trip over them. If you were not busy, you would stay within three feet of the tote but, if you became busy, you were supposed to put the tote some place while you worked with a customer, correct?
A. Yes.

MR. RICHARDS: No further questions, Your Honor.

THE COURT: Anything else?

MR. FRANKLIN: No, Your Honor.

THE COURT: Call your next witness.

MR. FRANKLIN: Andrea Jones.

MR. FRANKLIN: May it please the court.

THE COURT: You may proceed.

Direct Examination by Mr. Franklin

Q. State your full name.
A. Andrea Abigail Jones.

Q. And your address?
A. 580 Tampa Road, Oldsmar, Atlantis.

Q. Ms. Jones, you were formerly an employee of Nickel & Dime, correct?
A. Yes.

Q. What was your job?
A. I worked in ready-to-wear.

Q. Did you receive any training as an employee regarding totes and stocking?
A. They gave me a manual to read and told me not leave anything on the floor for people to trip on.

Q. Like these totes over here in the corner, correct?
A. Right.

Q. Were you given a piece of paper by Nickel & Dime that told you that?
A. It was either in the manual or by our time clock; I can't remember.

MR. FRANKLIN: That's all I have.

THE COURT: Cross-examination?

MR. RICHARDS: Yes, Your Honor. Thank you.

Cross Examination by Mr. Richards

Q. You said that you were told not to leave things out on the floor where people could trip over them but, if you were working with the totes, as long as you were within a few feet, it was permissible, correct?
A. As long as someone couldn't trip over it.

MR. RICHARDS: No further questions.

MR. FRANKLIN: Nothing further, Your Honor.

THE COURT: You're excused and free to leave. Next witness.

MR. FRANKLIN: Shannon Young.

Direct Examination by Mr. Franklin

Q. State your full name for the record.
A. Shannon Young.

Q. What is your address?
A. 4304 Highlands Avenue, Clearwater, Atlantis 33872.

Q. Prior to March 2000, were you an employee at Nickel & Dime?
A. Yes, sir.

Q. What was your job title?
A. Lead sales.

Q. Did you have any training on the policies and procedures regarding totes?
A. Yes.

Q. What kind of training did you have?
A. When you brought a tote into your department, you were supposed to store it away from the floor and work from that spot to put your purchases out on the floor.

Q. When you say "floor," do you mean where the customers are?
A. Yes.

Q. Did that training come from management?
A. Yes.

MR. FRANKLIN: Okay. No further questions.

THE COURT: Cross.

Cross Examination by Mr. Richards

Q. Ms. Young, were you instructed that you were to work out of the tote and not to leave it unattended?
A. Yes.

Q. Were you instructed to store them where people could see them and not trip over them?
A. Yes.

MR. RICHARDS: Okay. Thank you. No further questions.

MR. FRANKLIN: No further questions, Your Honor.

THE COURT: You're excused and free to leave. Next witness.

MR. FRANKLIN: Christy Davidson.

Direct Examination by Mr. Franklin

Q. State your full name for the record, please.
A. Christy Tait Davidson.

Q. What is your address?
A. 1211 Windmill Drive, Dunedin, Atlantis.

Q. In January 2000, were you an employee at Nickel & Dime?
A. Yes.

Q. What was your job title?
A. I was department manager of lingerie and accessories.

Q. Did you receive any training regarding inventory totes and restocking?
A. We were told not to carry more than three or four totes out at a time and to keep them close to the wall or where we were working at all times.

Q. Were you ever instructed on where within your department to place them?
A. Out of the customer's reach.

Q. How about in terms of walkways within your department?
A. We were told to put them up against the rack while we were working with them so they would not be in the aisle.

Q. Were you specifically instructed not to put the totes in the aisle?
A. We were told to make things safe so customers could get by.

MR. FRANKLIN: No further questions, Your Honor. Thank you.

THE COURT: Cross examination.

Cross Examination by Mr. Richards

Q. Ms. Davidson, you said safety was always a main concern.
A. Yes.

Q. Were you always supposed to keep the totes within a close proximity of where you were working?
A. Yes.

Q. And the totes were supposed to be out in the open, correct?
A. Yes.

Q. Not hidden?
A. Not hidden.

Q. Was stocking done during working hours?
A. Yes.

Q. Is that the way it's done in retail business?
A. Everywhere that I know of.

Q. In some departments, like lingerie and accessories, they may be out in the middle of the floor, right?
A. Right.

Q. Not up against the wall?
A. Right. They are up against where you are working. In the lingerie department, I had a table, and no one was supposed to go behind that table.

Q. Do you have any personal knowledge about the incident involving Scarlet Rose?
A. No.

Q. Did the accessory department have a table?
A. No.

Q. Did you have to work close to the racks in the accessories department?
A. Yes.

Q. Was it out in the open?
A. Yes, but someone always had to be attending to the tote.

Q. Someone would have to be attending?
A. Yes.

MR. RICHARDS: Thank you. No further questions.

MR. FRANKLIN: No further questions, Your Honor.

THE COURT: You're excused and free to leave.

THE COURT: Call your next witness.

Videotaped Testimony of Dr. Beebe

MR. FRANKLIN: Your Honor, we have a videotaped deposition to play.

THE COURT: Set it up and announce to the jury whose deposition this is, where it was taken and when. Does the court reporter need to take this down, or do you stipulate that the videotape is part of the record?

MR. FRANKLIN: For the plaintiff, Your Honor, the videotape can be part of the record.

MR. RICHARDS: The defense will so stipulate to the videotape and original transcript being part of the record.

THE COURT: Ladies and gentlemen of the jury, the sworn testimony of this witness given before trial in a deposition is going to be played for you now in a videotape. You are to consider and weigh this testimony as though this witness had testified here before you in person.

MR. FRANKLIN: May it please the court, plaintiff calls Dr. Von N. Beebe, who will testify by videotape.

THE COURT: You may proceed.

(Videotaped deposition is played) *[Author's note: see Chapter Six for the testimony of Dr. Beebe.]*

THE COURT: Ladies and gentlemen of the jury, at this time, we will recess for the evening. Do not discuss this case among yourselves or with other people, and do not permit anyone to say anything to you about this case. Any additional instructions?

MR. FRANKLIN: No, Your Honor.

MR. RICHARDS: No, Your Honor.

THE COURT: We'll be in recess until 8:30 in the morning. [The jury was escorted from the room by the baliff.]

MR. FRANKLIN: Before we dismiss for the day, I'd like to have a few things marked into evidence.

THE COURT: Mark everything into evidence that will go back with the jury when they deliberate. If you have any problem, I will be in my chambers.

MR. RICHARDS: For the record, as to the medical records, we've tried to eliminate all references to insurance. If Mr. Franklin finds any more references, I'd be glad to stipulate that he can remove them. Neither of us wants to create a mistrial by inadvertently allowing records that reference insurance to go to the jury.

THE COURT: Thank you for bringing this to my attention. Mr. Franklin, I will require you to make sure that none of the exhibits that are given to the jury refer to insurance.

MR. FRANKLIN: For the record, plaintiff's exhibits 1, 2, 3, 4 and 5 are stipulated into evidence as well as defendant's exhibit number 1 and 2.

THE COURT: Mark those and admit them.

Day Three of the Trial

THE BAILIFF: All rise.

THE COURT: Please be seated. Bring our jury back in.

THE BAILIFF: All rise.

THE COURT: Please be seated. Let the record reflect that the jury has returned to the jury box and each is in his or her proper seat. Counsel, you may continue.

MR. FRANKLIN: Thank you, Your Honor.

Testimony of Jane Morris, Plaintiff's Mother

MR. FRANKLIN: Plaintiff calls Jane Morris.

Direct Examination by Mr. Franklin

Q. Please state your full name for the record.
A. Jane Morris.

Q. What is your address?
A. 232 Oak Street, Tarpon Springs, Atlantis 34689.

Q. What is your relationship to Scarlet Rose?
A. I'm her mother.

Q. Ms. Morris, do you recall an incident that your daughter, Scarlet Rose, had in January 1998 when she fell on a tennis court?
A. Yes, I do.

Q. Did you assist her after that accident in terms of taking care of her?
A. I brought her to my house and did everything for her because she was in bed for a while.

Q. For what length of time were you her caregiver?
A. About a month.

Q. In terms of being her caregiver, did that include cooking for her?
A. I served her meals in bed.

Q. Was your daughter living with you during that time?
A. Yes, she was.

Q. Did there come a time when her condition improved and she was able to do everything for herself?
A. Yes.

Q. Was that prior to the January 31, 2000, incident at Nickel & Dime?
A. Yes.

Q. When did that happen?
A. I don't remember the month. She went back to her place a few weeks after the incident, but she was back again a few weeks after surgery.

Q. Do you recall the incident that occurred in January 2000 at the Nickel & Dime store?
A. Yes.

Q. Prior to going to Nickel & Dime that day, where were you planning to go with your daughter?
A. Scarlet and I were going to go to lunch, but she wanted to stop at Nickel & Dime before we ate.

Q. Was Ms. Rose having any problems that day that would have prevented her from driving, such as being disoriented, confused, or anything like that?
A. No.

Q. What was her purpose for going there?
A. Her daughter gave her shorts for Christmas, and she was going to exchange them.

Q. Please describe what happened that day at Nickel & Dime.
A. We drove up to the curb, and she got out. I stayed in the car. A young woman came out of the store and said, "You need to come inside because your daughter has had an accident."

Q. Did you go inside?
A. Yes, I did.

Q. What did you observe when you entered the store?
A. When I got to her, she was sitting on the floor crying, and her left leg was bleeding.

Q. When you say the front of the leg, are you talking about the part below or above the knee?
A. From the knee down to just above the ankle.

Q. That was on her left leg?
A. Yes.

Q. You said she was sitting on the floor. Was she sitting up on her buttocks?
A. Yes, she was sitting up.

Q. Were there any other people around your daughter?
A. Yes, several ladies were crowded around her.

Q. Was your daughter complaining of any discomfort or pain?
A. Yes, she was crying and said she was in pain.

Q. Did you hear her say where she was hurting?
A. She was complaining about her back.

Q. Did anyone provide medical assistance or call an ambulance?
A. Yes. I told them to call an ambulance, because I wanted her to go to the hospital right away.

Q. Did you observe anything in the area that might have caused her to fall?
A. No.

Q. Did you later see what caused her to fall?
A. Yes.

Q. What did you see?
A. There was a box with the lid open on one side of the aisle and a rack on the other. There were things on the floor, like slippers or socks, that had been knocked off of the rack. Scarlet said she had tripped over a box that had been left in the aisle.

Q. Did you actually see the box that Ms. Rose said she tripped over?
A. Yes, it was sitting in the middle of the side aisle.

Q. Was the box that she fell on in the middle of a customer walkway?
A. Yes, it was. The aisle was crowded with merchandise.

Q. After the fall, when you arrived, did you do anything with the shorts that Ms. Rose had brought with her into the store, or had she already exchanged them?
A. Somebody handed me the shorts and said the ambulance would be there in a few minutes. I took the shorts back to the customer service area. I started down the aisle where Scarlet had fallen, but I could not get through, so I turned around and went through another aisle to customer service.

Q. Was your daughter having any problems walking when she entered the store?
A. No.

Q. Once the ambulance arrived, did you follow it to the hospital?
A. Yes.

Q. Could you describe the kind of pain your daughter was in?
A. She was saying, "oh, my back," and was crying. She was in a lot of pain.

Q. How long were you and your daughter at the hospital that day?
A. About five hours.

Q. What did you do after leaving the emergency room?
A. She got in the back seat of my car, lay down, and I took her to my house.

Q. Describe for the jury what occurred over the next couple of weeks.
A. I was taking care of her, and she was in bed most of the time.

Q. Could she drive herself to her doctor appointments?
A. No, I drove her everywhere she went.

Q. Did you continue to assist her until the day of the surgery performed by Dr. Beebe?
A. Yes. She was able to do some things before the surgery, but I continued to provide assistance before the surgery and for a little while after the surgery.

MR. FRANKLIN: That's all the questions I have, Your Honor. Thank you, Ms. Morris.

THE COURT: Cross examination.

MR. RICHARDS: May it please the court.

Cross Examination by Mr. Richards

Q. Good morning, ma'am. After your daughter's fall on the tennis court, you were cleaning her place, washing clothes, doing grocery shopping, vacuuming the floor, and all of those types of things, correct?
A. Yes, but Scarlet had recovered and was able to do those things for herself, until the fall at Nickel & Dime, then I had to do it all over again.

Q. Was she in a wheelchair after the fall on the tennis court?
A. Yes, for a few weeks.

Q. Did she use a cane for awhile after that?
A. Yes, for a few months.

Q. How long was she with you after the fall on the tennis court?
A. Until she was walking without a cane.

Q. Do you remember what you saw when you found your daughter at Nickel & Dime?
A. Yes, I think so.

Q. Let me show you a photograph and ask you if you remember this scene?
A. No. I don't remember seeing that. As I recall, the box was more out of the aisle, and these lids were sticking out into the aisle.

Q. Does the box in this photo look like the box that you saw on the day of the incident?
A. I saw a large plastic container like the box that is sitting over there.

Q. Did your daughter tell you what she stepped into or got caught up in?
A. Not at the scene, because there was too much commotion.

Q. Did she ever tell you that she got her knees caught in this box?
A. I don't remember that. I remember her saying that she fell into a plastic container.

Q. Was the plastic container, which you see in the photograph, in the middle of the aisle?
A. I remember the plastic container being somewhere else than it is in the photo, so someone must have moved it.

Q. It is a pretty big box, isn't it?
A. Yes.

Q. You didn't have any trouble seeing it, did you?
A. No.

MR. RICHARDS: Thank you, ma'am. I have no further questions to ask you.

THE COURT: Redirect examination.

MR. FRANKLIN: No, Your Honor.

THE COURT: May the witness be excused?

MR. FRANKLIN: Yes, Your Honor, but I would ask that, since she will not be called again as a witness, she be allowed to stay in the courtroom.

THE COURT: Any objection, Mr. Richards?

MR. RICHARDS: No, Your Honor.

THE COURT: Call your next witness.

MR. FRANKLIN: Plaintiff rests, Your Honor.

THE COURT: Approach the bench.

Motions at the Close of Plaintiff's Case

At the close of plaintiff's case, Alan, outside of the presence of the jury, made a motion for directed verdict in favor of Nickel & Dime. He claimed that the facts of this case clearly established that it was an open and obvious condition, and the plaintiff was responsible for the incident and was the legal cause of the injury she sustained. The court denied the motion.

MR. RICHARDS: At this time, I would move for a directed verdict. The evidence is undisputed and shows that this was an open and obvious condition; therefore, Nickel & Dime is not negligent. I have some cases that indicate that the property owner's duty is to maintain their store in a reasonably safe manner and to not create a dangerous condition. Despite the argument that the tote shouldn't have been there, Ms. Rose testified that she failed to observe the large plastic tote, and it was her negligence, not Nickel & Dime's, that caused the incident.

The plaintiff has presented testimony from three store employees who said it was a violation of Nickel & Dime's internal policy and procedure. I have previously submitted case law and argument, by way of a Motion *in Limine*, which was denied, to the effect that the violation of an internal policy is not in and of itself negligence. In order to allow this case to move forward, Your Honor, you must find that plaintiff has met her burden of proving negligence on the part of the store at the close of their case. I argue that she has not done that because it was open and obvious and not a dangerous condition. For those reasons, I move for a Directed Verdict on behalf of the defendant.

MR. FRANKLIN: The standard jury instruction for a case like this,,which is a pure negligence case, reads that the jury must find that the defendant negligently failed to maintain its premises in a reasonably safe condition, negligently failed to correct a dangerous condition that the defendant knew or should have known of within the use of reasonable care, or that it negligently failed to warn plaintiff of a dangerous condition that the defendant had or should have had knowledge of. The open and obvious argument goes to the issue of whether or not there was any comparative negligence on the part of the plaintiff, which is an issue for the jury to decide. The duty to warn the plaintiff is a jury issue. The failure of the defendant to maintain its premises in a safe condition is an issue of negligence, Your Honor. It is inappropriate, under the circumstances, for a store to put a box in the middle of an aisle. That is a dangerous condition or, at the very least, it is a factual issue for the jury to decide. For those reasons, plaintiff asks the Court to deny the defendant's motion at this time.

MR. RICHARDS: I rely on the *Shapp* case, which basically states that a storeowner, such as Nickel & Dime, has no duty to warn a patron of an open and obvious condition unless that open and obvious condition is inherently dangerous. The box is not inherently dangerous, and we did not fail to warn plaintiff of a dangerous condition.

MR. FRANKLIN: I have nothing further to offer, Your Honor.

THE COURT: I will deny your motion at this time, Mr. Richards.

Chapter Twelve

**DEFENDANT'S CASE
IN CHIEF**

Testimony of Store Employees

THE COURT: Mr. Richards, call your first witness.

MR. RICHARD: Defendant, Nickel & Dime, calls as its first witness, Marjorie Murphy.

Direct Examination by Mr. Richards

Q. Good morning. If you would, please tell the jury your name.
A. Marjorie Meagan Murphy.

Q. Please state your address.
A. 870 Sunshine Lane, Clearwater, Atlantis.

Q. Were you employed at Nickel & Dime on January 31, 2000?
A. Yes, I was.

Q. How were you employed?
A. As a selling supervisor.

Q. Had you been an assistant store manager prior to that?
A. No, I was in the management team, but I was not an assistant manager or manager.

Q. Are you aware of an incident that occurred on January 31, 2000, involving the plaintiff, Scarlet Rose?
A. Yes, I am.

Q. Did you take this photograph that has been marked as an exhibit in this case?
A. Yes, I did.

Q. When did you take that photograph?
A. Within minutes after the incident occurred.

Q. Did you actually witness the incident?
A. No, I did not.

Q. When did you arrive at the scene?
A. I arrived at the scene moments after it occurred.

Q. Did you or anyone else move anything before that photograph was taken?
A. No.

Q. Is this an accurate picture of what you observed when you arrived at the scene?
A. Yes.

Q. Did you have conversations with the plaintiff, Scarlet Rose?
A. Yes, I did.

Q. Did she tell you what had happened?
A. Yes. She told me that she was trying to go to the customer service department to exchange a pair of shorts. She said she was in a rush because her mother was waiting for her outside, and she didn't see the box.

Q. Why did you take pictures?
A. It is store policy, when there is an accident, to take a picture of the scene and attach it to an incident report.

MR. RICHARDS: Your Honor, this photograph has been admitted into evidence. I request permission to publish it to the jury.

THE COURT: Any objection?

MR. FRANKLIN: No objection.

THE COURT: If you will, hand it to the Bailiff, and the Bailiff will publish it to the jury.

MR. RICHARDS: Yes, Your Honor.

Q. Let me show you another photograph, which has been marked as defendant's exhibit number 3, and ask you if you recognize what that photograph depicts?
A. It is a picture of the purse and accessory area.

Q. Is this the slippers rack that was involved in the incident?
A. Yes.

Q. Is that the aisle that Scarlet Rose walked down prior to reaching the slipper's rack?
A. Yes.

Q. What were those tables used for?
A. Displaying merchandise.

Q. Was it unusual for them to be there?
A. No.

Q. How wide is that walkway?
A. About five or six feet.

Q. How wide is that table?
A. About two feet.

Q. Please explain to the jury how a person, such as Scarlet Rose, would get to the slipper's department after entering the front door.

A. She would walk past the registers and a gift area. The aisle she fell in is a secondary aisle, so she would have walked down the main aisle about 50 feet and made a left turn.

Q. What is a tote?

A. A tote is a plastic container or cardboard box that merchandise is loaded in when being transported from store to store.

Q. Is this a tote?

A. Yes.

Q. Are you familiar with store policy and procedure regarding use of totes and restocking shelves?

A. Yes.

Q. Was there a written procedure, to your knowledge, in regard to the placement of totes?

A. No. Except for general safety precautions, there was nothing specific in writing.

Q. Is there anything in writing that states personnel may not use totes or cardboard boxes to restock the shelves?

A. No.

Q. The area where the incident occurred is called the accessories department?

A. Yes.

Q. In the accessories department, was there a workstation that was blocked off where totes or boxes could be placed while personnel restocked shelves?

A. No.

Q. What would employees, who worked in the accessories department, do to restock their shelves?

A. They would keep the totes as close to them as possible.

Q. Was restocking done after the store was closed?

A. No.

Q. Do you know how other department stores restock their shelves?

A. Yes, other stores do it the same way.

Q. On January 31, 2000, was there a sales person working close to the totes when you arrived?

A. Yes, the department supervisor, Caitlin Palmer and a salesperson were there.

Q. Were employees permitted to have more than one tote out on the floor at one time?

A. The more experienced workers were allowed to.

Q. Were these employees experienced enough to do so?

A. Yes, but no matter how experienced an employee was, she had to work only a few feet away and wasn't supposed to take care of customers or leave the totes unattended.

Q. Is that a verbal policy?
A. Yes.

Q. Have you ever worked in that department?
A. Yes.

Q. Was there a policy in regard to where totes should be placed when working in an open area?
A. Yes. You were to keep them as close to you as possible, preferably up against something so people would see them.

Q. Were employees supposed to keep the totes where they could be seen or out of sight?
A. Where they could be seen, not hidden, because that would be a hidden hazard.

Q. Since employees had to restock shelves during business hours and there was no area near the accessories department to place the totes, was it absolutely necessary for totes, on occasion, to be in the aisles?
A. Yes.

Q. When totes were placed in an aisle, the employee had to be within a few feet of the totes, and people had to be able to see them?
A. Right.

MR. RICHARDS: Thank you. I have no further questions.

THE COURT: Cross.

MR. FRANKLIN: Yes, Your Honor.

Cross Examination by Mr. Franklin

Q. Ms. Murphy, when you came to the scene of this particular fall, Ms. Rose was on the floor, is that correct?
A. Yes.

Q. And she was complaining of some pain and discomfort?
A. Yes.

Q. At that time, what was she complaining of?
A. First it was her shin, and then she said her lower back hurt.

Q. Was there a display rack that had been knocked down near the scene of the fall?
A. No, I don't remember one.

Q. You indicated that Ms. Rose told you that she was in a hurry because her mother was waiting, correct?
A. Yes.

Q. And she didn't see the tote, correct?
A. That is correct.

Q. Could she have walked around the tote to get by it?
A. The way the box was positioned, she could have walked around the corner of the tote to get around it.

Q. This is the picture you took immediately after the accident?
A. Yes.

Q. This picture shows the plastic tote as it was when you first saw it, correct?
A. That is correct.

Q. The tote that is pictured is the same tote as the one here in the courtroom, correct?
A. Yes, it is.

Q. If the tote is three feet wide, the aisle is six feet wide, and the tote was in the middle of the aisle, there would be approximately one and a half feet on either side, correct?
A. Right.

Q. Is it your testimony, as a former Nickel & Dime supervisor, that there is nothing wrong with someone blocking an aisle in that fashion?
A. That is my testimony.

Q. Someone, such as Ms. Rose, who had the intention of walking through that area would either have to walk over this tote or squeeze around it, is that right?
A. Yes, or go another route.

Q. Did Ms. Rose ever tell you that she intentionally tried to walk over the tote?
A. No.

Q. Do you remember when I took your deposition a few months ago?
A. Yes.

Q. I'll refer counsel to page 92, line 17; and I'll ask you, ma'am, if you remember this question and your answer to it.

> Question: "Tell me what you recall about this particular accident."
> Answer: "I was not present when it happened. When I got there, the woman had fallen and hurt her leg. She told me instead of walking around the tote she wanted to take a shortcut and tried to step over it and fell."

Do you remember that question and answer?
A. No.

Q. You don't? Do you remember giving a deposition on November 19, 2000?
A. Yes, I do.

Q. Do you think you might have said that in the deposition?
A. Well, if it's there, I did.

Q. Let me ask you again. Do you remember Scarlet Rose ever saying that she was trying to step over the tote to get to the customer service area as fast as she could?
A. No, I don't. I'm sorry.

Q. Did you remember it in November?
A. Apparently I did.

Q. It was store policy to keep the totes near you?
A. Right.

Q. Was it because they were obviously out in the open and you wanted to make sure that you had control over them?
A. Yes.

Q. Would you want to keep a tote away from the middle of the walkway?
A. Yes.

Q. While keeping it near you?
A. Yes.

Q. In looking at this photograph, there's a walkway that is defined by the edge of the tote, right?
A. Yes.

Q. The tote was in the middle of the walkway, correct?
A. Yes.

MR. FRANKLIN: No further questions, your Honor.

THE COURT: Redirect.

MR. RICHARDS: Briefly, your Honor.

Redirect Examination by Mr. Richards

Q. Ms. Murphy, in an open area of a retail department store, is there any floor space that is not an aisle or walkway?
A. No.

MR. RICHARDS: Thank you. No further questions.

MR. FRANKLIN: No further questions, Your Honor.

THE COURT: May the witness be excused?

MR. FRANKLIN: She may.

THE COURT: You're excused and free to leave. Next witness.

MR. FRANKLIN: Caitlin Palmer, please.

THE COURT: Please have a seat.

Direct Examination by Mr. Richards

Q. Please tell the jury your name.
A. Caitlin Christine Palmer.

Q. Please state your address.
A. 4620 Marsh Lane, Clearwater, Atlantis.

Q. In January 2000, were you employed at Nickel & Dime department store?
A. Yes.

Q. What was your position?
A. Sales supervisor.

Q. Please take a look at these two photographs that have been admitted into evidence. Do you recognize those photographs?
A. Yes, sir.

Q. Do you remember that an incident occurred in that location on January 31, 2000?
A. Yes, sir.

Q. Do you remember any other incident occurring in that location?
A. No, sir.

Q. How long have you worked at Nickel & Dime?
A. Fourteen years.

Q. Did you see the incident occur?
A. Yes.

Q. Where were you standing when the incident occurred?
A. I was in the corner in another section.

Q. How far from the lower right corner of this photograph?
A. Not too far.

Q. Approximately, how many feet?
A. About ten feet.

Q. What were you doing at that time?
A. I was straightening up.

Q. Tell the jury what you saw.
A. I saw a lady come in. She was walking fast in the corner over there, and then she fell.

Q. What did you see her do, specifically?
A. I don't know what she was doing. It looked like she was trying to climb over the box.

Q. When you saw her fall, what did you do?

A. I called Ms. Murphy, and we went over to where she was lying on the floor to assist her.

Q. Let me show you this picture that is defendant's exhibit number 2. Do you recognize that picture?

A. Yes. It's the tote we use to restock shelves.

Q. Does that photograph depict the scene as it was when plaintiff fell?

A. Yes, sir.

Q. Do you remember if there was a stockperson or salesperson working in the vicinity of that tote?

A. Yes, sir.

Q. Do you remember who that was?

A. Carol Westwoman.

Q. Do you remember any other incident occurring in the vicinity of where this incident occurred?

A. No.

Q. What did Ms. Rose say to you after you arrived?

A. We asked how she was and determined it was best to leave her on the floor until the paramedics arrived. She said she was sorry, because she was in a rush to get to the bathroom.

Q. Did you move anything before the picture was taken?

A. No, sir.

Q. Did anybody move anything?

A. No, sir.

Q. Did you see a rack pulled down?

A. No, sir.

MR. RICHARDS: I have no further questions. Thank you.

THE COURT: Cross-examination?

MR. FRANKLIN: Yes, Your Honor. May it please the court.

Cross Examination by Mr. Franklin

Q. Ms. Palmer, did you say that you saw Ms. Rose come into the store?

A. Yes.

Q. Did you say that she was walking in a hurried fashion?

A. Yes.

Q. Do you watch all patrons when they enter the store?

A. No.

Q. Please tell the jury how you happened to watch Scarlet Rose as she entered the store on this particular day and walk all the way through the store, in a hurried fashion, until you saw her fall.

A. I don't know. I happened to be looking in her direction and saw her. I wasn't paying a lot of attention, but I saw her enter the store and fall.

Q. You told Mr. Richards that this picture, exhibit 2, is a picture of the scene as you recall it, correct?

A. Yes.

Q. Do you remember when I took your deposition back on November 19, 2000?

A. Yes, sir.

Q. And do you remember when, at page 15, line 22, I asked you these following questions, and you answered as follows:

> Question: "Let me ask you, does this appear to be a photograph of the scene when this occurred?"
> Answer: "I don't remember."

My question is: do you remember it or not?

A. Well, I answered "I don't remember" at that time, but I remember what I told you.

Q. And you also remember that Ms. Rose was trying to climb over the tote, is that correct?

A. Yes, sir.

Q. Is the walkway, where Ms. Rose fell, for employees and patrons to use?

A. Yes, sir.

Q. Is it dangerous to place totes within a walkway?

A. Not in my opinion. They are out in the open and aren't dangerous at all.

Q. Why would you put something where someone would be walking and might trip over?

A. We have to restock our shelves, and there is no other place to put the totes. We do it when it is not too busy and, to my knowledge, no one else has ever fallen.

Q. In other words, it is all right to put things in a walkway as long as no one falls, is that it?

A. We do the best we can.

Q. Is that a display rack pictured in this photograph?

A. Yes.

Q. It looks as though the tote is in the middle of the walkway. Is that an accurate depiction of what the picture shows?

A. Yes.

Q. Is it all right to put the tote in the middle of the walkway?

A. Yes, a tote can be left out in the open so everyone, including our staff, can see it.

Q. In order for Ms. Rose to use that walkway, she would have had to have stepped over that tote, is that correct?
A. She might have been able to walk around it.

Q. You testified that she indicated to you that she was trying to step over it, is that correct?
A. Yes, sir. When we were picking her up, she said she was in a hurry, she was sorry and it was her fault because she was trying to go to the bathroom.

Q. Did she have any merchandise in her hands?
A. I don't recall.

Q. Did she complain of any injuries at the time?
A. She hurt her leg or ankle.

Q. Let me refer you back to your deposition that we took on November 19, 2000. I refer you to page 16, line 12. Do you recall this question and answer?

> Question: "Did she complain to you about any injuries or pain?"
> Answer: "Not to me. She said she was in a hurry and was trying to get to the bathroom."
> Question: "What else did she say?"
> Answer: "That she had hurt her back and scraped her knee."

Do you remember that question and answer?
A. Yes, I remember saying that.

MR. FRANKLIN: That is all the questions I have, Your Honor.

THE COURT: Redirect?

MR. RICHARDS: No, Your Honor.

THE COURT: May the witness be excused?

MR. RICHARDS: She may, Your Honor.

THE COURT: You are excused and may leave. Next witness.

Testimony of IME Doctor

MR. RICHARDS: Dr. Christopher Paul, please.

Direct Examination by Mr. Richards

Q. Good morning, Dr. Paul. Please tell us your full name.
A. Christopher Brockton Paul.

Q. Describe your medical background and training.
A. I have an M.D. and a master's of science in pathology from the Medical College of West Virginia. I have three years of general surgery, one of which was as a general surgery fellow. I

have four years of orthopedics. I'm board certified in orthopedic surgery with a sub-specialty certificate in feet.

Q. Explain to the jury what it means to be board certified in orthopedic surgery.
A. It means I've completed an approved residency, had two years of practice experience, and passed the board exam.

Q. Are all doctors who practice medicine in the field of orthopedics members of the Board of Orthopedic Surgery?
A. No.

Q. Doctor, you have been called upon at the request of defendant, Nickel & Dime, Inc., to conduct an examination of the plaintiff, Scarlet Rose, have you not?
A. Yes, I did see her for the purpose of conducting an examination at your request.

Q. Do you consider yourself to be the defendant's expert in this case?
A. No, my opinion is based solely on the medical records and my medical knowledge of Ms. Rose's exam and history.

Q. Do you consider what you performed to be an independent medical examination?
A. Yes.

Q. Have you ever worked for me, my law firm, or Nickel & Dime in the past?
A. No.

Q. If you would, describe what you have reviewed in this particular case.
A. I was supplied with Ms. Rose's medical records from 1989 to 2000. The records, which I prepared at the IME, were relative to orthopedic problems. I also examined Ms. Rose and conducted some limited testing.

Q. To the best of your knowledge, have you reviewed all medical records that relate to her orthopedic problems from 1989 to the time Dr. Beebe performed surgery?
A. Yes.

Q. What else did you do in this particular case?
A. I took a history from Ms. Rose and performed a physical exam.

Q. How much time did you spend with Ms. Rose?
A. Probably 45 minutes to an hour.

Q. Have you generated a written report?
A. Yes, I have.

Q. And have you a copy of that report in front of you?
A. Yes, I do.

MR. RICHARDS: At this point, Your Honor, I would offer Dr. Paul as an expert witness and ask to allow him to render expert opinions.

MR. FRANKLIN: The plaintiff will stipulate that Dr. Paul is an expert witness.

THE COURT: The witness is qualified as an expert. You may proceed, counsel.

Q. Dr. Paul, as a result of the records that you have reviewed, your physical examination of the plaintiff and your conversation with the plaintiff, have you formed any opinions on this case?

A. Yes.

Q. Within a reasonable degree of medical probability, were the findings and the symptoms that Dr. Beebe reports in his records present in Ms. Rose prior to January 31, 2000, when she fell in Nickel & Dime?

A. Yes, I've examined the records and the reports, and it seems to me that the patient had an extensive work-up on her back prior to her fall. She had an MRI in July 1998 that showed she had problems at L4-L5 with involvement of both the L4 root and spinal stenosis involving the L5 root. She had some discussion about surgery with Dr. Patrick, who is the orthopedic surgeon who performed the ankle surgery on Scarlet. If you compare the findings of the 1998 MRI with the 2000 MRI, as well as Dr. Beebe's operative notes, you find that the result in 1998 showed a bulge. In 2000, the area had degenerated with root compression on the left, spinal stenosis, and a general process of degeneration of the discs in Ms. Rose's lumbar spine. The issue is whether the fall caused the herniation or it was a result of the natural progression of a disease process that existed prior to the fall.

Q. You mentioned that surgery was considered before March 2000. Was surgery discussed in the records that you reviewed before the fall?

A. Yes. Ms. Rose's back problem was serious enough for her to warrant discussions with Dr. Patrick, an orthopedic specialist. He thought that she had an L5 radiculopathy and did not feel that she was a surgical candidate.

Q. Based upon your review of the records, do you have an opinion as to whether or not conservative treatment was appropriate for Scarlet Rose's low back problem from the time she fell in 1998 and the next few months?

A. Yes. The patient had complaints of back pain, which may have arisen from her ankle injury, but her back became a focal point of treatment after her ankle was healing. She had heat packs, whirlpools, massages, medication, and an MRI. Some spinal stenosis, mild disk bulges, and herniations will respond to nonsurgical intervention. She received adequate nonsurgical invention, anti-inflammatories, and physical therapy.

Q. Is there any other conservative treatment that could have been done for Scarlet Rose before January 31, 2000?

A. No. She had improved with conservative treatment, but the problems that caused her back pain had not gone away.

Q. Did she recover from her ankle surgery?

A. Yes, according to the records, what she told me, and from my examination, she did; however, it was a fracture that required surgery to reattach ligaments, and it takes time to fully recover. It affects ambulation, which did not help her back.

Q. Did the back surgery go well?

A. Yes.

Q. Before the January 31, 2000, fall at Nickel & Dime and prior to Dr. Beebe's surgery, do you find any indication as to whether or not the symptoms that Ms. Rose was complaining of changed significantly, or did her symptoms seem the same?

A. Ms. Rose says the pain was in the same place in terms of her low back, but the pain became more intense.

Q. Did you get a description from Ms. Rose on how the January 31, 2000, incident at Nickel & Dime occurred?

A. Yes.

Q. Did Ms. Rose tell you she fell to the ground, or did she get stuck in a box?

A. She got tangled up in a box and couldn't get down to the floor or get up by herself.

Q. Was the fall similar to a person falling on the street?

MR. FRANKLIN: Object to the form. That is an improper question. It lacks predicate in terms of the facts of either fall sufficient to give the doctor basis to compare the two.

THE COURT: Overruled.

A. A sidewalk is a hard surface, and there is potential for injury, but it depends on how she landed. If she fell back over and landed on her buttocks, that would be different from falling forward and landing on her face. When she fell into the box at Nickel & Dime, that could be called a fall even though she didn't land on the ground.

Q. After 1998, were Ms. Rose's problems constant, episodic or both?

A. Although she said it was worse after the fall at Nickel & Dime, she had some constant level of pain and episodic exacerbations for almost six months after the fall in 1998.

Q. Did you notice evidence of degenerative disk disease prior to the January 31, 2000, fall at Nickel & Dime?

A. Yes, but degenerative disk disease doesn't mean you have to have surgery.

Q. Do you have an opinion as to what percentage of problems requiring surgery existed prior to the January 31, 2000, fall at Nickel & Dime?

A. Yes.

Q. Would you please tell the jury what percentage of the medical problems required surgery?

A. I would say 95 to 100 percent. If you compare the MRI done by Dr. Beebe with the 1998 MRI, there's not a whole lot of difference. The same levels and problems are involved.

Q. Can you identify anything objective in the records that would indicate a medical condition or problem that existed after the January 31, 2000, fall that did not exist prior to that fall?

A. No.

MR. RICHARDS: Thank you, Dr. Paul. I have no further questions.

Cross Examination by Mr. Franklin

MR. FRANKLIN: Good morning, Dr. Paul.

A. Good morning.

Q. You testified that you treat back injuries and intervertebral disk injury, whether degenerative in nature or from an injury, operatively and nonoperatively, correct?

A. Yes.

Q. A nonoperative treatment is favored over an operative treatment unless it is an emergency situation?

A. Not exactly. If there were paralysis or rapidly progressing symptoms, then you would perform surgery.

Q. The success of conservative treatment is obviously reduction in pain or increase in mobility, correct?

A. It should be both.

Q. If a patient with a disk disorder, whether it be degenerative in nature or from trauma, gets to the point, through conservative treatment, where the pain level is manageable and acceptable to the patient and mobility is increased, then conservative treatment would be favored over operative therapy, right?

A. Yes. Conservative management has fewer complications than surgery.

Q. And surgery is designed to relieve or remove symptomology, not to correct a process, correct?

A. No. If the patient's symptoms are not under control after five years, surgery might be warranted.

Q. Getting it under control, would that be the level of pain that a patient can tolerate?

A. No. If you could get the patients back to where they had minimal pain without having surgery, then you would consider that a success. However, once you damage your spine, there is always some damage. Because Ms. Rose had a previous injury, we would recommend that she avoid things like heavy lifting and repetitive bending.

Q. Is it a fair characterization that from about one year after the 1998 accident Ms. Rose's back complaints were nonexistent until the January 31, 2000 fall?

A. Yes.

Q. Would you agree that Ms. Rose saw Dr. Patrick, Dr. Mullan, and Dr. Beebe as a result of the fall at Nickel & Dime, and their treatment was reasonable and necessary?

A. Yes.

Q. She was not complaining of back pain six months prior to the fall, correct?

A. That is accurate.

Q. She did not see Dr. Patrick, who was the doctor administering the conservative therapy, for that entire period, correct?

A. That's correct.

Q. Did you see anything in the records that indicated Ms. Rose required a surgical fusion prior to the fall at Nickel & Dime?

A. No. Surgery was not considered a viable option at that time.

Q. You say that she had a bulge, not a herniation, on the 1998 MRI, but you do not attribute the herniation to the fall because the bulge is close to where the herniation occurs. Did you view the actual films?

A. No, I didn't look at the film. The radiologists are more reliable than I am, and I rely on their reports and descriptions.

Q. Did you review Dr. Patrick's records where he read the MRI?

A. Yes.

Q. He doesn't mention that there was an L4 nerve root compression, does he?

A. No, he doesn't. Dr. Patrick says that there is no compression seen on the film.

Q. In reviewing Dr. Beebe's surgery record and the MRI results of March 2000, did you notice that Dr. Beebe read the films, not the radiologist's records?

A. Yes.

Q. He notes that there is evidence of a lateral disk protrusion at L4-5 on the right. Is that what you're referring to when you say disk herniation?

A. Yes.

Q. Wouldn't you agree that a doctor who performs surgery on the herniated disk and reads the MRI film is better qualified to render an opinion about a bulge, herniation, or impingement on the nerve root rather than a doctor who simply reads the radiologist's report?

A. Dr. Beebe operated on the disk, but he didn't see it before the fall in question, and Dr. Patrick agreed with the radiologist's report. I don't think my opinions differ substantially from those of Dr. Beebe or Dr. Patrick except as to when and why the disk herniated and began to impinge on the nerve root, which is a matter of opinion because no one knows for sure.

Q. You've already mentioned that you agree that her low back pain got better prior to January 31, 2000, correct?

A. That's correct.

Q. Pain is not something you can judge, is it?

A. That is correct.

Q. Given Ms. Rose's condition up until January 2000, do you have an opinion as to whether or not she is someone who would be more susceptible to injuring her back than a normal person who did not have the back history she had?

A. Any time you have a previous injury, you're more susceptible to a secondary injury.

Q. Is a twisting injury to the back, in a woman with her history, more significant than falling on one's buttocks?

A. They are different kinds of injuries. If you land on your buttock, that's a flexion compression injury. You tend to get compression fractures, not disk herniations, with that injury. Twisting tends to affect the disk and the soft tissues more because the force is directed differently, so if you already have a weak spot and it is in the soft tissues, then the problem is going to be worse.

Q. A twisting injury might have more of an impact on someone with a pre-existing condition, correct?

MR. RICHARDS: Objection.

THE COURT: Overruled.

A. It depends on the spine. There are too many variables to say for sure.

Q. You indicated that after the fall in 2000 Ms. Rose's pain became worse?
A. It was more intense, although in the same places.

Q. It was more intense after the fall, correct?
A. She had trouble with it in 1998 after the fall where she injured her ankle but, according to her, it was more intense after she fell in 2000.

Q. Before she fell at Nickel & Dime, was she a surgical candidate, in your opinion?
A. Probably not. But, even without the fall at Nickel & Dime, I think her back would have eventually gotten worse and, if she didn't improve on conservative measures, she would have been reevaluated for surgery.

Q. You testified that the 2000 fall increased the intensity of pain, which pushed her into surgery.
A. I think it pushed her into seeing Dr. Beebe and making the decision, but some of it was because Dr. Patrick had previously discouraged surgery; whereas, Dr. Beebe said, "I can make you better."

Q. Does Dr. Beebe's report indicate that there is the risk that it could get worse?
A. Right. He told her that and must have explained the potential risks involved.

Q. Doctor, do you know what Dr. Beebe actually told her?
A No. I was not there, but I do know what's in the record. Ms. Rose said that the impression she was given was that Dr. Patrick told her she had a good chance of getting worse with surgery and not a very good chance of getting better. When she talked to Dr. Beebe, he gave her the impression that she would probably get better, although there was still a chance she could get worse.

Q. After the 2000 fall, was she back in bed?
A. Yes.

Q. Your opinion, Doctor, is that the fall at Nickel and Dime had an effect on her pre-existing condition, but the effects were minimal in terms of her overall condition, right?
A. That's right.

Q. You believe that the disk had already herniated before she fell at Nickel & Dime through a natural progression of her pre-existing degenerative disk disease, correct?
A. That's right.

Q. You disagree with Dr. Beebe and Dr. Patrick, correct?
A. Everyone has an opinion. I am sure there are many qualified medical practitioners who would agree with me and many who would agree with Dr. Beebe.

Q. But Dr. Beebe is a neurosurgeon and he performed the surgery, correct?
A. That is true, but it is still a matter of opinion. Dr. Beebe would not likely disagree with his own diagnosis. I am an independent medical practitioner offering my opinion on the subject.

Q. And you are being paid for your testimony?

MR. RICHARDS: Objection.

THE COURT: Overruled.

Q. Please tell this jury what you are being paid for your testimony.
A. My fee is $500 per hour for deposition or trial testimony, and $600 to conduct a medical examination and render a written report.

Q. And what percentage of your practice does this involve, Dr. Paul?
A. Ten percent.

Q. Every examination you perform is for the defendant in a lawsuit, correct?
A. Yes. Plaintiffs generally use the treating physicians to testify.

Q. A defense attorney is not likely to use you again if you render an unfavorable report, correct, Dr. Paul?

MR. RICHARDS: Objection.

THE COURT: Sustained.

MR. FRANKLIN: No further questions, Your Honor.

THE COURT: Any redirect examination, Mr. Richards?

MR. RICHARDS: No, your Honor.

THE COURT: Call your next witness.

MR. RICHARDS: The defense rests.

THE COURT: Ladies and gentlemen, we're going to recess for lunch. During this recess, you will be permitted to go about your separate and personal affairs. Do not discuss the case among yourselves or anyone else, and do not permit anyone to say anything to you about the case. Do not have a conversation with the parties, attorneys, or witnesses who have appeared or who are listed to appear in this case. Any additional instructions, Mr. Franklin?

MR. FRANKLIN: No, Your Honor.

THE COURT: Mr. Richards?

MR. RICHARDS: No, Your Honor.

THE COURT: We'll be in recess until 1:30. If you would, please return to the conference room at or by 1:30, and the bailiff will call for you when we're ready to proceed. Take our jurors out.

THE BAILIFF: All rise.

MR. RICHARDS: I would renew my motions at this point.

Motions at the Close of Defendant's Case-in-Chief

At the close of defendant's case, Alan made a Motion for Directed Verdict, arguing the same position, but suggesting that the standard of proof was different. When plaintiff rested, the court was required to make every reasonable inference in favor of the plaintiff. After the defense rested, the court could interpret the evidence without allowing favorable inferences to the plaintiff.

The court could not make any factual determinations on the evidence, but the judge could rule that the evidence was such that the only determination that a reasonable person would make on the evidence presented was that Scarlet Rose was negligent and Nickel & Dime was not. The judge denied the motion.

The plaintiff's attorney made a similar motion. He was asking the court to rule that it was the plaintiff who was entitled to the entry of a directed verdict because Nickel & Dime was negligent. It had violated its own internal stocking policy and should not have left the box unattended where Scarlet Rose could trip over it.

THE COURT: I'll deny your motions at this time.

Rebuttal Testimony

Plaintiff's Rebuttal Testimony

Plaintiff's attorney recalled Scarlet Rose to the witness stand to rebut, or deny, everything that Ms. Murphy and Ms. Palmer had said about where and how she fell. Before Ms. Rose took the witness stand, at a sidebar conference, which is a meeting that takes place at the bench, Alan argued that this would be improper rebuttal testimony because Ms. Rose had already told the jury her side of the case. The judge, however, allowed Scarlet Rose to testify.

THE COURT: Rebuttal?

MR. FRANKLIN: Your Honor, I would call Scarlet Rose as rebuttal.

THE COURT: I remind you, Ms. Rose, that you're still under oath.

Direct Examination by Mr. Franklin

Q. Ms. Rose, you heard testimony today about some statements that you allegedly made at the time of the fall in January 2000?
A. Correct.

Q. When you were on the floor or after you fell, did you tell the Nickel & Dime employees that you were trying to climb over the tote?
A. No, I did not.

Q. Were you trying to climb over the tote?
A. No, I never saw the tote.

Q. Were you in such a hurry on January 31, 2000, that you didn't pay attention to where you were going?
A. No, sir. I was just exchanging the shorts.

Q. Were you walking fast?
A. After you break an ankle, you don't walk fast and you pay attention to where you are going. I was looking up and ahead, not down.

MR. FRANKLIN: No further questions, Your Honor.

THE COURT: Cross?

MR. RICHARDS: No, Your Honor. No questions.

THE COURT: You may step down and have a seat. Next witness?

MR. FRANKLIN: No further rebuttal, Your Honor.

THE COURT: Ladies and gentlemen, at this time there are some matters that the court needs to discuss with the attorneys. The bailiff will take you to the conference room. If you want to go outside for a few minutes, you may do so, but I would ask that you return promptly. We will call for you as soon as we're ready to proceed. Please take the jurors out.

THE BAILIFF: All rise.

Motions at the Close of All Evidence

In the event that the case was appealed, the parties must preserve the argument that the evidence was legally insufficient. If the trial court had not been asked to rule upon the matter, then the party could not raise the issue on appeal; therefore, both attorneys made another Motion for a Directed Verdict, based on the evidence, but the motions were denied. The court told them that the case involved factual issues, which could only be decided by a jury.

THE COURT: I believe you still have your motions?

MR. RICHARDS: Yes, Your Honor.

THE COURT: Do you have any additional arguments?

MR. RICHARDS: I do, Your Honor. I cite the case of *Dixie v. Peters*. It says that the law is clear on two basic duties owed by a landowner to invitees. The first is to use reasonable care and to maintain the premises in a reasonably safe condition and to give the invitee warning of concealed perils that are or should be known to the landowner but are unknown to the invitee. In addition, some conditions are so open and obvious that they can be held, as a matter of law, not to constitute a hidden danger.

Our argument is that the placement of the tote, in the manner depicted by the photograph and the testimony given, is open and obvious and not a dangerous condition. The fact that the tote was left in the aisle did not cause the accident because it's an open and obvious condition, and the plaintiff should have seen and been aware of it.

The case of *Bennett v. Mart*, cited at 491 A.2d 1248, indicates that the store was not an insurer of the customer's safety but did have a duty to exercise ordinary care and to keep its aisles in a reasonably safe condition. This included eliminating dangerous conditions that it had actual or constructive notice. It's normal for retailers to restock their shelves using boxes in the walkways, so it's not negligence to have boxes out when people are restocking unless it constitutes a danger.

The conditions shown in the photographs illustrate an open and obvious condition. As a matter of law, liability does not exist when the act complained of falls on a sudden and unexpected action of the tortfeasor because there is no prior indication that the tortfeasor will engage in conduct that causes the injury. Nobody expected the plaintiff to walk down the aisle and get trapped in the tote.

The Supermarket v. Sanchez, cited at 22 *Atlantis Law Weekly* D 2173, involves a situation where the store had a demonstration table with small pieces of cake left out in the open. The store's internal policy says that somebody should be at that table at all times. At the time the plaintiff came along, nobody was at the table. The argument was that some cake had fallen onto the floor. The plaintiff slipped on the cake and fell. The plaintiff sued, claiming negligence. The court said defendant's demonstration table was not inherently dangerous, and even though the store violated its own internal rule, it didn't make the store negligent because the woman hurt herself.

In the *Olsen* case, 561 A.2d 319, the court holds that an owner is entitled to assume that the invitee perceives an open and obvious condition by using his or her own senses and is not required to give the invitee notice or warning of an obvious danger. If the Court were to say that it is dangerous to leave a box out in the open, the store wouldn't have to warn invitees of the dangerous condition because it is open and obvious.

Therefore, I move for a directed verdict at the close of plaintiff's case and a directed verdict at the close of my case. I submit that, as a matter of law, we are entitled to summary judgment because this is not a dangerous condition. It was an open and obvious condition, and Nickel & Dime isn't responsible for Ms. Rose's injury.

THE COURT: Mr. Franklin.

MR. FRANKLIN: The defense is basically saying that putting a tote in the middle of the aisle, where it's reasonably foreseeable that patrons will walk down, is not dangerous but an open and obvious condition, and they don't have a duty to warn anybody. The evidence in this case is that Nickel &

Dime had a policy that employees had to keep the totes close to them and never put them in the middle of an aisle.

The issue is that, by putting a tote in the middle of the aisle, a dangerous condition was created, and the defendant could have foreseen someone walking over it and getting injured. There's evidence in the record sufficient enough on that question to go to a jury.

The cases Mr. Richards discussed talk about the duty to warn in terms of an open and obvious condition. Usually those cases talk about something that can't be moved like a curb, stairway, or speed bump. These things are so open and obvious that a reasonable person should see it, and the defendant has no duty to warn the plaintiff, but that does not relieve the defendant from the obligation to maintain the premises in a reasonably safe condition.

I cite the case of *Marb v. Dixie Stores* at 472 A.2d 891. If the defendant had actual knowledge of a dangerous condition and failed to maintain the premises in a reasonably safe manner, then it would be inconsistent with the philosophy of *Hoffman v. Jones* to bar the plaintiff from recovery. The defense is trying to argue in their Motion for Directed Verdict that Ms. Rose's alleged comparative negligence of not seeing the condition is grounds for a directed verdict. That is not sufficient grounds for a directed verdict, and the jury has to decide, based upon the evidence, who is at fault.

I would also cite the case of *Bryant v. Lucky Stores*. In this case, the lower court rendered a summary judgment based upon the grounds that a speed bump was open and obvious, and the defendant had no duty to warn. The appellate court reversed the summary judgment and held that the fact that the bump was open and visible is not determinative of whether Ms. Bryant's negligence in failing to see the speed bump was the sole cause of her injury. The question is whether she used due care in her own safety, and it must be taken into consideration all of the relevant factors as to whether Ms. Bryant should have seen the speed bump.

There's clearly enough evidence in this record to allow the jury to consider whether the defendant's employees maintained their premises in a reasonably safe condition, whether there was a dangerous condition that they should have been aware of and corrected, and whether they had a duty to warn the plaintiff of the dangerous condition.

THE COURT: Any response, Mr. Richards?

MR. RICHARDS: As I said before, this is a negligence case, and we need to determine what the standard of negligence is for this department store as compared to what other reasonably prudent department stores would do under similar circumstances. I don't think there are facts in this record to say that Nickel & Dime deviated from the standard of care of all other department stores.

The second issue is whether or not Nickel & Dime maintained the store in a reasonably safe condition. We know that the box is three feet wide, two feet high and a foot deep and that it was in the middle of an aisle. Mr. Franklin makes the argument that it was in a walkway, but in a department store, everything is a walkway.

The final point I want to make is in response to the comparative negligence argument. It's my argument that, as a matter of law, the box did not cause the accident. The plaintiff walking into the box caused the accident. Before you apply the comparative negligence standard, you have to find negligence against Nickel & Dime and then decide whether or not Scarlet Rose was negligent. So, I think, on this record, we're entitled to a directed verdict. Thank you.

THE COURT: I'll deny your motion. Does the plaintiff wish to argue her motions or rely on the argument previously made?

MR. FRANKLIN: We will rely upon our prior argument, Your Honor.

THE COURT: Plaintiff's Motions for Directed Verdict are denied. This is a factual issue to be decided by the jury. So, we have some jury instructions to discuss.

Jury Instructions

THE COURT: Gentlemen, I have plaintiff's requested jury instructions, which I believe are from the standard jury instructions. Mr. Richards, please let me know whether or not you have any objections to these, as we go through them. I have the following:

2.1   the introductory instruction
2.2(a)   the believability of witnesses
2.2(b)   expert witness
3.1   standard instruction on the issue of duty to use reasonable care.

Mr. Richards, is there a question in this case about whether or not Ms. Rose was a business invitee? It seems to me that the preemptive charge covers that, correct?

MR. RICHARDS: Yes, Your Honor, it does. I have no objection to that instruction being given.

THE COURT: Then I have 3.5 negligence issues; it looks like that's the standard.

MR. FRANKLIN: Yes, Your Honor, it is.

THE COURT: I then have:

3.5(f)   the appropriate charge, duty of the landowner toward a business invitee
3.6   issues to legal cause and damages, standard
3.7   greater weight of the evidence and burden of proof, standard
3.8(a)   defense issues regarding comparative negligence on the part of the plaintiff, standard
3.9   greater weight of the evidence, standard
4.1   negligence defined, standard
5.1(a)   legal cause, standard
6.1(c)   comparative negligence, standard
6.2(a)   injury, pain, disability, disfigurement, loss of capacity for the enjoyment of life, standard
6.2(b)   aggravation of a pre-existing condition, standard
6.2(c)   medical expenses, standard
6.9(a)   personal injury, mortality tables, standard
6.10   reduction of damages to present value, standard
7.1   prejudice and sympathy, standard
7.2   election of the foreperson, standard
7.3   jury deadlock, standard.

Any other standard instructions, gentlemen?

MR. RICHARDS: Did you mention 6.3 on collateral source? It's the standard and says that you should not reduce the amount of compensation that the plaintiff is entitled to for wages, medical insurance payments, or other benefits that the plaintiff may have received from her employer, insurance company, or some other source, and the court will make any necessary reduction.

MR. FRANKLIN: I would ask Mr. Richards if we could give a medical record summary along with these instructions.

MR. RICHARDS: I have no problem with the medical bill summary.

THE COURT: I will give it. If there are no other standard jury instructions, that takes us to the defendant's special negligence. Do we need that since we have the standard on negligence?

MR. FRANKLIN: I would point out that the committee notes indicate that it's inappropriate to give an instruction on negligence if the standard is adequate, and I suggest it is.

THE COURT: We have an instruction that covers that, don't we, Mr. Richards?

MR. RICHARDS: This instruction states that the plaintiff must pay attention and notice open and obvious conditions. We don't have standard jury instructions that say what the law is in regard to the open and obvious condition. I think I need this instruction in order to argue to the jury the open and obvious issue.

MR. FRANKLIN: This is a simple case of negligence. The issue is whether or not Nickel & Dime and Scarlet Rose failed to exercise reasonable care, and I see no need for a special instruction.

THE COURT: Do any of these cases say that this instruction must be given?

MR. RICHARDS: No, but I suggest that the appellate opinions indicate that the instruction should be given if the trial court believes it is an accurate statement of the law and that it will help a jury understand the issues better.

THE COURT: I'm going to give defendant the specially requested instruction. How about the verdict form?

MR. FRANKLIN: I think that there are some changes to be made. The aggravation pre-existing instruction says that, if the jury cannot separate the pre-existing condition from the aggravation, they have to award all the conditions. However, if they can separate it, then they can apportion damages. I think number eight was our attempt to try to deal with the total damages and ask the jury to apportion what they are attributing to a pre-existing condition versus an aggravation.

MR. RICHARDS: Mr. Franklin wants to put down the amount in terms of money, and I wanted it in terms of percentage. I would like a percentage rather than an amount on what was the pre-existing problem and what was the aggravation problem because the evidence indicates that the cost of the surgery was the aggravation.

THE COURT: My secretary will make the necessary change. We'll leave in the dollar amount and let the jury determine the amount instead of using percentages.

MR. FRANKLIN: We have agreed on everything else, and here it is for your approval.

Form 12.1 — Verdict Form

IN THE CIRCUIT COURT OF THE SIXTH
JUDICIAL CIRCUIT IN AND FOR
PINEAPPLE COUNTY, ATLANTIS

SCARLET ROSE,
Plaintiff,

v.   Case No. 00-125-PDD

NICKEL & DIME, INC.,
Defendant.

Verdict

WE, THE JURY, return the following verdict:

Question no. 1: Was there negligence on the part of the defendant, Nickel & Dime, Inc., which was a legal cause of loss, injury, or damage to the plaintiff, Scarlet Rose?
___YES
___NO

If your answer to question no. 1 is "NO," your verdict is for the defendant, and you date and sign this verdict form and return it to the courtroom. If your answer to question 1 is "YES," please answer Question no. 2.

Question no. 2: Was there negligence on the part of the plaintiff, Scarlet Rose, which was the legal cause of her injury or damage?
___YES
___NO

If your answer to question no. 2 is "NO," then put "100%" next to the defendant, Nickel & Dime, Inc., in Question no. 3 and proceed to answer Question no. 4. If your answer to Question no. 2 is "YES," then answer Question no. 3.

Question no. 3: State the percentage of any negligence that was the legal cause of the loss, injury or damage to the plaintiff that you charge to:

Defendant, Nickel & Dime, Inc.   ____%
Plaintiff, Scarlet Rose   ____%
Total must be 100%

Question no. 4: What is the amount of any damages sustained for medical expenses in the past?
$_____

Question no. 5: What is the amount of any future damages for medical expenses?
$_____

Question no. 6.: What is the amount of any damages for pain and suffering, mental anguish, inconvenience, or loss of capacity for the enjoyment of life in the past.

$_____

Question no. 7: Total Damages of Scarlet Rose (add lines 4, 5 and 6)

$_____

Question no. 8: Please state the amount of the medical damages sustained by Scarlet Rose that you attribute to a medical condition that preexisted the incident complained of.

$_____

SO SAY WE ALL, this ___day of July, 2000.

_____
FOREMAN/FOREWOMAN

THE COURT: This verdict form is acceptable to the Court.

Allotting Time for the Closing Arguments

THE COURT: How much time do you need for closing? 20 minutes per side?

MR. RICHARDS: Yes, Your Honor, that's fine with me.

MR. FRANKLIN: I need more than that, your Honor.

THE COURT: 25 minutes?

MR. FRANKLIN: At least 30 minutes.

THE COURT: Okay. 30 minutes. Mr. Franklin, you'll have the opening and closing.

MR. FRANKLIN: If the Court could let me know when I have reached 20 minutes, I would appreciate it, because I'd like to reserve about ten minutes for rebuttal.

THE COURT: We'll take a ten-minute break and go straight to closing arguments.

Chapter Thirteen

CLOSING ARGUMENTS, JURY DELIBERATIONS, AND THE VERDICT

Closing Arguments

The attorneys' final summations remained. Most attorneys think that a case is won or lost during closing arguments. Some think that the attorney who is the last to speak has the best opportunity to persuade the jury to vote in his or her client's favor.

THE COURT: Please bring back the jury.

THE BAILIFF: All rise.

Instructions by the Court Prior to Closing Arguments by the Attorneys

THE COURT: Let the record reflect that the jury has returned to the jury box and each juror is in his or her proper seat. Please be seated.

Ladies and gentlemen of the jury, both the plaintiff and the defense have rested their case. At this time, the attorneys will present to you their final arguments. Please remember that you should not consider what the attorneys say as evidence. Closing arguments are intended to assist you in understanding the issues of the case, so listen closely to their arguments.

Under the rule, each side has equal time. First, Mr. Franklin will address you on behalf of Ms. Rose, then Mr. Richard will address you on behalf of Nickel & Dime followed by a short rebuttal from Mr. Franklin. Mr. Franklin.

Closing Argument by Plaintiff's Attorney

MR. FRANKLIN: Thank you, your Honor. May it please the Court. Ladies and gentlemen of the jury, I want to thank you for your service. You have heard a lot of testimony but, basically, you are concerned with two issues in this case. The first issue is who is responsible for the fall, and the second issue is what injury and damage did Ms. Rose sustain as a result of the fall.

In this case, Scarlet Rose alleges that Nickel & Dime was negligent and caused her injury and damage. The judge will instruct you that negligence is defined as "the failure to use reasonable care." "Reasonable care" is the degree of care that a reasonable person would use under similar circumstances. Negligence occurs when a person fails to do something or does something that a reasonable person would or would not do under similar circumstances.

As to the issue of liability or who is responsible for the fall, the testimony you've heard is undisputed. The tote was in the middle of the aisle and caused Ms. Rose to fall. You heard testimony from a number of Nickel & Dime employees that the store had a policy to bring totes onto the floor when stocking items, but they were to keep totes close to them so that customers and employees wouldn't step on or trip over them. You also heard that they were not to put totes in the middle of walkways.

This picture was taken by Marjorie Murphy just minutes after the incident. There is no question that it shows a walkway, and a tote is in the middle of the walkway. So, when you decide the issue of who is responsible for this accident, I would ask you to remember what the standard of negligence is and what a reasonable person would do under similar circumstances. Is it reasonable for a person to place a tote, a box of this size, in the middle of a walkway where it's foreseeable that someone might walk down that aisle? We ask you to find that it was not reasonable to leave the tote in the middle of the aisle unattended, and Nickel & Dime was negligent.

You are going to be asked to decide what responsibility Ms. Rose must bear for this accident. You will be instructed that Ms. Rose should have exercised reasonable caution. You heard testimony that, after she fell, Ms. Rose told some employees that she was in a hurry to get to the bathroom and tried to walk over the tote. In addition, you heard about Ms. Rose's prior ankle and back problems.

Ladies and gentlemen, you will have to decide who and what to believe. Is it reasonable to expect that Ms. Rose would climb over a tote in order to get to the bathroom when she had these prior physical problems? Ms. Rose testified that she did not see the tote. She told you that she was walking down the aisle and, in the middle of the aisle, there were racks that made it difficult for her to walk past. She decided to walk through another department. She turned and fell into the tote. We suggest to you that what Ms. Rose did was reasonable, and she was not negligent.

As far as damages and what happened after the fall, the evidence shows that Ms. Rose had pre-existing ankle and back problems. We have not suggested to you that she didn't have these problems before the incident; however, when she fell in Nickel & Dime, she was asymptomatic. You're going to be asked to decide whether Ms. Rose's medical problems, specifically her back surgery, were caused, as a matter of law, by the negligence of Nickel & Dime.

You will be instructed to decide if Nickel & Dime's negligence was the legal cause of Ms. Rose's loss or damages. Legal cause exists when negligence, in a natural and continuous sequence, directly produces or contributes substantially to produce such loss, injury or damage so that it can be reasonably said that but for the negligence the loss, injury or damage would not have occurred, which is or may be an aggravation of a pre-existing condition. The judge will instruct you that, when you are trying to apportion the pre-existing problem with the aggravation of that problem, you must make allowances for her condition and how it was aggravated.

If you are unable to distinguish her preexisting problems from the problems that resulted from the incident and you find Nickel & Dime legally responsible for the incident, then you must award all medical problems, conditions, and damages against Nickel & Dime. The primary issue is, would Ms. Rose have had back surgery if this incident hadn't occurred? We suggest to you that the answer to that question is "no," because that is what Dr. Beebe and Scarlet Rose told you.

Ms. Rose's special damages are $50,000. This figure includes lost wages and the actual financial damages. It does not include the pain and suffering that Ms. Rose endured or will endure for the rest of her life. She has two rods in her spine and was told to see an orthopedic specialist once a year for the rest of her life. She is doing well now, but no one knows what the future holds. There is anxiety and uncertainty about her health and future because of the negligence of Nickel & Dime.

When one thinks about justice, the most common symbol is the blindfolded lady holding the scales of justice. She determines whether the plaintiff or defendant places more weight on the scales. Ms. Rose must prove her case by a preponderance of the evidence, which means that the scales tip slightly in favor of one party and against the other. On behalf of Scarlet Rose, I submit that there is substantially more weight on Scarlet Rose's scales, and we ask you to return a verdict in her favor of $250,000. I thank you for your careful consideration.

THE COURT: Mr. Richards.

Closing Argument by Defendant's Attorney

MR. RICHARDS: May it please the Court. Ladies and gentlemen of the jury, both Nickel & Dime and Scarlet Rose come before you to ask for justice. None of you knew anything about Scarlet Rose before you came to court on Monday, nor did you have any feelings about Nickel & Dime that would affect the way you decide this case. You will weigh the evidence and do the job the best you can. All that we can ask for is a fair and impartial jury and, on behalf of Nickel & Dime, we thank you for your time and attention, and for being a fair and impartial jury.

Your job is not an easy one. Somebody is going to go home happy, and somebody is going to be disappointed. You are the ones who will decide who that will be. As Mr. Franklin stated, this case involves two issues, who is responsible and what happened as a result. Basically, that involves liability and damages.

There is a conflict in the testimony with regard to what Ms. Rose said and what the employees testified to, but the single most important piece of evidence in this case is the photograph that was taken five to ten minutes after the incident occurred. Look at this tote. It is one foot deep, by two feet high, by one foot wide. Somehow Ms. Rose got stuck in there. How did that happen? We know that she was walking down the main aisle, which is approximately six feet wide. Mr. Franklin says she made a left-hand turn and somehow she fell into the tote. If she were paying attention, she would be looking ahead. Where was she looking? Where does any reasonable person look when he or she is walking down an aisle at a department store? Is she looking ahead? Is she looking down? Is she looking at the merchandise on the racks? Or is she not paying any attention to where she is going because she is in a hurry to use the restroom?

On behalf of Nickel & Dime, we suggest that the only reason this incident occurred was because Ms. Rose wasn't paying attention to where she was walking. The judge will instruct you that a person has a duty to watch out for himself or herself and to act in a reasonably safe fashion. For Nickel & Dime to be negligent, it must have created a dangerous condition. To return a verdict against Nickel & Dime, you must find that the tote in the aisle was an unsafe condition. Nickel & Dime suggests to you that it was not a dangerous condition, and it was not negligent for a tote to be in the aisle when a sales clerk restocks the shelves.

Mr. Franklin told you that Nickel & Dime was negligent by violating its standard of care and proper procedure. You heard five or six former and current Nickel & Dime employees talk about this incident and tell you about the policy and procedure for restocking shelves. Every department store must restock their items, bring boxes onto the floor, and get their items out of the boxes onto the shelves. Where is the evidence that Nickel & Dime did something that a reasonably prudent department store would not have done? There was none. We submit that Nickel & Dime didn't do anything different from other department stores and was not negligent in this case.

Nickel & Dime has a duty to do the best it can in a reasonable manner. Nickel & Dime's position is that its employees were doing their jobs. They were stocking items in a way that reasonably prudent department store owners would. Carol Westwoman, an employee who was stocking a shelf, was within a few yards of where the incident occurred. A supervisor was standing nearby and would have seen if something were wrong and done something about it. This was not a dangerous condition or a violation of a standard of care. This was an open and obvious condition, and the plaintiff is responsible for what happened.

You will be given a verdict form to take with you when you retire to deliberate. After you elect a foreperson, you will need to answer the first question on the verdict, which is, do you find that Nickel & Dime was negligent in this matter? If you answer "no," you come back from the jury room, return your verdict, and the trial is over.

If you find that Nickel & Dime was negligent in some fashion, then you must decide if Scarlet Rose is responsible. If you do, then you must decide what percentage of responsibility to attribute to Nickel & Dime and what percentage of responsibility to attribute to Scarlet Rose. That's the liability aspect of the case. We suggest that Scarlet Rose was entirely responsible for this incident but, if you decide otherwise, we ask that you find Scarlet Rose primarily responsible for this incident.

As for the damages portion of the case, you must decide what damages resulted from this accident. I think it's important not to lose sight of the fact that this incident involved her scraping her leg after she hit the one-foot-by-two-feet tote and got her knees stuck in there. There was no fall. She said she pulled a rack down, although no one saw the rack, and people helped her out of the tote. She got on the floor and went to the hospital. Did this cause her to have surgery involving the insertion of two rods in her spine to stabilize a destabilized situation? On behalf of Nickel & Dime, I would suggest to you that it did not.

Ms. Rose had a pre-existing back problem. Although it was not bothering her as much as it had in 1998, she had been having chronic pain and difficulty in ambulation from her left ankle and back. The question is, was her back worse after the incident at Nickel & Dime? You heard Dr. Paul's and Dr. Beebe's testimony. Dr. Paul testified that 95 to 100% of Ms. Rose's back problems pre-existed the fall at Nickel & Dime. From an objective medical point of view, Dr. Beebe was unable to determine for certain if the herniated disc, which he found on the MRI, occurred as a result of the fall at Nickel & Dime. If Ms. Rose had seen Dr. Beebe prior to the incident, would he have operated on her? If you think so, then the surgery is not the result of the incident at Nickel & Dime.

In conclusion, you must now decide who is at fault and assess the damages. Because Ms. Rose had back problems prior to the incident on January 31, 2000, and would have probably needed surgery anyway, Nickel & Dime asks that you not find it legally or financially responsible for Scarlet Rose's claim for money damages. Thank you.

Plaintiff's Rebuttal of Defendant's Closing Argument

THE COURT: Mr. Franklin, you have ten minutes.

MR. FRANKLIN: This is my opportunity to rebut Mr. Richards' closing argument. The defense would have you believe that Dr. Beebe said Ms. Rose's back condition was the same as it was prior to the incident at Nickel & Dime. That is inaccurate. Dr. Beebe testified that, based on a reasonable degree of medical probability; Ms. Rose aggravated a pre-existing condition in the fall. He described it as a twisting fall.

Remember Ms. Rose's description of how she grabbed the rack and pulled it down as she fell? The mechanics of the fall are important. Before the fall, she had never been recommended for back surgery. Dr. Beebe said that a severe twisting injury caused or necessitated the surgery. He reviewed the prior MRI and told you that what he saw was different. He attributed his inability to be certain as to whether the condition preexisted to the poor quality of the MRI but, in his opinion, there is a greater than 50 percent chance, which is the standard of proof in this case, that she aggravated a pre-existing condition. The defense failed to provide any competent medical evidence that the fall did not aggravate a pre-existing condition. Ms. Rose suffered as a result of the fall and has $50,000 in special damages in addition to pain and suffering.

As to the liability aspect in this case, Ms. Rose never told you that she was trying to climb over the tote. She said she didn't see it. How would she get an abrasion on her shins if she saw the tote and tried to climb over it? She didn't see it. More importantly, was it high enough to see? Is it reasonable for a store to put boxes like this in the middle of a walkway? Employees told you it wasn't. They told you that it was against policy to put them in the middle of the aisle. Where was Carol Westwoman, who was supposed to be standing less than three feet away? She didn't testify before you. Was she negligent? You bet she was. Did that cause Ms. Rose to aggravate her back condition and require surgery? You bet it did.

On behalf of Scarlet Rose, I submit that the preponderance of the evidence in this case overwhelmingly establishes that Nickel & Dime was negligent and that Ms. Rose was injured as a result of that negligence. Preponderance of the evidence does not mean absolute certainty. It means that if the weight of the evidence, considered as a whole, tends to prove her case, then you have to return a verdict for Ms. Rose.

You're going to be instructed on apportioning or determining what her pre-existing condition was and how that relates to the damages she incurred as a result of the incident at Nickel & Dime. You will take back to the jury room a list of all the medical bills, which total $50,000. The majority of those bills are related to the surgery. When you ask yourself what Ms. Rose's condition was prior to the incident and how it was aggravated in the fall, ask what treatment did she have to go through as a result of that fall in 1998. Not surgery! The surgery, the $50,000 in special damages, and all the past and future pain and suffering are a result of Nickel & Dime's negligence.

THE COURT: You have two minutes remaining.

MR. FRANKLIN: Thank you, Your Honor. Mr. Richards has repeatedly mentioned the size of the tote and said it was an open and obvious condition and that Ms. Rose is responsible for the fall. When you look at the evidence, ladies and gentlemen, please remember that Scarlet was a patron, a customer at Nickel & Dime. The aisles were crowded, and there were items on display that distracted customers from looking at the floor. Ask yourself was it reasonable for the defendant to put that box in the middle of the walkway.

After you have decided that it was negligence on the part of Nickel & Dime, on behalf of Scarlet Rose, I ask that you return a verdict in her favor of $250,000—$50,000 for her special damages, or monetary damages, $50,000 for future damages, and $150,000 for the pain and suffering she has experienced and will continue to experience for the rest of her life as a result of this unfortunate incident.

I thank you, again, for your careful attention to the facts of this case and the applicable law, which Judge Doherty is about to instruct you. Because of your efforts and the efforts of fellow citizens just like you, our judicial system is the best in the world.

Jury Deliberations

Instructions by the Court

It was time for Judge Doherty to give the jury the instructions. To make sure the judge read the jury instructions correctly, Marlene and Chris followed the instructions as the judge read them. The court reporter took down what was said, but if a mistake was made and caught in time, it could be corrected. No one wanted to retry a case because of a minor technicality.

THE COURT: Ladies and gentlemen of the jury, I will now instruct you on the law in deciding this case. The evidence in this case consisted of sworn testimony by witnesses, exhibits received into evidence, facts that may have been admitted or agreed to by the parties, and any fact of which the court has taken judicial notice.

In determining the facts, you may draw reasonable inferences from the evidence, but you should not speculate on any matters outside the evidence.

In determining the believability of a witness and the weight to give the testimony, you may consider the demeanor of the witness, the frankness or lack of frankness, intelligence, any interest the witness may have in the outcome of the case, the means and opportunity the witness had to know the facts, the memory of the witness, and the reasonableness of the testimony.

You have heard testimony from expert witnesses on technical subjects. Some of the testimony was in the form of opinions. You may accept this testimony, reject it or give it the weight you think it deserves considering the knowledge, skill, experience, training or education of the witness, and the reasons given by the witness for the opinion expressed.

The court has determined and instructs you, as a matter of law, that Nickel & Dime, Inc., had a duty to use reasonable care for Scarlet Rose's safety. The issues for you to determine on the claim of Scarlet Rose, the plaintiff, against the defendant, Nickel & Dime, Inc., are whether the defendant negligently failed to maintain its premises in a reasonably safe condition, failed to correct a dangerous condition that the defendant knew of or should have known about, or failed to warn the plaintiff of a dangerous condition that the defendant had or should have had knowledge greater than the plaintiff. There is no duty to warn a patron against blatant or obvious conditions that are not dangerous per se. A patron is under a corresponding duty to exercise reasonable care for his or her own safety and to observe the obvious.

To constitute a hidden danger, it must be hidden from knowledge or sight, and could not be discovered by using reasonable care. If the greater weight of the evidence does not support the claim of the plaintiff, then your verdict should be for the defendant.

If, however, the greater weight of the evidence does support the claim of the plaintiff, then you should consider the defenses raised by the defendant. The first issue of defense for your determination is whether the plaintiff, Scarlet Rose, was negligent and, if so, whether the negligence was a contributing legal cause of the injury or damage.

If the greater weight of the evidence does not support the defense of the defendant, then your verdict should be for the plaintiff and the total amount of her damages. If the greater weight of the evidence shows that both plaintiff and defendant were negligent, you should determine the percentage of the total negligence of each party.

"Greater weight of the evidence" means the more persuasive, convincing force and effect of the entire evidence in the case. "Negligence" is the failure to use reasonable care. "Reasonable care" is that degree of care that a reasonably careful person would use under similar circumstances.

Negligence may constitute either doing something that a reasonably careful person would not do under like circumstances, or failing to do something that a reasonably careful person would do under like circumstances. Negligence is a legal cause of loss, injury or damage if it directly and in natural and continuous sequence produces or contributes substantially to producing the loss, injury, or damage, it can reasonably be said that but for the negligence the loss, injury or damage would not have occurred.

If your verdict is for the defendant, you will not consider the matter of damages but, if you find for the plaintiff, you should determine the total amount of loss, injury or damage that the greater weight of the evidence shows she sustained as a result of the incident, including any damage that the plaintiff may experience in the future. The court will enter a judgment based on your verdict.

If you find that the plaintiff was negligent in any degree, the Court, in entering judgment, will reduce the total amount of damages by the percentage of negligence that you find chargeable to the plaintiff, Scarlet Rose.

You shall consider the following elements of damages: pain and suffering, disability or physical impairment, disfigurement, mental anguish, and inconvenience or loss of capacity for the enjoyment of life experienced in the past or to be experienced in the future. There is no exact standard for measuring these damages. The amount should be fair and just in light of the evidence.

If you find the injury aggravated a pre-existing disease or physical defect, you should determine what portion of the plaintiff's condition resulted from the aggravation and make allowance in your verdict only for the aggravation. But if you cannot make the determination, or it cannot be said that the condition would have existed apart from the injury, you should consider and make an allowance in your verdict for the entire condition.

You should not reduce the amount of compensation the plaintiff is entitled to on account of any other benefits that the evidence shows the plaintiff received from any other sources. The court will reduce, as necessary, the amount of compensation the plaintiff is entitled to on account of these payments.

Your verdict must be based on the evidence that has been received and on the law that I have instructed you. In reaching your verdict, you are not to be swayed by prejudice, sympathy or any other sentiment for or against the parties.

When you retire to the jury room, select someone to act as the foreperson to preside over your deliberations and to sign your verdict. Your verdict must be unanimous. You will be given one form of verdict. Has the plaintiff reviewed the proposed verdict?

MR. FRANKLIN: Yes, Your Honor, and it is acceptable.

THE COURT: Mr. Richards?

MR. RICHARDS: Yes, Your Honor, it is acceptable to the defendant.

THE COURT: You have one verdict form that is three pages in length. I instruct you to read the instructions, follow the instructions and answer the appropriate questions carefully. After you have reached your verdict, on the third page, there is a place for your foreperson to sign and date. Any additional instructions or corrections by the plaintiff?

MR. FRANKLIN: No, Your Honor.

THE COURT: By the defense?

MR. RICHARDS: No, Your Honor.

THE COURT: At this time, I will send you a review of the items that have been admitted into evidence. During your deliberations, if you have any questions or any problems, please reduce them to writing and notify the bailiff.

You may now retire to deliberate your verdict.

Mr. Bailiff, please take the jury to the jury room.

The Jury Retires

At 4 p.m., the bailiff escorted the jury, except for the alternate juror, into the jury room. The bailiff gave them the evidence that had been received by the clerk and the verdict form. When the jury left the room, Judge Doherty told the alternate juror, Ms. Ashley, that she was free to leave and thanked her for her service to the community and legal system. He told her that, after the verdict was returned, she could discuss the case with anyone.

The Verdict

By 6 p.m., the jury had reached a verdict. The bailiff informed the court, and the court instructed the bailiff to bring the jury back into the courtroom.

The bailiff brought the jury back into the courtroom, and the judge asked if the jury had reached a verdict. The foreperson stood up and said, "Yes, we have, Your Honor."

The judge asked the bailiff to give the verdict form to the clerk, who read the verdict, word for word. The jury returned a verdict of either:
1. $250,000 in favor of the plaintiff, finding plaintiff to be 50% negligent
2. In favor of the defendant, with plaintiff 100% negligent

3. $250,000 in favor of plaintiff, finding Nickel & Dime to be 100% negligent
4. Other.

Learning the Verdict

THE BAILIFF: All rise. You may be seated.

THE COURT: Let the record reflect that the jury has returned to the jury box and each juror is in his or her proper seat. Ladies and gentlemen of the jury, have you reached your verdict?

MR. PUMPERNICKEL: Yes, sir.

THE COURT: Would you hand it to the bailiff who will deliver it to the court.

The clerk will publish the verdict.

THE CLERK: *Scarlet Rose v. Nickel & Dime, Inc.*, case number 00-125: We, the jury, return the following verdict:

Question no. 1. Was there negligence on the part of the defendant, Nickel & Dime, Inc., that was a legal cause of the loss, injury or damage to the plaintiff, Scarlet Rose?
Answer: *[The verdict is to be decided by the class.]*

Author's note: At this point in the class, I suggest instructors have the class vote, just as a jury would vote, to determine the outcome. I would appreciate it if the results were sent to the publisher at 9614 Greenville Avenue, Dallas, Texas, 75243.

Polling the Jury

After the verdict was read, the judge asked the attorneys if either attorney wanted the jury polled. Both said yes. The judge proceeded to ask each juror if that was his or her verdict, and each replied that it was.

THE COURT: Counsel, would you like the jury polled?

COUNSEL: Yes, Your Honor.

THE COURT: Ms. Snark, is this your verdict?

MS. SNARK: Yes, sir.

THE COURT: Mr. Flynnsky, is this your verdict?

MR. FLYNNSKY: Yes, Your Honor.

THE COURT: Ms. Elizabeth, is this your verdict?

MS. ELIZABETH: Yes, sir.

THE COURT: Mr. Pumpernickel, is this your verdict?

MR. PUMPERNICKEL: Yes, sir.

THE COURT: Mr. Christian, is this your verdict?

MR. CHRISTIAN: Yes, sir.

THE COURT: Ms. Bardsley, is this your verdict?

Ms. BARDSLEY: Yes, sir.

THE COURT: Ladies and gentlemen of the jury, I wish to thank you for the time and consideration that you've given to this case. I also wish to advise you of a special privilege enjoyed by jurors. Although you are at liberty to speak to anyone about your deliberations, no juror can ever be required to talk about the discussions that occurred in the jury room except on court order. A request may come from those who are simply curious or from those who might seek to find fault with you, and it will be up to you to decide whether or not to preserve your right to privacy as a juror. Any additional instructions before we discharge our jury panel?

MR. FRANKLIN: No, Your Honor.

MR. RICHARDS: No, Your Honor.

THE COURT: Again, ladies and gentlemen of the jury, we thank you for your time, your patience and your service to our judicial system. You are now discharged from this case. Would you take our jurors out, Mr. Bailiff, and see that they are escorted out of the building to their vehicles, please.

THE BAILIFF: All rise. [The bailiff escorts the jurors from the courtroom]

THE COURT: Gentlemen, this trial is now concluded pending post-trial motions and other matters, which you can schedule with my judicial assistant. I compliment both of the attorneys for representing their respective clients, presenting the case to this jury in a professional and competent fashion and for the courtesies displayed to each other, as well as the court and all court personnel. At this point, we are adjourned.

Chapter Fourteen

POST-TRIAL MOTIONS

Depending on the verdict, either side might wish to seek further relief from the court. Before either side can initiate an appeal, several actions must take place. Following is a list of some of the post-trial motions that can be filed after the trial is concluded and other activity that will occur, regardless of the outcome.

Motion for Taxation of Costs

Cost is an issue that arises in every lawsuit that goes to trial. An Atlantis statute provides for the imposition of costs upon the nonprevailing party. This rule takes effect regardless and independent of the proposal for settlement rule and statute. Not all costs are recoverable. Some costs are awarded at the discretion of the trial judge. There are guidelines for the enforcement of costs, which are found in the Atlantis rules of civil procedure.

Motion to Tax Attorney's Fees

In general, unless there is a contract or a statute that provides for attorneys' fees to the prevailing party, attorneys' fees are not recoverable. In the case of *Scarlet Rose v. Nickel & Dime*, there was neither a contract nor a statute providing for attorneys' fees; therefore, attorneys' fees could only be recovered if either party were entitled to fees based upon the offer of judgment statute or rule regarding proposals for settlement.

Proposal for Settlement or Offer of Judgment

Depending on what verdict the class returned, one party could be entitled to recovery of attorneys' fees. The rule and statute reflect the procedure to be followed. The original of the proposal for settlement would be filed with the court only if the outcome of the trial permitted recovery by either side. The attorney for the prevailing party would, unless an agreement is reached, schedule a hearing before the court upon a motion for attorneys' fees.

Motion for Attorneys' Fees

If a verdict is returned that is within 25% of what either side offered, one party may be entitled to attorneys' fees, based on the offer of judgment statute and the proposal for settlement rule. Unless a settlement can be reached, the attorney seeking fees will prepare an itemization of hours expended, include his or her hourly rate, and request an award of fees. Both parties may be required to retain an attorney as an expert witness to testify to the reasonableness and necessity of the amount of the attorneys' fees.

In general, the opposing party will not agree to the total fee amount or the hourly fee sought nor will it agree that all the legal activities undertaken were reasonable and proper. If Scarlet Rose prevails, her attorney will ask the court for a "multiplier." Since the case was accepted on a contingency fee basis, the fee should be increased because of the uncertainty of the outcome. Because the defense is not seeking anything from the other side, the defense is never entitled to a multiplier unless the defendant has filed a counterclaim, in which case the defendant might be entitled to a multiplier.

Generally, the plaintiff will seek a multiplier of 2.5 to 3, and the defense will try to keep the multiplier at zero to 1.5. In *Scarlet Rose v. Nickel & Dime*, only Bruce can recover a fee and a multiplier. Alan could not obtain an increased fee, but he could recover, for his client, the amount of fees paid to his firm after the time the proposal for settlement was effective. The defense would vigorously argue that a multiplier is inappropriate in this type of case.

The prevailing party will ultimately obtain an order from the court awarding fees. The order says fees or costs are subject to appellate review as well as the verdict from the trial.

Motion for New Trial

Before an appeal is filed, the party initiating the appeal generally files a motion for new trial. The motion is based on the grounds that the court or the jury erred before or during the trial. Although there are many ways that a judge can err, unless there is juror misconduct, a jury can err only in its verdict. If the verdict is erroneous, as a matter of law, because the evidence is legally insufficient, which is determined by the trial judge or the appellate court, to support the verdict, than the verdict will be overturned.

If a motion for new trial is not filed, it can affect issues that could be raised on appeal. The theory behind the rule is that the lower court, or trial court, should be given the opportunity to correct an error before an appellate court reverses the judgment.

The losing party will assert that the court's error was so significant that it deprived the party of a fair trial. The court can err by admitting facts into evidence, failing to prevent an attorney from making improper comments to the jury, failure to grant motions at any stage of the proceeding, or if the judge makes improper comments during the trial.

Two of the most frequent grounds for appeal are improper argument of counsel and the instructions that were given to the jury before the jury deliberated. However, a party must object to the action or inaction of the court that is the basis for the motion for new trial *when the incident or event occurs*. Failure to do so is generally seen as a waiver of the right to complain.

Motion for Entry of Judgment Not Withstanding the Verdict

The motion for judgment *non obstante veredicto* requests the trial judge to overturn and reverse the jury's verdict. If a judge is convinced that the evidence is lacking and the verdict is wrong, the motion is granted. A trial judge usually allows an appellate court to make this determination instead of substituting his or her view for the jury's.

To file this motion, the advancing party must have made this argument at all stages of the trial and at the close of the case. Otherwise the argument will not be properly preserved, and the party will be prevented from making the argument on appeal.

Motion to Allow Post-Trial Questioning of Jurors

When jurors are excused, the court will tell the jurors, as Judge Doherty did in this case, that they may choose whether to talk with anyone about the case. Some attorneys will file a motion requesting permission to interview a juror. If an attorney has a reason to believe there may have been juror misconduct, the motion would be filed, and a hearing would be scheduled. Either attorney would attempt to talk to jurors informally before filing a motion.

Motion for Addittur or Remitittur

It is the province, or power, of the jury to determine liability and the amount awarded, but if a jury makes a mistake and awards too much or too little, the court has the power to correct the verdict or judgment. Either the court adds to the judgment, "addittur," or reduces the judgment, "remitittur."

Motion for Bond Pending Appeal

Before an appeal can be filed with the clerk's office in the appellate court, a court may require a bond to be posted with the clerk of the county in which the trial took place, if the court requires the appellant to post a bond, as is usually done. This bond is called a "supersedeas bond." There are specific guidelines in determining the amount of the bond. The party seeking the appeal will typically seek a bondsmaker to post the bond. A bondsmaker generally charges 10% of the verdict as a fee and requires some collateral.

Continued Negotiations

At any stage in the proceedings, the parties can agree to settle. Either side can agree to waive his/her right to appeal in exchange for a lesser payment or the waiver of attorney's fees or costs. It is almost always the client's decision, but when the attorney's fee is the sole issue, the attorney may decide whether to settle a case without consulting the client. In most cases, the court will retain jurisdiction over a civil matter to enforce a settlement.

Post-Trial Report

A defense attorney will be required to submit a complete report on the trial regardless of the outcome, even if a representative attended the trial. The following is an outline of such a report.

1. Trial Result
   a. Expected? If not, why not?
   b. Discussions with the judge/jury, if applicable.

2. Evaluation of result
   a. Evaluation of judge/jury
   b. Evaluation of experts
   c. Evaluation of favorable evidence
   d. Evaluation of unfavorable evidence
   e. Potential for appeal
   f. Recommend motion for new trial/remittur or settlement?
   g. Appealable error/issues
   h. Pros/cons and evaluation of probabilities for success of appeal

    i.   Estimated expenses to appeal

    j.   Present settlement recommendations.

Recording Judgment

Even though the verdict has been reduced to judgment and the judge has signed the order, the judgment cannot be enforced until the prevailing party's attorney "records the judgment." Recording is accomplished by obtaining a certified copy of the judgment from the civil division of the clerk's office and filing it at the real property division of the clerk's office. The certified judgment is officially recorded when it is placed in the official court records and is given a folio and page number, but the judgment cannot be enforced until the time for filing an appeal has expired.

Motion to Set Aside Judgment

In some circumstances, after an appeal has been filed, concluded, or is pending, the court may set aside the judgment. The motion must be filed as soon as the legal reasons are discovered, or a party will have waived the opportunity to challenge a judgment. By rule, there are circumstances under which this motion can be filed. They usually involve allegations of fraud, newly discovered evidence that was withheld by the other side, or other grievous matters.

Motion to Stay Execution if Judgment Pending Appeal

If an appeal is taken, normally a defendant must request a stay of execution of the judgment and post a supersedeas bond in the amount of the judgment was discussed above. Once the judgment is recorded, it could be enforced; therefore, a defendant who wishes to appeal an adverse verdict will seek an order from the court preventing the judgment from being enforced until after the appeal is concluded.

Notice of Appeal

The formal notice of appeal must by filed within 30 days after the entry of judgment and requires notification to the court and opposing counsel that an appeal will be taken. If post-trial motions are filed, these would delay the time for filing a Notice of Appeal until after the trial judge had ruled upon the motions.

TIMETABLE OF EVENTS IN
ROSE V. NICKEL AND DIME

January 31, 2000   Incident at Nickel and Dime
March 17,2000   Surgery performed by Dr. Beebe
May 1, 2000   Initial consultation with law firm by Scarlet Rose
June 19, 2000   Demand letter to Nickel and Dime
July 1, 2000   Lawsuit filed, together with discovery requests
July 25, 2000   Answer and affirmative defenses filed
July 25, 2000   Discovery requests filed by defendant
September 9, 2000   Defendant answers plaintiff's discovery
September 25, 2000   Plaintiff answers defendant's discovery
November 15, 2000   Plaintiff's deposition
November 19, 2000   Depositions of defendant's employees
December 29, 2000   Offer of judgment filed by defendant
January 6, 2001   Proposal for settlement filed by plaintiff
January 14, 2001   Depositions of treating physicians
January 27, 2001   Deposition of plaintiff's surgeon
February 20, 2001   Compulsory physical examination of plaintiff
March 3, 2001   Deposition of cpe (IME) doctor
March 5, 2001   Notice filed with court that case is at issue
March 25, 2001   Trial order issued, plus order to mediate
April 2, 2001   Motion in limine filed by defendant
April 2, 2001   Motion for summary judgment filed by defendant
May 4, 2001   Hearing on motion in limine and summary judgment
May 29, 2001   Mediation
June 9, 2001   Witness and exhibit lists filed with court
June 19, 2001   Pretrial conference
July 6, 2001   Trial

Book Order Form

Please send _____ book(s) at $38.50 each to:

Name: _____

Address: _____

City: _____ **State:** _____ **Zip:** _____

Sales Tax: Please add 8.25% for books shipped to Texas address.

Shipping: $4.00 per book.

Payment: Check or money orders only. Make payable to "Pearson Publications Company."

Mail to: Pearson Publications Company
9614 Greenville Avenue
Dallas, TX 75243

E-mail: pearsonpub@aol.com

Website: Pearsonpub-legal.com

Total: Book(s) @ $38.50 each $_____

Texas Sales Tax (8.25%), if applicable $_____

Shipping ($4.00 per book) $_____

Total Due $_____